NHL HOCKEY

Picture Credits:
All pictures by Bruce Bennett Studios, except *.
C. Anderson: 27, 66, 67; Paul Angers: 41; T.
Beigan: 19; *Brian Bennett: 71; *Gary Bettman: 17;
D. Carroll: 70; M. Di Giacomo: 92, 122; J. Di
Maggio: 121; H. Dirocco: 63; A. Foxall: 20, 96; D.
Giacopelli: 29; J. Giamundo: 33, 40, 48, 65, 76, 84,
93, 107; *Hockey Hall of Fame: 8, 118, 119; G.
James: 57; P. Laberge: 21, 26, 30, 35, 44, 52, 68;
Scott Levy: 22, 23, 46, 54, 56, 72, 85, 89, 104, 105,
113; R. Lewis: 28, 38, 60; R. McCormick: 37; Jim
McIsaac: 25, 34, 47, 51, 55, 64, 82; L. Murdoch: 42;
W. Robers: 43; Nick Welsh: 94; B. Winkler: 3, 4,
39, 69, 106; B. Wippert: 24.

First published in Canada in 1996 by
Raincoast Book Distribution Ltd.
8680 Camble Street
Vancouver, B.C. V6P 6M9
(604) 323-7100

ISBN 1-55192-047-6

Printed and bound in Italy

NHL HOCKEY

The Official Fans' Guide

John MacKinnon

RAINCOAST BOOKS

Vancouver

CONTENTS

The Next One: Wayne Gretzky is the Great One,
Mario Lemieux is the Magnificent One,
and Eric Lindros (left), the Philadelphia Flyers' giant-
sized center, is the next dominant force in the NHL.

INTRODUCTION

The transformation of the National Hockey League from a parochial league into an organization with a global vision began with the 1972 Summit Series between Canadian stars and the great national team of the Soviet Union—the Big, Red Machine.

After years of seeing their understaffed team whipped by the Soviets at the Olympics and World Championships, Canadians were finally given the chance to see their best players, their professionals, the stars of the NHL, supposedly deliver an overdue lesson to the big, bad Russians. It didn't work out quite that way.

The Canadians won, but it took some desperate, last-minute play and a goal by Paul Henderson with 34 seconds remaining in the final game to give Canada a 6-5 victory in the game and a slender series triumph—four games won, three lost, one game tied. The Canadian-invented sport—and the NHL—would never be the same.

NHL teams soon began to copy the superior Russian training methods, to blend their intricate, purposeful drills into often unimaginative North American practices, to pay more attention to the game's technical aspects.

The Russians, and other European teams, grafted the North Americans' never-say-die competitiveness and physical courage onto their highly skilled brand of hockey.

As the NHL expanded, first from six to 12 teams, then to 14, then 18 and up to its current roster of 26 teams, the teams cast their nets wider and wider in search of major-league talent, hauling in U.S. high-schoolers and collegians, Russians, Finns, Swedes, Germans, Czechs and Slovaks.

The NHL, dominated for its first half-century by Canadian stars like Frank McGee, Howie Morenz, Aurel Joliat, George Hainsworth, Maurice (Rocket) Richard, Gordie Howe, Glenn Hall, Bobby Hull, Bobby Orr and Frank Mahovlich, was adjusting to an influx of European talent.

NHL fans grew to admire players like Borje Salming, Anders Hedberg, Ulf Nilsson, Peter, Anton and Marian Stastny and, in the 1990s, Sergei Fedorov, Pavel Bure, Jaromir Jagr and Teemu Selanne.

As the NHL moves toward the 21st Century, it has grown from a six- to a 26-team league, with teams in 12 U.S. states as well as the District of Columbia, and four Canadian provinces. The league has been expanding, with two teams in Florida, one in Texas, three in California, another in Arizona, one in Colorado, along with its traditional strength along the Eastern Seaboard.

Twelve of the 26 teams have opened brand new arenas within the last four years and the league is heading into the third year of a five-year national TV contract with Fox.

This fall marked the inaugural World Cup hockey tournament, a joint venture involving the NHL and the NHL Players' Association that featured games in Europe and North America. And in 1998, NHL stars will represent their countries at the Winter Olympics in Nagano, Japan, which will further boost exposure for the league, particularly its enviable roster of international stars.

Today's NHL stars, players like Paul Kariya, Trevor Linden, Joe Sakic, Peter Forsberg, Brian Leetch, Martin Brodeur, Saku Koivu, Brendan Shanahan, Petr Nedved et al, have the opportunity to display their talents on a world stage as no generation of players before them has.

The NHL, long the forgotten child among the major North American professional sports, is poised as never before to raise its profile and jostle baseball, football and basketball for a larger share of the sports marketing pie.

The NHL has come a long way indeed since Henderson's legendary goal on a cold September night in Moscow in 1972. The ongoing progress—including Hockey Night in Nagano in 1998—should be great fun to witness.

Grounded Rocket: A knee injury sidelined Vancouver's Pavel Bure for 67 games in 1995-96 but the Russian Rocket is set to fly again in 1996-97.

BIRTH OF A HOCKEY LEAGUE

The whole world was not watching when a small cluster of men met in a downtown Montreal hotel on November 22, 1917 and formed the National Hockey League. The National Hockey Association, a forerunner of the NHL, had suspended operations, so the heads of the Montreal Canadiens, Montreal Wanderers, Ottawa Senators and Quebec Bulldogs attended a founding meeting and formed a new league.

A single reporter—Elmer Ferguson, of the Montreal Herald—reported on the somewhat shaky launch. For starters, the Bulldogs, a poor draw in Quebec City, decided not to operate in the NHL's first season, so the Toronto Arenas were admitted to the league as a replacement.

The league was down to three teams early into the first season, though, after the Westmount Arena, home to the Montreal Wanderers, burned down. With nowhere to play, the Wanderers, too, dropped out. The NHL, then, featured the Original Three for most of its initial season, not the Original Six, a term that would gain common usage years later.

The first president of the NHL was Frank Calder, a soccer-playing British emigree to Canada who had grown to love the Canadian game of hockey. His name would eventually be etched onto a trophy given annually to the best first-year, or rookie, player in the NHL.

In that first season, the league held the first of many dispersal drafts to distribute the players from the Bulldogs, including their scoring star, Joe Malone, who was chosen by the Canadiens.

In one of two opening-night games for the new league on December 19, 1917, Malone scored five goals as the Canadiens defeated Ottawa 7-4. Malone went on to score 44 goals during the 22-game regular season, easily winning the scoring title and setting a scoring pace never equalled in NHL history. The new league had its first superstar.

The league suffered its first major setback the following season, 1918-19. An influenza epidemic enfeebled many of the players on both finalists in the Stanley Cup playoffs—the Montreal Canadiens and Seattle Metropolitans of the Pacific Coast Hockey Association. Joe Hall, one of Montreal's star players died of the disease and so many players were stricken that the series was cancelled with no winner declared.

Building a Following

Interest in NHL hockey grew appreciably through the 1920s and 1930s, but the popularity curve was far from smooth.

In 1919, the Mount Royal Arena was built as the home of the Montreal Canadiens and five years later, the Montreal Forum was constructed to house the Maroons, the other NHL team in that hockey-mad city. In Ottawa, Frank Ahearn built a 10,000-seat arena called the Auditorium in 1923. And in Toronto, Maple Leaf Gardens was completed in 1931.

When Ottawa met the Canadiens in the 1923-24 playoffs,

11,000 jammed into the Auditorium to see the Canadiens, with Howie Morenz, defeat the Senators 4-2. The Canadiens went on to defeat Vancouver to win the Stanley Cup, the first of 24 they would win in the NHL's 80 years.

The Forum, the Canadiens' home for most of the century, was actually built as the home of the Maroons. But a warm spell spoiled the natural ice at the Mount Royal Arena in the Fall of 1924, so the Canadiens asked to play at the Forum, which had artificial ice. So it was that the Canadiens opened the Forum on November 29, 1924, whipping the Toronto Maple Leafs 7-1.

The 1924-25 season witnessed the first labor-management dispute when the players of the Hamilton Tigers, where the Quebec Bulldogs had shifted in 1920, went on strike before the playoffs. They wanted to be paid an extra $200 Cdn. per player for work during the playoffs, a seemingly reasonable request since Hamilton had made a record profit.

Fans' Target: NHL president Clarence Campbell enraged Montreal fans in March 1955 when he suspended their hero, Maurice (Rocket) Richard.

League president Calder, though, acted in support of the owners, in the belief that giving in to the players would put at risk the owners' "…large capital investment in rinks and arenas, and this capital must be protected."

Accordingly, Hamilton was disqualified from the playoffs, and the players were suspended and fined $200 Cdn. each. The Hamilton players' stand on playoff pay would be echoed in a similar stand later in the century by all NHL players, but at the time it seemed a minor obstacle on the league's pathway to success.

By the 1927-28 season, the NHL had grown from three teams to ten, split into two divisions: the Canadian and American. The Canadian division included the Toronto St. Patricks, the Ottawa Senators, the New York Americans, the Montreal Maroons and Montreal Canadiens. The American division consisted of the Boston Bruins, the New York Rangers, the Pittsburgh Pirates, the Chicago Blackhawks and the Detroit Cougars. This two-division alignment remained intact for 12 seasons, although this era was hardly immune from franchise shifts.

After winning the Stanley Cup in 1927, the Ottawa Senators, increasingly cashstrapped as the Great Depression approached, slid downhill. In 1930, the Senators sold star defenseman Frank (King) Clancy to the Toronto Maple Leafs for $35,000 Cdn., the largest sum ever paid for a hockey player. But even that cash infusion couldn't staunch the financial hemorrhage and, after suspending operations for the 1931-32 season, the Senators moved to St. Louis. The Eagles, as they were called, staggered through one season, before folding. Franchises also sprung up, struggled and folded or moved, in Pittsburgh and Philadelphia.

There was no shortage of star players in this era, which featured the scoring exploits of Nels Stewart, Cy Denneny, Aurel Joliat, Babe Dye, Montreal's incomparable Morenz, Harvey (Busher) Jackson, Charlie Conacher, Bill Cook and Cooney Weiland.

The game was evolving, finding itself, through the NHL's early days. Forward passing of the puck was not permitted at all until the 1927-28 season, when a rule change legalized this radical change in the defensive and neutral zones. When another rule change in 1929-30 gave players the green light to pass the puck ahead to a teammate in all three zones, goalscoring doubled. Ace Bailey led the league with 22 goals in 1927-28, compared to 43 goals for the league-leading Weiland the following season.

Play in the NHL was often vicious in the early days, but no incident horrified fans quite like Eddie Shore's attack on Ace Bailey on December 12, 1933 at the Boston Garden. Shore had been bodychecked into the boards by Red Horner and got up seeking revenge. He skated up to Bailey, who had his back to him, and knocked his feet out from under him. Bailey's head smacked against the ice and he went into convulsions. Horner responded by knocking Shore out with one punch, opening up a seven-stitch cut. Surgeons had to drill a hole in Bailey's skull to remove a blood clot that had formed near his brain. He remained unconscious, near death for 15 days and never played again.

The NHL of the 1930s produced many sublime evenings, also, but none like the Longest Game, a playoff encounter that began March 24 and ended March 25 in 1936.

That night, the Montreal Maroons and the Detroit Red Wings faced off in a Stanley Cup semifinal series opener that lasted 176 minutes 30 seconds. The only goal was scored by Detroit's Modere (Mud) Bruneteau at 16:30 of the sixth overtime period, provoking momentary stunned silence among the 9,000 fans at the Montreal Forum, followed by a huge ovation of relief. The game that began at 8:34 pm had ended at 2:25 am the following morning and all in attendance were utterly exhausted. None deserved a rest

more than Detroit goaltender Norm Smith, a Maroons castoff, who stopped 90 shots in his first NHL playoff game.

The Forum was also the scene for one of the saddest days in NHL history—the funeral of Canadiens great Howie Morenz on March 10, 1937. Morenz had died from complications arising from a broken leg. More than 25,000 fans filed past the coffin at center ice in the Forum.

As the 1930s progressed, teams began to die as well, as the NHL shrank from a ten-team, two-division league to a one-division league with seven teams by 1940.

The War Years

In the early 1940s, a rule change introduced a center red line to the NHL ice surface. The idea was to speed up play and reduce offside calls. The change marked the onset of the league's so-called Modern Era.

As the NHL moved into this new phase, one player dominated the transition—Maurice (Rocket) Richard. Playing

Mr. Hockey: Gordie Howe's marvellous career stretched over five decades. His legendary longevity permitted him to play in the NHL with his sons, Mark and Marty.

Russian Bear: Anatoli Tarasov has been called the father of Soviet hockey. In fact, he studied the hockey writings of Toronto's Lloyd Percival.

Rubbing salt in the fans' wounds, he replaced Drillon with Don Metz, a raw rookie, putting him on a line with Nick Metz, his brother, and Dave (Sweeney) Shriner. The trio dominated the rest of the series as the Leafs, who got spectacular goaltending from Turk Broda, did the seemingly impossible and won the Stanley Cup. Drillon never played for the Leafs again.

Many NHL stars of this era enlisted in the Canadian armed forces and served in the war, including Broda, Syl Apps, Bob Goldham, the Metz brothers, Jimmy Orlando, Sid Abel, Mud Bruneteau and Bucko McDonald. The league operated throughout the wartime era, but the quality of competition was thinned by military service.

It was in the 1940s, too, that the NHL stabilized as a six-team league, its constituent members coming to be known as the 'Original Six.' The general managers, the sporting architects of those teams, became as legendary as the players: Frank J. Selke in Montreal; Toronto's Smythe; Jack Adams, who built the great Detroit Red Wings teams of the 1950s; Tommy Ivan with the Chicago Blackhawks.

right wing with center (Elegant) Elmer Lach and left winger Hector (Toe) Blake, Richard was the scoring star for the Montreal Canadiens, a symbol of competitive excellence for all French-Canadians and one of the most fiery, combative athletes ever to play any professional sport.

In the 1944-45 season, Richard scored 50 goals in 50 games, setting the standard for scoring brilliance for years to come. Lach (80 points), Richard (73) and Blake (67) finished 1-2-3 in the scoring race, earning the nickname, the 'Punch Line'.

Richard set a single-game scoring record that season, too, by scoring five goals and adding three assists as the Canadiens whipped the Red Wings 9-1 in Montreal on December 28.

The Stanley Cup highlight of the World War II period had to be the Toronto Maple Leafs' dramatic comeback victory in 1942, the only time in NHL history that a team overcame a 3-0 deficit in games to win a seven-game final series.

The Maple Leafs, second-place finishers during the 48-game regular season, found themselves in that predicament against the Detroit Red Wings, who had finished fifth in regular-season play.

At that point in the series, Maple Leafs' manager Conn Smythe, the man who built Maple Leaf Gardens and whose hockey credo was: "If you can't beat 'em in the alley, you can't beat 'em on the ice," took extreme measures.

Smythe benched right winger Gordie Drillon, the Leafs' top scorer, provoking outrage among Maple Leafs' supporters.

The Richard Riot

Sports journalist Rejean Tremblay once said: "The Rocket once told me that when he played he felt he was out there for all French Canadians."

Accordingly, all of French Canada was outraged in March 1955 when NHL president Clarence Campbell suspended Richard from the final three regular-season games and the entire playoffs for slugging a linesman in a fracas during a game in Boston.

Campbell, who embodied Anglophone dominance for many French-Canadians, attended the Canadiens' next game, against Detroit, at the Montreal Forum and quickly became a target for the irate Montreal fans seeking revenge for what they perceived as unjustly severe treatment of their hero.

At the end of the first period, a young man approached the NHL executive, extending his hand. But when Campbell held out his for an expected handshake, the man slapped his face. Moments later, a tear-gas bomb was set off behind one of the goals and soon after, the city's fire chief stopped the game, which was forfeited to Detroit.

The 15,000 fans filed out onto Ste-Catherine Street and a procession of pillaging unfolded along the street for several blocks.

The next day, Richard went on radio and television to appeal for calm in Montreal. The incident resonates to this day in Quebec. Many cite it as the spark that touched off the so-called Quiet Revolution, a period of profound and peaceful social change in the early 1960s.

The league entered the 1950s with its depth of talent restored, its membership rock solid and the quality of play impressive.

The Rocket and Mr Hockey

If the overall quality of play was high, two teams stood out head and shoulders above the pack—the Detroit Red Wings and the Montreal Canadiens. Between them the Red Wings and Canadiens won ten of 11 Stanley Cups from 1950-1960. From 1951 through to 1960, the Canadiens made the Stanley Cup finals ten straight times, winning the Cup six times, including five in a row from 1956-60.

Beginning with the 1948-49 season and ending with the 1954-55 campaign, the Red Wings finished first in the regular season seven straight times, topping things off with a Stanley Cup victory four times during that run of excellence.

The Red Wings were constructed around Gordie Howe—Mr Hockey, a prolific scorer and physically powerful player with a legendary mean streak he often expressed by delivering a pile-driver elbow to an opponent.

The Canadiens' leader was Maurice (Rocket) Richard, a passionate star with a burning desire to win at all costs. Richard's eyes, it was said, lit up like a pinball machine as he crossed the opposition blue line and homed in on the net to score.

In the Stanley Cup semifinals against Boston in 1952, Richard scored one of his most memorable goals. After a thunderous check by Boston's Leo LaBine, Richard left, semi-conscious, for the Forum clinic to have a nasty gash to the head stitched. He returned to the game late in the third period, with the score tied 1-1. His head bandaged, still groggy, Richard fashioned an end-to-end rush that he completed by fending off defenseman Bill

Quackenbush with one hand and shovelling a one-handed shot past goaltender Sugar Jim Henry.

With two spectacular stars like Howe and Richard, the NHL's popularity soared, and television broadcasts of NHL games only added to its appeal.

It was a period of consistently fat profits for the club owners: Conn Smythe in Toronto; the Norris family, which owned or controlled the Detroit Red Wings, Chicago Blackhawks and New York Rangers; Weston Adams in Boston; and the Molson family in Montreal.

Some of the players, notably Ted Lindsay of Detroit and Doug Harvey of Montreal, did some figuring and estimating and concluded that they were reaping a small slice of a revenue pie that was much larger than the owners let on.

In 1957, Lindsay was the driving force behind the formation of the National Hockey League Players' Association. The group wanted to take control of the players' pension fund, and channel broadcast revenues from the All-Star game directly into the fund.

The owners were, to say the least, hostile to the players' efforts. Jack Adams, the Red Wings' GM, traded Lindsay and goaltender Glenn Hall, both first-team All-Stars, to the Chicago Blackhawks. The Canadiens, unwilling to lose their best defenseman, waited three years before trading Harvey to the New York Rangers. Ownership battled the players every step of the way and in 1958 the players dropped their attempt to form a legally recognized association.

The exciting on-ice wars between the Red Wings, Canadiens, Bruins and Maple Leafs obscured the decade-ending labor-management skirmish. Far more prominent in the public imagination was the dominance of the Canadiens, who won a record five straight Stanley Cups to close the decade.

The Canadiens of that era were so proficient on the power play they forced a rule change. In 1956-57, the NHL ruled that a penalized player could return to the ice if the opposing team scored a goal in his absence. Previously, a player had to sit out the full two minutes, during which time the potent Canadiens power-play unit sometimes scored two or even three times.

As the league moved into a new decade, Richard retired, but another brilliant player emerged with the Chicago Blackhawks—Bobby Hull. Actually, it was Bernie Geoffrion, one of Richard's ex-teammates, who became the second player to score 50

The Fog: Fred Shero coached the Philadelphia Flyers to two straight Stanley Cups in the 1970s but couldn't rekindle that magic as coach of the New York Rangers.

Skill Set: Along with Hedberg, Hull and Lars-Erik Sjoberg, the flashy Winnipeg Jets had plenty of skill and helped change the way hockey is played in North America.

ICE TALK

"THERE IS NO WAY (THE CANADIENS) CAN BEAT US WITH A JUNIOR B GOALTENDER,"

GEORGE (PUNCH) IMLACH, TORONTO MAPLE LEAFS' GENERAL MANAGER AND HEAD COACH ON ROOKIE MONTREAL GOALIE ROGATIEN VACHON ON THE EVE OF THE 1967 STANLEY CUP FINAL SERIES

goals in a season. Of course, Geoffrion recorded the feat in the 1960-61 season, a 70- not a 50-game season. Hull recorded the first of his five 50-plus goal seasons the following year.

Hull and teammate Stan Mikita were at the top of an impressive list of 1960s scoring stars that included Frank Mahovlich, the still-impressive Howe, Jean Beliveau, Andy Bathgate, Red Kelly, Alex Delvecchio, Rod Gilbert, Ken Wharram, John Bucyk and Norm Ullman.

The Toronto Maple Leafs supplanted the Canadiens as the dominant team in the early 1960s, winning three straight Stanley Cups from 1962-64, but the Canadiens won four in five years from 1964-69. They might have won five straight, except for Toronto's stunning upset victory over Montreal with an aging team in 1967.

That Stanley Cup final was truly the last of an era, because the NHL was preparing for unprecedented growth as the decade wound down.

A Victory for the Aged—Toronto's 1967 Stanley Cup Win

The Montreal Canadiens had won two straight Stanley Cups and seemed a solid bet to win a third as they prepared to meet the Maple Leafs in the final pre-expansion final series.

The Maple Leafs, third-place finishers during the season, had surprised lots of people by knocking off the first-place Chicago Blackhawks in the semifinals, but the younger, speedier Canadiens had swept the New York Rangers in four games, going with rookie goalie Rogatien Vachon.

The Maple Leafs' lineup had an average age of more than 31 years that included 42-year-old goalie Johnny Bower, and 41-year-old defenseman Allan Stanley. Twelve members of the roster were over 30—seven of them over 35.

When the Canadiens won Game 1, 6-2, with Henri Richard recording the hat-trick and Yvan Cournoyer scoring twice, it seemed to confirm the experts' analysis—the younger, quicker Canadiens were simply too good for the aging Leafs.

Then the ageless Bower went out and shut out the Canadiens as Toronto won Game 2, 3-0. The Leafs won Game 3 in overtime 3-2, with Bower brilliant again, making 60 saves. But when he strained his groin in the Game 4 pre-game warm-up, Maple Leafs' coach Punch Imlach had to insert Terry Sawchuk in goal.

The Canadiens seemed to solve Sawchuk, winning 6-3 to even the series 2-2. But Sawchuk only gave up two goals in the final two games—as Toronto stunned the hockey world by winning the series 4-2. The ageless wonders had turned back the clock and rediscovered their prime.

"I felt sick for a month afterwards," said Montreal defenseman Terry Harper. "To lose the Stanley Cup, that was horrible, but to lose to Toronto and have to live in Canada afterwards, oh man—everywhere you'd go you'd run into Leafs' fans, well, that was like losing twice."

ICE TALK

"A MISTAKE HAS BEEN MADE."

NHL PRESIDENT CLARENCE CAMPBELL, AFTER MISTAKENLY ANNOUNCING THAT THE EXPANSION VANCOUVER CANUCKS WOULD SELECT FIRST OVER THE BUFFALO SABRES IN THE 1971 ENTRY DRAFT

So Long, Original Six, Hello Expansion

The success—artistic and financial—of the Original Six had attracted interested investors as early as the mid-1940s. In 1945-46, representatives from Philadelphia, Los Angeles and San Francisco had applied for franchises. The Original Six owners, jealously guarding their rich profit margins, were hostile to the notion for years.

But envious of the lucrative TV contracts U.S. networks were signing with the National Football League, American Football League and Major-League baseball, and recognizing that such riches were definitely beyond the grasp of a six-team, Canadian-

Broad Street Bounty

"We take the shortest distance to the puck and arrive in ill humor." That was the Philadelphia Flyers credo, as enunciated by head coach Fred Shero. He wasn't kidding.

The Flyers were constructed around a core of stellar players: goaltender Bernie Parent; defensemen Jim Watson and Bob Dailey; centers Bobby Clarke and Rick MacLeish; and wingers Bill Barber and Reggie Leach.

The supporting cast included some honest checkers like Bill Clement, Terry Crisp and Ross Lonsberry and a platoon of enforcers like Dave (The Hammer) Schultz, Bob (Houndog) Kelly, Don (Big Bird) Saleski, Jack McIlhargey and Andre (Moose) Dupont.

The blend of goaltending brilliance, team defense, toughness and scoring punch helped make the Flyers the first expansion club to win one Stanley Cup, let alone two.

Shero was nicknamed 'The Fog' by his players because he was given to cryptic sayings.

On the day of Game 6 in Philadelphia's Stanley Cup victory over the Boston Bruins in 1974, Shero wrote this message on the chalkboard in the dressing room: "Win together today and we'll walk together forever."

The Flyers won, and carved their names into the Stanley Cup.

based league, the league governors decided to proceed with expansion. The decision was spurred, in part, by aggressive efforts by the Western Hockey League, a development league, to push for major-league status.

The NHL governors received 15 applications for new franchises and in February, 1966, granted teams to Los Angeles, San Francisco, St. Louis, Pittsburgh, Philadelphia and Minnesota. The new franchises cost $2 million U.S. each.

The new teams were grouped together in the West Division, which enabled them to be competitive amongst themselves, even if they weren't really competitive with the six established teams in the East Division. The first three years of expansion, the St. Louis Blues, coached by Scotty Bowman, and staffed with aging stars like Glenn Hall, Jacques Plante, Doug Harvey, Dickie Moore and others, advanced to the Stanley Cup final. Each year, the Blues lost in four straight games.

The third of those three four-game sweeps of the Blues was administered by Bobby Orr and the Boston Bruins. Orr had become the first defenseman in NHL history to record 100 points in 1969-70, when he scored 33 goals and added 87 assists for 120 points to win the scoring championship. Many thought it was the first Stanley Cup of a Boston dynasty, but Orr's career was foreshortened by a series of knee injuries. He left the NHL before he was 30, with just two Stanley Cup rings—1970 and 1972.

Expansion coincided with the establishment of the NHL Players' Association—ten years after Ted Lindsay's effort had failed. A Toronto lawyer named Alan Eagleson had helped striking players on the minor-league Springfield Indians win their dispute with Eddie Shore, the club's miserly, ogre-like president and manager.

That victory helped him win the players' support when, led by a core group of Toronto Maple Leafs players, the association was established in 1967, with Eagleson as its executive director.

King of Kings: After Wayne Gretzky was traded to Los Angeles in 1988, it suddenly became chic to be seen at an NHL game in La-La Land.

Players' salaries, kept artificially low for decades, were about to increase dramatically, but it was a rival league—the World Hockey Association—far more than the Eagleson-led NHLPA that would be responsible.

The Winnipeg WHA franchise provided instant credibility for the rival league by signing Bobby Hull for $1 million Cdn.. Then they borrowed Hull's nickname—The Golden Jet—to name their own club. Other high-profile players who followed included J.C. Tremblay, Marc Tardif, Gerry Cheevers and Derek Sanderson.

Many clubs signed players to lucrative contracts rather than lose them to WHA teams.

To combat the upstart league, the NHL kept on expanding, adding Vancouver and Buffalo in 1970. That year, the great Gilbert Perreault was the prize available for the expansion club fortunate enough to choose first in the entry draft. To decide between the Sabres and Canucks, the league brought in a wheel of fortune apparatus, the kind popular at country fairs. The Sabres were assigned numbers one through ten, with the Canucks getting 11-20. The wheel was given a spin and came to rest at the number 1—or so it seemed. Clarence Campbell, the league president announced that the Sabres had won, prompting elation among the Buffalo supporters. But the wheel had stopped at 11. Campbell stepped back to the microphone and uttered this phrase: "A mistake has been made."

Perreault played 17 seasons for the Sabres and scored 512 goals, while Dale Tallon, selected by the Canucks, had a solid, but unspectacular career with Vancouver, Chicago and the Pittsburgh Penguins. Expansion continued in 1972 , when Atlanta and the New York Islanders were added, and in 1974 the Kansas City Scouts and the Washington Capitals joined the league. The NHL had tripled in size in just seven years, severly depleting the talent base.

The dilution was made more apparent by the 1972 Summit Series between Canada and the Soviet Union. Canadians expected their pros, who had been banned for years from competing in World Championships or Olympic competitions, to drub the Soviets, but were stunned when the Soviets beat Canada 7-3 in the opening game at the Forum. The Soviet game, with legendary coach Anatoli Tarasov directing its development, had caught up to and, in many areas, passed the Canadian style. That realization stunned a country which prided itself on producing the best hockey players in the world.

Canada, playing on pride, guts and determination, won a narrow series victory with four victories, three losses and one game tied. But the game had changed forever.

On the expansion front, meanwhile, not all the franchises took root where they were first planted. The California Golden Seals moved to Cleveland in 1976, then merged with the struggling Minnesota North Stars in 1979. The Kansas City Scouts moved to Denver, Colorado in 1976 and then in 1982 to East Rutherford, New Jersey, where they remain as the Devils.

In the early expansion days, Montreal general manager Sam Pollock took advantage of expansion to build a 1970s dynasty in Montreal. The Canadiens, rich in solid talent throughout their farm system, swapped good young players, and sometimes established but aging players, to talent-starved expansion clubs for high draft picks.

Swedish Import: Anders Hedberg was Bobby Hull's linemate in his WHA days with the Winnipeg Jets, but he became a Ranger when the Jets entered the NHL in 1979.

In this fashion, the Canadiens obtained Guy Lafleur, Steve Shutt, Bob Gainey, Doug Risebrough, Michel Larocque, Mario Tremblay—the building blocks of the six Stanley Cup champions during the 1970s.

Many complained that the rapid expansion drastically diluted the talent in the NHL. The Philadelphia Flyers, the first post-expansion club to win the Stanley Cup, certainly weren't overloaded with talent. Their canny coach, Fred Shero, made the most of a small nucleus of excellent talent, led by goalie Bernie Parent, center Bobby Clarke, and wingers Bill Barber and Reggie Leach, and a belligerent style of play that intimidated the opposition.

That formula led the Flyers to back-to-back Stanley Cup championships in 1974 and 1975. By 1976, the Canadiens load of drafted talent—particularly Guy Lafleur—had matured, and Montreal rolled to four straight Stanley Cup championships to close out the 1970s.

ICE TALK

"I REALLY LOVED EDMONTON. I DIDN'T WANT TO LEAVE. WE HAD A DYNASTY HERE. WHY MOVE?"

WAYNE GRETZKY, ON HIS BEING TRADED TO THE LOS ANGELES KINGS IN 1988, A TRANSACTION THAT SENT ALL OF CANADA INTO A STATE OF MOURNING

The turn of the decade also saw the ten-year war with the WHA resolved, when the only four surviving teams from the rival league—the Quebec Nordiques; Hartford Whalers; Edmonton Oilers; and Winnipeg Jets joined the NHL. The teams were stripped of the talent they had recruited, often in bidding wars with NHL clubs, and denied access to TV revenue for five years after joining the NHL.

As a result, the Jets lost stars Anders Hedberg and Ulf Nilsson, both of whom played for the New York Rangers thereafter. The Oilers were permitted to keep Wayne Gretzky, who had signed a personal services contract with Oilers owner Peter Pocklington. And the Whalers iced a lineup that included 50-year-old Gordie Howe, playing with his sons, Mark and Marty.

The Nordiques' response was be to creative in its recruiting efforts. Club president Marcel Aubut arranged for Slovak stars Peter and Anton Stastny to defect from Czechoslovakia, and the pair were joined one year later by older brother Marian. The Stastnys, especially Peter and Anton, became the scoring stars on the rebuilt Nordiques.

The success of the Stastnys helped convince NHL managers that there were rich veins of talent in Europe that had to be tapped. Communism was one major obstacle to doing so immediately, however.

There were few large impediments to importing Scandinavian talent, though, as the New York Islanders found out. They won four straight Stanley Cups, beginning in 1980, with some talented Scandinavians, like Tomas Jonsson, Stefan Persson, Anders Kallur and Mats Hallin, playing important roles.

The European influence really took hold in the NHL, though, with the Edmonton Oilers, who supplanted the Islanders as the NHL's pre-eminent team in 1984, when they won the first of five Stanley Cups in seven years.

Glen Sather, the Oilers' general manager and coach, sprinkled some talented Europeans like Jari Kurri, Esa Tikkanen, Reijo Ruotsalainen, Kent Nilsson and Willy Lindstrom around the Edmonton lineup, with good results.

But Sather went one step further, borrowing much from the flowing, speed-based European style and adapting it to the NHL.

Sather once described the Oilers" style as the Montreal Canadiens (of the 1970s) updated for the 1980s.

The style of play—executed by great players like Gretzky, Mark Messier, Glenn Anderson, Paul Coffey and Kurri—helped Sather construct a Canadiens-like 1980s dynasty.

Thinking Globally

As the NHL moved toward the 1990s the governors began to develop a larger vision. This was not an easy process. The traditions and mind-set of the Original Six had continued to dominate the league well after expansion had transformed a small, regional league into a continental one, albeit a weak sister compared to major-league baseball, football and basketball.

The NHL had evolved into a 21-team league but was controlled by the triumvirate of league president John Ziegler, Chicago Blackhawks owner Bill Wirtz and NHLPA executive-director Alan Eagleson.

The league had traditionally been gate-driven, dominated by shrewd entrepreneurs like Smythe, the Norrises, the Wirtz family and the Molsons, who owned their own arenas and knew how to fill them but had little feel for or interest in marketing the league as a whole.

A series of linked events began to change this. By the summer of 1988, Wayne Gretzky had led the Edmonton Oilers to four Stanley Cups and established himself as the best player in hockey. But to Oilers owner Peter Pocklington he was a depreciating asset whose value had peaked.

Pocklington traded Gretzky to the Los Angeles Kings—sending Edmontonians, and Canadians in general, into mourning, and stunning NHL ownership.

Bruce McNall, then the Kings' owner, promptly raised Gretzky's salary. He reasoned that Gretzky would generate far greater revenues for the Kings, both at the gate and through advertising and he was proved right.

Two years later, the St. Louis Blues used similar logic when they signed Brett Hull, their franchise player, to a three-year contract. Then they signed restricted free agent defenseman Scott Stevens to a four-year deal.

While salaries were rising, there were other parts of the hockey business taking off as well. In the United States more people watched NHL hockey on Fox and ESPN than ever before. In Canada, Saturday became a double dream as *Hockey Night in Canada* began running doubleheaders. And in the U.S. and Canada the NHL found success in five new markets. Anaheim, Ottawa, San Jose, Miami Florida and Tampa Bay all greeted the game with excitement and big crowds. The value of an NHL franchise rose and the level of people wanting to own a team grew.

As the economics of major professional hockey changed, the NHL realized that the old, gate-driven model would not work anymore. Hockey entrepreneurs began to build new, larger arenas, which featured scores of so-called luxury suites, hotel-plush boxes designed to enable corporate executives and guests to enjoy a game in high style.

Merger Man: Quebec Nordiques president Marcel Aubut was a key player in the NHL admitting four former WHA franchises to the NHL in 1979.

Labor Man: Under executive-director Bob Goodenow, the NHL Players' Association has become more proactive about getting its share of the NHL revenue pie.

New forms of advertising opportunities—on scoreboards, rink boards, even on the ice itself—were deployed to generate more money. And the NHL, long a marketing luddite among major professional leagues, got into the merchandising business in a concerted way.

As the hockey business grew more sophisticated, the players became more assertive about their interests, also. Dissatisfaction with NHLPA executive-director Alan Eagleson's autocratic, company-union style had been growing and, in 1990, the players selected former agent Bob Goodenow, the man who had negotiated Brett Hull's blockbuster contract, as their new director.

At the end of the 1992 season, the players staged an 11-day strike, demanding, among other things, the marketing rights to their own likenesses. They wanted a chunk of the revenue pie, in other words, and were prepared to fight to get it. The players also sought more relaxed free agency guidelines enabling them to sell themselves on the market.

As the league adjusted to a new economic and labor reality, it sought new leadership capable of achieving peace with the players and the league's on-ice officials, and proactively directing its newly ambitious business aspirations.

In 1992, a search committee selected Gary Bettman, a lawyer and former executive with the marketing-slick National Basketball Association to become the league's first commissioner.

Early in his tenure, Bettman made a business statement by recruiting two powerful new partners to set up NHL franchises—the Disney Corporation and Blockbuster Entertainment.

Michael Eisner, the Disney CEO, named his company's team the Mighty Ducks of Anaheim, after a commercially successful movie of the same name. Wayne Huizenga, head of Blockbuster,

established a second team in Florida, the Panthers, based in Miami.

It had long been a cliche that pro sports was an entertainment business, but recruiting the likes of Eisner and Huizenga suggested that NHL head office had actually begun to believe this maxim.

One team—the Ottawa Senators—misread the market and grossly overestimated the promotional opportunities available to young stars when they signed untried No. 1 draft pick Alexandre Daigle to a five-year contract in June 1993. The deal included a marketing component that was unrealistically generous for an unproven rookie.

If the Gretzky, Hull and Stevens contracts had lifted the salary ceiling, the Daigle deal significantly raised the entry level and helped cause an ownership backlash. The notion of a rookie salary cap took hold and a second owner-player showdown in three years loomed.

The result was a lockout that cancelled 468 games from October 1, 1994 to January 19, 1995, shrinking the regular season to 48 games with no inter-conference play. The deal finally struck included a rookie salary cap and provided somewhat greater freedom of movement for older players.

The new, five-year deal couldn't help franchises stuck with outmoded arenas, however, and two Canadian teams, the Quebec Nordiques and Winnipeg Jets, moved south to Denver and Phoenix, respectively—Quebec for 1995-96, Winnipeg for the 1996-97 season. The move proved successful for Colorado when they won the Stanley Cup in their first year.

The Next One

Eric Lindros was so dominant as a junior hockey player that he was dubbed 'The Next One'—Wayne Gretzky being 'The Great One'—well before he was drafted No. 1 overall by the Quebec Nordiques in 1991.

He was also supremely confident in his ability and secure in the knowledge that his extraordinary skill and potential as a marketing vehicle gave him unprecedented leverage to negotiate.

He warned Nordiques president Marcel Aubut, with whom he did not get along, not to draft him, saying he would refuse to report if he were selected. Sure enough, Quebec drafted him and Lindros, true to his word, did not report. He played another year of junior and for Canada's Olympic team at the 1992 Olympics in Albertville, France.

In June 1992, Aubut invited a bidding contest for Lindros and thought he had made a blockbuster deal with the New York Rangers. But the Philadelphia Flyers also had an offer on the table that included $15 million U.S., six players and two first-round draft picks.

An arbitrator was called in and he awarded Lindros to the Flyers in one of the most bizarre transactions in NHL history.

Going For Gold

Joint venture is a buzz phrase in the NHL of the 1990s, with two significant projects at the forefront of the business plan: the World Cup of Hockey, held for the first time this Fall; and the Dream Teams concept, NHL pros playing in the Winter Olympics in Nagano, Japan in 1998. The NHL and NHLPA are working together on both projects and expect to reap even greater exposure for their league.

Having buried—and not without a struggle—the parochial, Original Six mentality that predominated just 30 years ago, the NHL heads toward the year 2000 poised not only to deregionalize the sport in the U. S., but to compete on the international sporting market.

The league moves forward with franchises established in most key markets in North America and a five-year TV deal with the Fox network to build on. The collapse of the Soviet Union and its Communist satellites in the 1980s and 1990s gave the NHL access to a wealth of young talent, players like Alexei Yashin, Alexei Zhamnov, Alexei Zhitnik, Jaromir Jagr, Roman Hamrlik and many others. It represented an infusion of skill into the NHL when it badly needed new young stars to sell in its new markets.

Hockey remains the No. 4 sport in most U.S. market but it has marshalled its marketing forces as never before to move up the pecking order. Success will require hard work. Though NHL franchises have failed in non-traditional markets like Oakland, California, Denver, and Atlanta in the past, the future looks good for expansion teams since the Colorado Avalanche and the Florida Panthers played in the 1996 Stanley Cup finals.

It does seem clear, though, that the sport has forever left behind its image as a regional game, interesting only to Canadians and American fans in select, northern areas.

The NHL has truly gone global and there's no turning back now.

Mightiest Duck: Disney Company CEO Michael Eisner transposed cinematic marketing techniques to help sell the sport of hockey in Southern California.

TEAMS IN THE NHL

With the growth of the National Hockey League in North America and the influx of bright international stars like Jaromir Jagr, Sergei Fedorov and Peter Forsberg, the NHL is showcasing more individual talent in the 1990s than it ever has. Yet the team concept continues to endure as the bedrock principle of the sport. It's a cliche in hockey that no player—no matter how spectacular his contribution—is bigger than his team.

Consider the case of goaltender Patrick Roy. For a decade, Roy was the undisputed superstar and leader of the Montreal Canadiens, which has produced the greatest teams in the history of the sport.

But early in the 1995-96 season, humiliated about being left in goal to suffer during a one-sided loss, Roy had a public tiff with Mario Tremblay, the Canadiens coach, and told the club president he had played his last game for the team. Four days later, Roy, a sporting icon in hockey-mad Montreal, was traded to the Colorado Avalanche.

Hockey fans certainly identify with the stars of the sport, but they root for their team, above all. Within days of Roy's departure, the Montreal fans were chanting the name of their new goaltending hero: Tee-bo, Tee-bo, 21-year-old Jocelyn Thibault.

The ultimate standard

Successful hockey teams are an amalgam of coaching acumen, solid team defense, great goaltending, timely scoring, leadership, fan support and the most elusive factor of all—team chemistry.

Coaches set the tone for success and none was more successful than Hector (Toe) Blake, the legendary coach of the Montreal Canadiens in the 1950s and 1960s.

In his first meeting with his team, in October 1955, Blake told his players: "There are some guys in this room who play better than I ever did. I have nothing to teach them. But what I can show you all is how to play better as a team."

Blake obviously succeeded. In 13 years as coach of the Canadiens, the team finished first in the regular season nine times and won eight Stanley Cups, including five straight from 1956-60.

Scoring titles and individual awards may be the measure of a player's excellence, but NHL teams are measured by one standard only—their ability to win the Stanley Cup.

An entire generation of Toronto Maple Leafs fans has grown

World Class: Alexei Kovalev's speed and array of moves make him one of the most dangerous forwards in the National Hockey League.

to adulthood without seeing their club win the Cup, yet the legend of an aging Leafs club that did win it in 1967 lives on.

In the early 1970s, the New York Islanders entered the NHL as an expansion club and were carefully crafted into a formidable group by general manager Bill Torrey. The validation of Torrey's genius in drafting Denis Potvin, Mike Bossy, Bryan Trottier, Clark Gillies and others was the four straight Stanley Cups the Islanders won, beginning in 1980.

As great as those stars were, though, the Islanders championship chemistry didn't click until Torrey traded for Butch Goring, a speedy, gritty,centerman. Goring checked the opposing team's top center and, a keen student of the game, designed the Islanders' penalty killing system.

The Edmonton Oilers of the 1980s were loaded with offensive firepower, boasting the likes of Wayne Gretzky, Jari Kurri, Glenn Anderson, Paul Coffey and Mark Messier. But they didn't become a champion until coach Glen Sather had taught them to play solid, if not necessarily brilliant, team defense.

Mario Lemieux, the game's best player, led Pittsburgh to two straight Stanley Cup triumphs in the early 1990s, but a key member of both teams was Trottier, who brought invaluable playoff experience to those Pittsburgh teams.

New York fans of a certain age have fond memories of stars like Jean Ratelle, Rod Gilbert and Vic Hadfield, the famous GAG (Goal-a-game) line of the 1970s. But none of those players ever won a Stanley Cup.

The Rangers faithful had to wait until 1994, after Messier, who learned how to be a champion with the Oilers, had moved to New York and instilled team values in his new teammates.

Cruising Speed: At 35, Detroit defenseman Paul Coffey is still one of the fastest players in the game, and the defensive leader on the Red Wings.

Saving goals

And no team can succeed without great goaltending: the Islanders' Billy Smith; Grant Fuhr of the Oilers; the Rangers' Mike Richter; Tom Barrasso of the Penguins.

No goalie can boast a Stanley Cup performance chart quite like Roy. He led the Canadiens to a Stanley Cup as a rookie in 1986 and backstopped them to another in 1993, when he coolly closed the door on the opposition as Montreal won ten games in overtime.

From 1990 through 1995, the Detroit Red Wings compiled a winning percentage of .594, second in the league over that span only to Pittsburgh. Yet the closest the Red Wings got to the Stanley Cup was a losing performance, in four straight games, to the New Jersey Devils in 1995.

In 1995-96, the talent-rich Red Wings, won a record 62 games, breaking the old record for most victories in a season (60) set in 1976-77 by the Canadiens. But that Montreal team was in the process of winning four straight Stanley Cups. The Wings knew their regular-season success, by itself, still rang hollow.

"We've got a great team here," said Red Wings defenseman Paul Coffey. "But we don't rank with the others until we win a Stanley Cup."

MIGHTY DUCKS OF ANAHEIM

By careful aquisition of top talent to complement their existing skills, the young Ducks are building toward league stardom.

The Mighty Ducks of Anaheim probably wouldn't exist if it hadn't been for Emilio Estevez and a rag-tag bunch of skaters who turned a low-budget Disney production into a celluloid success.

"The movie was our market research," recalls Disney chairman Michael Eisner, who approached the NHL about an expansion franchise after the screen version of the Mighty Ducks grossed almost $60 million.

In the fall of 1993, the real-life Mighty Ducks became the NHL's third California-based member, joining the Los Angeles Kings and San Jose Sharks.

There have been no sappy Hollywood endings since the Ducks took to the Pond, a 17,174-seat facility that's had an SRO sign since the team's inception. But the Mighty Ducks, perhaps using some of Tinker Bell's savvy, have quickly built a playoff-contending club.

No rag-tags

They were the league's big surprise that first year, tying an NHL first-year team record with 33 victories, including 19 road wins, the most ever by a first-year club.

In the lockout-shortened 1994-95 season, they remained in the playoff hunt until the final two games of the schedule.

The Ducks also began developing their first star players in left winger Paul Kariya and defenseman Oleg Tverdovsky.

Kariya, the team's first choice in the 1993 amateur draft, has blossomed into one of the NHL's top goal scorers, despite his 5-foot-11, 175-pound stature. That is two inches shorter and 21 pounds lighter than the average NHL player. "He is deceptively fast," says St. Louis coach Mike Keenan. "He anticipates and reads plays exceptionally well."

Tverdovsky, the Ducks' top draft pick in 1994, was the price the club had to pay on February 7, 1996, when the opportunity arose to obtain high-scoring Teemu Selanne from the Winnipeg Jets. They also had to part with No. 1 1995 draft pick Chad Kilger, a center.

"It's a trade we couldn't pass up," said Anaheim general manager Jack Ferreira. "You don't get the chance to get a guy like Teemu Selanne every day of the week."

With Selanne, a 76-goal scorer in 1992-93, joining Kariya the Mighty Ducks have a formidable 1-2 offensive punch. A jovial, fun-loving Finnish player, Selanne will also take some of the pressure off Kariya, who admits to having a strained relationship with the media.

That's entertainment

Even with these two snipers, the Mighty Ducks are in the bottom five in most league offensive categories. That's been the case from their birth, as coach Ron Wilson stresses containment hockey, effectively using a cast of grinders to neutralize opponents.

Finnish Duck: Teemu Selanne was stunned to be traded to Anaheim last season, but quickly settled into a scoring groove with linemate Kariya.

★ ROLL OF HONOR ★

Conference/Division	Western/Pacific
First NHL Season	1993-94
Honor roll	Share record for most wins (33) by first-year team
Home rink/Capacity	Arrowhead Pond/17,174
Stanley Cups	0

Playing Record

	W	L	T	Pts
Regular Season	84	112	18	186
Playoffs	0	0		

With Disney backing, the Ducks can undoubtedly afford to supplement their player development by trading for high-priced talent such as Selanne when the opportunity arises. But there are no signs that the Pond faithful are getting restless about the way Wilson and Ferreira are building their club.

From a marketing and merchandising standpoint, the Mighty Ducks are among the NHL elite. Their logo—a goalie mask resembling an angry duck—and team colors of purple, jade, silver and white are big sellers well beyond the Magic Kingdom.

An annual FanFair fundraiser held by the Mighty Ducks at Disneyland has raised over $1 million U.S. in three years for disadvantaged children.

"We're in the business of entertainment and we want to always give our fans their money's worth," says Mighty Ducks president Tony Tavares. "While we are always looking for new ways to improve the team on the ice, the same can be said for how we approach our overall entertainment package."

Gretzky's Heir: Many hockey observers believe that the speedy Paul Kariya is the 1990s version of Wayne Gretzky, combining speed, skill and an uncanny ability to anticipate how plays will develop.

BOSTON BRUINS

Bobby Orr and the Big, Bad Bruins are long gone, but Ray Bourque leads a gritty, competitive team.

It is a photograph that still sends shivers of excitement up the spines of the Boston Bruins' loyal supporters. The forever frozen image is of young defenseman Bobby Orr gliding through the air after he was tripped at the goalmouth while in the process of scoring the Stanley Cup-winning goal against St. Louis Blues netminder Glenn Hall.

It was May 10, 1970. The sweetest moment for an NHL franchise that had gone 29 years without a championship and, after another Orr-led triumph in 1972, is still waiting for its next sip from the NHL mug.

Solid past

Not that the Bruins haven't been productive. They have the longest current streak of winning seasons with 29, and Harry Sinden has been around as the coach or general manager for all but two of them.

Prior to the arrival of Sinden and the emergence of Orr—arguably the best defenseman ever, until his knees gave out after ten years in Boston—the Bruins had missed the playoffs for eight straight seasons.

One of the original six NHL teams, the Bruins started play in the 1924-25 season. They had several glittering performers grace their roster over the years—notably tough guy defenseman Eddie Shore, right winger Dit Clapper and center Milt Schmidt. But they had only three Stanley Cups to their credit before Orr, slick center Phil Esposito and (Chief) Johnny Bucyk combined their talents for two Cups in the early 1970s.

Orr was the first NHL defenseman to win the scoring championship, achieving the feat in 1969-70. Esposito won five scoring championships in just over eight seasons with Boston. In 1968-69, he became the first NHL player to compile more than 100 points in a season.

After the two Cup triumphs in the early 1970s, there were plenty of heartbreaks in ensuing years, including the deciding game of the Adams Division final against Montreal in 1979. The Bruins held a one-goal lead until the closing minutes, when Boston, coached by colorful Don Cherry, was penalized for having too many players on the ice. The Canadiens tied the score on the power play and won in overtime. Sinden has forever maintained that the old Montreal Forum was inhabited by ghosts who turned the tide for the Canadiens.

Working ethic

The Bruins continue to be a competitive squad. Nothing flashy but a collection of largely unsung players instilled with a solid work ethic, which is the hallmark of Bruins' teams.

That hasn't changed, even though the club has moved out of dingy

Dollar Bill: The Bruins repatriated Bill Ranford via a trade with Edmonton last season and he figures to be the Bruins' goalie for years to come.

Boston Garden and its bandbox ice surface for the plush Fleet Center, a $160 million U.S. complex with a seating capacity of 17,565.

Again, a defenseman is the team leader. Ray Bourque, a life-long Bruin, has made the NHL all-star team 14 times, the only player in league history named a first- or second-team all-star in each of his full seasons in the NHL.

Center Adam Oates, a gifted playmaker who contributed to Brett Hull's success when the two were with St. Louis, is the Bruins' linchpin offensively, especially with hard-nosed Cam Neely's career threatened by chronic injury.

Right winger Rick Tocchet, whose own body has taken a pounding over the years, fit nicely into the Boston style after Sinden sent disappointing hometowner Kevin Stevens to Los Angeles for Tocchet late in the 1995-96 season.

The Bruins also seem to have solved a migraine by repatriating Bill Ranford as their goaltender. Ranford brings experience and stability to a position that's been a revolving door for more than a decade.

"We're a team that thrives on hard work," said Bourque, who despite his personal success is still seeking his first Stanley Cup.

Passing Grade: Center Adam Oates is one of the slickest playmakers in the NHL.

★ ROLL OF HONOR ★

Conference/Division	**Eastern/Northeast**
First Season	**1924-25**
Honor roll	**29 straight winning seasons**
Home rink/Capacity	**Fleet Center/17,565**
Stanley Cups:	**5 (1929, 1939, 1941, 1970, 1972)**

Playing Record

	W	L	T	Pts
Regular Season	**2280**	**1753**	**697**	**5257**
Playoffs	**228**	**242**		

BUFFALO SABRES

Once-proud Sabres adopt new image, seek new talent as they rebuild to regain their now-faded former glory.

The Buffalo Sabres scored a major coup months before they took to the ice for the first time in the 1970-71 season. Through a stroke of luck—actually the spin of a numbered wheel—the Sabres got the first draft pick ahead of their expansion cousin, the Vancouver Canucks.

George (Punch) Imlach, the wily former Toronto Maple Leafs coach who was the Sabres' first coach and general manager, used the selection to pluck a franchise player from the junior ranks—a rangy, swift-skating magician named Gilbert Perreault. The high-scoring center was an anchor for more than a decade, especially when teamed with youngsters Rick Martin and Rene Robert to form the French Connection line.

Perreault and Martin still rank 1-2 in club history for goals scored, with 512 and 382, respectively.

Best start

No pushover expansion club, the Sabres reached the Stanley Cup final in 1975, only to lose in six games to the Philadelphia Flyers, a series memorable for the fog at the Buffalo Auditorium and the brilliant goaltending of the Flyers' Bernie Parent.

Hardrock: Brad May (right) is a tough winger who can score, the kind of package most NHL general managers drool over.

It was a sobering end to what still ranks as Buffalo's best NHL season. The Sabres had won their first Adams Division title with a team-high 113 points.

Six Sabres topped 30 goals in that watershed season. Besides the French Connection trio, Rick Dudley, Danny Gare and short-handed-goal specialist Don Luce surpassed the milestone. In goal, Roger Crozier, an original Sabre, continued to shine in the twilight of a solid NHL career.

The Sabres have never again got that close to winning a championship, despite the promise of the Scotty Bowman years in the early 1980s, a period which saw the club draft such players as defenseman Phil Housley, forwards Dave Andreychuk and Adam Creighton and goaltender Tom Barrasso.

Bowman, who led the Montreal Canadiens to five Stanley Cups, did become the winningest NHL coach while in Buffalo. He surpassed Dick Irvin's 690 career coaching victories on December 19, 1984.

New venue, new hopes

The Sabres are no longer synonymous with gilt-edged scoring specialists, as was the case in the Perreault era and, more recently, the Alexander Mogilny era. It is a robust, strong-checking team built on solid goaltending—two-time Vezina Trophy winner Dominik Hasek and former Moscow Dynamo standout Andre Trefilov.

Pat LaFontaine, courageously returning to action from career-threatening knee surgery, is the only heralded sharpshooter, although Donald Audette, injured much of last season, is also a factor.

"Missing the playoffs last year was disappointing," said LaFontaine. "But I think we are building the nucleus of a contending club."

There are plenty of Sabres who aren't afraid to flex their muscles. Three players—Brad May, Matthew Barnaby and Rob Ray—accumulated more than 200 penalty minutes in 1995-96.

The Sabres, under sophomore coach Ted Nolan, a member of the Ojibway nation, are moving from the Memorial Auditorium to the Marine Midland Arena, a 19,500-seat facility along the Buffalo waterfront for the 1996-97 season. The cramped, ancient Auditorium had housed the Sabres from their inception.

The Sabres are also changing their image, abandoning their old crest which depicts a stampeding buffalo above crossed sabres. The new logo is the head of a red-eyed buffalo casting an angry, sidelong glance— "a buffalo with an attitude," explain team officials.

Hasek, for one, hopes the fresh approach rubs off.

"We didn't do enough last year," he explained. "I've heard my teammates say that we worked hard. But that wasn't enough."

Buffalo Backstop: Many believe that Dominik Hasek has been the league's best goalie for the last two years.

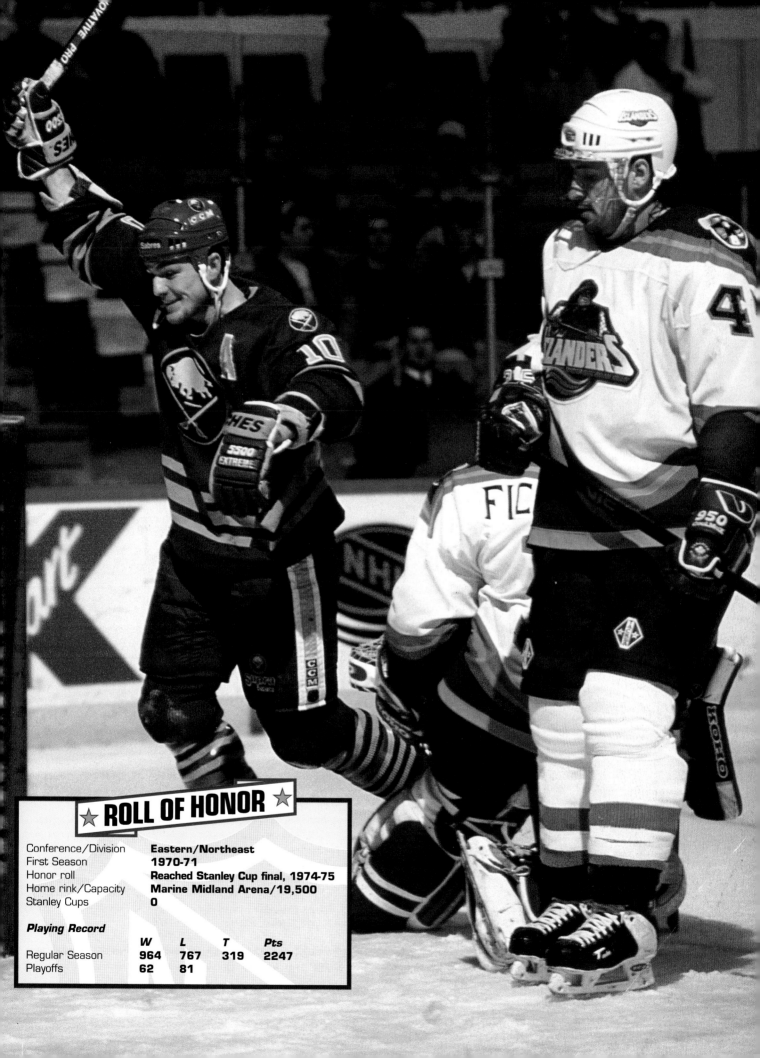

★ ROLL OF HONOR ★

Conference/Division	**Eastern/Northeast**
First Season	**1970-71**
Honor roll	**Reached Stanley Cup final, 1974-75**
Home rink/Capacity	**Marine Midland Arena/19,500**
Stanley Cups	**0**

Playing Record

	W	L	T	Pts
Regular Season	964	767	319	2247
Playoffs	62	81		

CALGARY FLAMES

A lot of history is crammed into the almost quarter-century existence of the Calgary nee-Atlanta Flames. They were the NHL's first venture into the Deep South of the United States, an experiment that lasted seven years after the June 6, 1972 day that Georgia businessman Tom Cousins was granted a franchise.

And what a honeymoon it was, with former Montreal Canadiens star Boom Boom Geoffrion, the French Canadian hockey legend, serving as coach and showman in the early years of the franchise, wooing fans in an accent as sweet as a Georgia peach.

Fans would flock to the 15,000-seat rink known as The Omni to watch Geoffrion direct an ice symphony that included performers such as goaltender Daniel Bouchard and flashy forwards Jacques Richard, Eric Vail and Guy Chouinard.

Goodbye Atlanta

Alas, the novelty soon wore off. Geoffrion was gone by 1975 and so was the franchise five years later, purchased by Vancouver real-estate magnate Nelson Skalbania and transferred to Calgary.

It was a humble beginning in the Flames' new abode, the 7,000-seat Stampede Corral, where the club remained until moving into the 20,000-seat Saddledome in 1983.

The move to Calgary meant changing the team's logo from a fiery 'A' to a flaming 'C'. But things also changed on the ice, where the Flames would win one Stanley Cup, two Conference titles and two best-overall crowns over the next 15 years.

And new heroes emerged. (Badger) Bob Johnson arrived from the University of Wisconsin to coach the Flames in 1982. Two years later, he guided the team to its first-ever 40-victory season, a feat he would surpass in each of the next three seasons.

Johnson, who coined the phrase, "It's a great day for hockey," took the Flames to the Stanley Cup final in 1985-86. Three years later, with wisecracking Terry Crisp at the helm, Calgary won its first Cup, becoming the first visiting team to do so against the Canadiens at the venerable Montreal Forum. Fittingly, it was the final bow for Lanny McDonald, the bushy-lipped co-captain who had come to epitomize the heart and soul of the team.

Rejuvenation

The current Flames are still imbued with plenty of character, starting with feisty 5-foot-6, 160-pound right winger Theoren Fleury, and newcomer Jarome Iginla, a hulking 19-year-old power forward the club hopes will replace left winger Gary Roberts who retired in June 1996.

Roberts had contemplated retirement after missing the last half of the 1994-95 season. But following two neck operations to repair nerve and disc damage in his spine, Roberts returned to the lineup

Comeback Year: Gary Roberts came back after two bouts of surgery on his neck to score 22 goals in 35 games in 1995-96.

on January 10, 1996 and quickly regained his scoring touch.

"You don't really know how good you have it until something has been taken away from you," says Roberts. "I'm rejuvenated. I feel like a kid again."

Rejuvenated would also describe Calgary coach Pierre Page, who admits he allowed the pressure to get to him while he was coach and general manager of the Nordiques. Page seemed like a goner when the Flames won only three of their first 20 games last season, a start that cost general manager Doug Risebrough his job.

Page persevered and implemented a system. Combined with the return of Roberts, the Flames became a force in the regular season. Unfortunately, Roberts reinjured his neck late in the season, missed the playoffs and was forced to retire.

The future is promising, with No. 1 1992 draft pick center Cory Stillman and goaltender Trevor Kidd, a 1990 first-rounder, starting to make an impact.

Big things, too. are expected from Iginla, acquired from the Dallas Stars in a mid-season trade that sent Joe Niemsendyk to Texas.

"I think we were the best team in the NHL in the second half of the schedule last season," says Page. "We accomplished what we set out to do."

Mighty Mite: Theoren Fleury is the league's smallest player but he may well have the biggest heart, also.

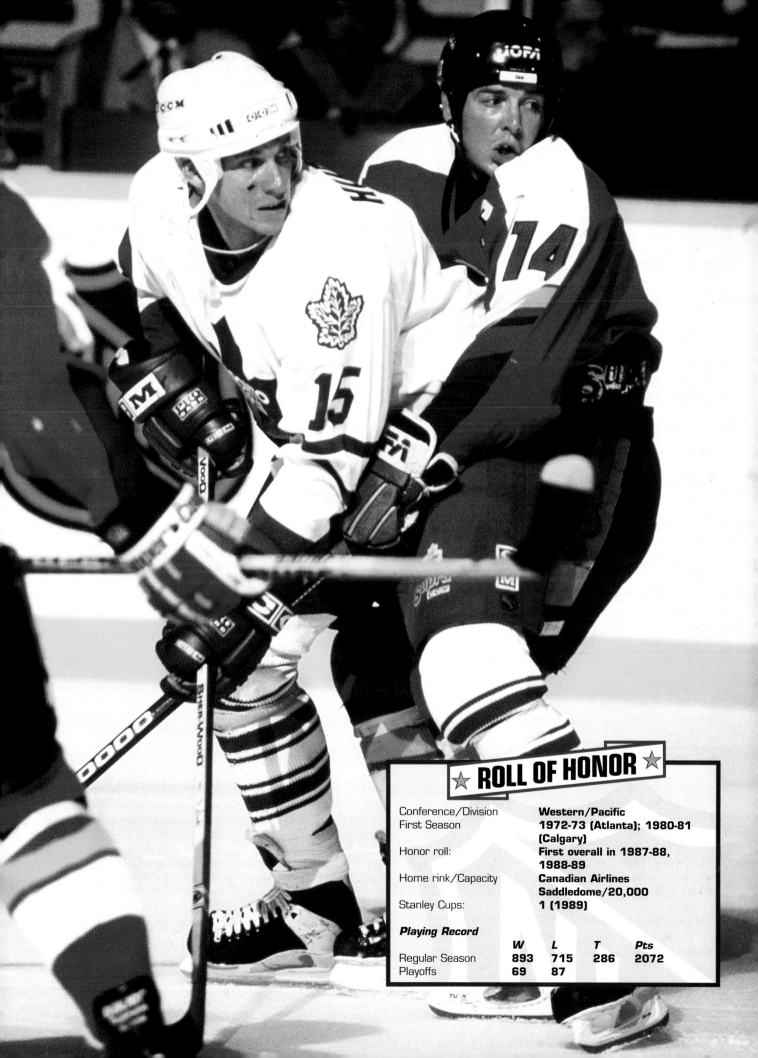

★ ROLL OF HONOR ★

Conference/Division	**Western/Pacific**
First Season	**1972-73 (Atlanta); 1980-81 (Calgary)**
Honor roll:	**First overall in 1987-88, 1988-89**
Home rink/Capacity	**Canadian Airlines Saddledome/20,000**
Stanley Cups:	**1 (1989)**

Playing Record

	W	L	T	Pts
Regular Season	893	715	286	2072
Playoffs	69	87		

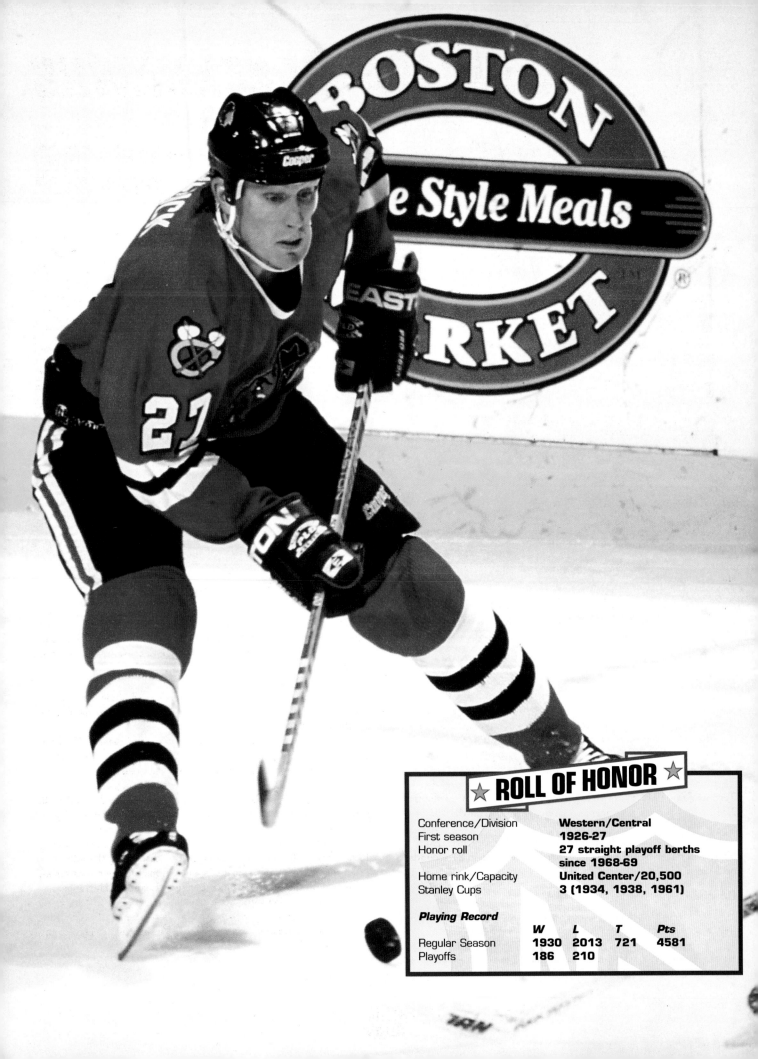

★ ROLL OF HONOR ★

Conference/Division	**Western/Central**
First season	**1926-27**
Honor roll	**27 straight playoff berths since 1968-69**
Home rink/Capacity	**United Center/20,500**
Stanley Cups	**3 (1934, 1938, 1961)**

Playing Record

	W	L	T	Pts
Regular Season	1930	2013	721	4581
Playoffs	186	210		

CHICAGO BLACKHAWKS

Although rarely an NHL champion, the talent-rich Blackhawks remain a legitimate contender in almost every season.

Stanley Cups have been few and far between for the Chicago Blackhawks, who joined the NHL back on September 25, 1926. At the time, their first head coach was a man named Pete Muldoon, who would lose the job after one abysmal season. But he didn't go gently. He is alleged to have placed a curse on the team, saying it would never finish first because it had treated him so ignominiously.

The Muldoon curse lasted 40 years, as Chicago didn't finish first until the 1966-67 season. In Stanley Cup play, the Blackhawks have escaped the curse only three times—they won in 1934, 1938 and 1961. In between, they endured long stretches of finishing out of the playoffs or being toppled in an early post-season round.

Talent vs curse

Yet, it is this franchise which has been blessed with some wonderful talent who, before moving into the spacious United Center in the 1994-95 season, played at Chicago Stadium, a raucous building where crowd noise reached decibel levels that intimidated many a visiting player.

Bobby Hull, the 'Golden Jet' who shellshocked goaltenders with his patented slap shot, was a Blackhawks star when he became the first NHLer to score more than 50 goals in a season, in 1966.

Stan Mikita, the gifted center immortalized not only in the Hockey Hall of Fame but in the movie *Wayne's World*, sparkled for 21 seasons, scoring 541 goals, second to Hull's 604. Both Hull and Mikita are regarded as the unofficial 'inventors' of the curved stick.

Then there was 'Mr. Goalie', Glenn Hall, whose coolness under fire belied a pre-game nervousness that routinely caused him to bring up his supper. Ever the innovator, Hall introduced the butterfly style of goaltending much in vogue today.

After Hall, it was Tony (O) Esposito making some history—his 15 shutouts in 1969-70 are a modern-day single-season record.

And the Blackhawks established some firsts on other fronts. They were the first NHL team to use a chartered flight, flying to Toronto for a 1940 Stanley Cup playoff game. They were the first NHL team to stage an afternoon game, with Detroit the visitor on March 19, 1933.

One of their forwards, Bill Mosienko, holds a record that likely will never be broken—he scored three goals in 21 seconds on March 23, 1952.

Continued challenge

While the Blackhawks no longer have the likes of Hull & Co., they remain a Stanley Cup threat, buoyed by center Jeremy

Hawks' Sniper: Jeremy Roenick averaged 47 goals a season in the early 1990s for Chicago.

Best in the Business: Chris Chelios has won the Norris Trophy as the NHL's best defenseman with both the Montreal Canadiens and Chicago Blackhawks.

Roenick, rookie forward Eric Daze, perennial Norris Trophy candidate Chris Chelios on defense and Vezina Trophy candidate Ed Belfour in goal.

Roenick returned admirably from an injured-marred 1994-95 season to again approach the scoring pace of his four previous seasons with Chicago, when he averaged 47 goals per season.

Chelios, who excels in all phases of the game, plays with a mean streak, which is bad news for opposing forwards who try to jam the net in front of Belfour. With Chelios and veteran Gary Suter the Blackhawks have two top-notch defensemen.

The 6-foot-4, 215-pound Daze, the Hawks' fifth pick in the 1993 entry draft, has blossomed quickly, displaying the talents that produced 206 points in 123 games in his final two seasons as a junior with the Quebec Major League's Beauport Harfangs.

"He's just beginning to adapt to the league," said Chicago coach Craig Hartsburg, a former NHL defenseman in his rookie year as the Blackhawks coach. "I think he's starting to challenge himself more."

★ ROLL OF HONOR ★

Conference/Division	**Western/Pacific**
First Season	**1979-80 (Quebec);**
	1995-96 (Colorado)
Honor roll	**104-point season in 1992-93**
Home rink/Capacity	**McNichols Sports Arena/**
	16,061
Stanley Cups	**1996**

Playing Record

	W	L	T	Pts
Regular Season	505	624	170	1180
Playoffs	51	51		

Financially stable in the Mile High City, the Avalanche rode their eye-popping talent to a first-year Stanley Cup.

This is NHL, Part 2 in Colorado, and the sequel promises to be far better than the original. Unlike 1976-77, when Colorado inherited the mediocre Kansas City Scouts, the Rocky Mountain region enticed the Quebec Nordiques, a rising NHL power whose owners felt they could no longer financially survive without a revenue-generating new rink in Quebec City.

Nordiques president Marcel Aubut and his ownership group sold the franchise to COMSAT, an entertainment company headed by Charlie Lyons, in the summer of 1995. That returned the NHL to Colorado, without a franchise after the Rockies moved and became the New Jersey Devils in 1982.

Recipe for change

The Rockies missed the playoffs every season but one while they were in Colorado. That won't happen to the Avalanche, who brought not only a solid foundation but virtually a completed house when they set up shop in the fall of 1995.

Not that they hadn't encountered several years of frustration in Quebec City, an area with passionate and discerning hockey fans.

One of four World Hockey Association teams absorbed by the NHL in 1979, the Nordiques made the playoffs seven straight years after their initial season. They were always competitive, with strong motivator Michel Bergeron behind the bench, the grit of pesky Dale Hunter and the goal-scoring touch of Peter Stastny and Michel Goulet.

But as their star players aged and key draft picks failed to deliver, lean times arrived for the Nordiques. The club missed the playoffs for five straight seasons. In 1991, No. 1 draft pick Eric Lindros refused to sign with Quebec, setting off a year-long battle that culminated in the Nordiques trading him to both the New York Rangers and Philadelphia Flyers. An arbitrator had to intervene, awarding him to the Flyers.

The trade was seemingly a turning point for the franchise. Among the players Quebec acquired was Swedish forward Peter Forsberg, the league's top rookie in 1994-95 and likely an all-star for years to come.

The Nordiques also used one of the draft picks acquired in the same trade to select goaltender Jocelyn Thibault. Once they were settled in Colorado, the transplanted Nordiques sent Thibault to Montreal for three-time Vezina Trophy winner Patrick Roy.

Lofty aims

The next few seasons should be satisfying for the Avalanche and coach Marc Crawford, who guided his team to a division title in each of his first two years behind the bench. Besides Forsberg, there's a wealth of offense from Joe Sakic, a rejuvenated Valeri Kamensky and hard-working Claude Lemieux.

Quiet Superstar: Joe Sakic quietly, unassumingly accumulates his 100 points every season, like clockwork.

As a player in the Swedish Elite League, Peter Forsberg was known as the best player not in the NHL. Now he's one of the best players in the league.

Curtis Leschyshyn and Sylvain Lefebvre are strong stay-at-home defensemen, while Sandis Ozolinsh, whom general manager Pierre Lacroix acquired from San Jose for Owen Nolan, has helped the power play.

Sakic, who survived the lean years, is a model of consistency. He collected more than 100 points in 1995-96, the fourth time in eight seasons that he's cracked the century mark.

Part of Colorado's success might be attributed to geography. Playing their home games at McNichols Sports Arena, in a city that is a mile above sea level, the club has learned how to handle the rarefied atmosphere. Visiting teams haven't been so quick to adapt.

"I think playing at such a high altitude has a lot to do with our success at home," said Lemieux. "I can see teams coming into our building and really feeling the effects—especially late in the game."

★ ROLL OF HONOR ★

Conference/Division	**Western/Central**
First season	**1967-68 (Minnesota); 1993-94 (Dallas)**
Honor roll	**Reached Stanley Cup final, 1981 and 1991**
Home rink/Capacity	**Reunion Arena/16,924**
Stanley Cups	**0**

Playing Record

	W	L	T	Pts
Regular Season	**843**	**1064**	**369**	**2055**
Playoffs	**86**	**94**		

Star-crossed Stars are regrouping in Dallas after a season rife with injuries and personal tragedy.

The franchise burst on the NHL scene in 1967-68, along with five other expansion brethren. It was the Minnesota North Stars back then but early tragedy would make star-crossed a more appropriate description.

On January 13, 1968, about halfway through the North Stars' inaugural season, a helmetless Bill Masterton struck his head violently on the ice and immediately lost consciousness. He was carried off the ice on a stretcher and died in hospital from brain injuries two days later.

It was the first and, to this day, the only NHL on-ice death. In Masterton's memory the Professional Hockey Writers' Association established an annual award in 1968 to honor a player who exemplifies "perseverance, sportsmanship and dedication to hockey."

While Masterton's work in that first season was largely unsung, that of his teammate Bill Goldsworthy was more noticeable. Goldsworthy blossomed into the North Stars' first big goal-scorer. He was the first player from a post-1967 team to score 250 goals, 48 of which came in the 1973-74 season. Masterton and Goldsworthy, who died in 1996 after a lengthy battle with the AIDS disease, are the only two players in franchise history to have their numbers retired.

First in Texas

On the ice, the North Stars' success seemed to run in ten-year cycles. Buoyed by the scoring of Bobby Smith, Steve Payne and Dino Ciccarelli and the goaltending of Gilles Meloche, coach Glen Sonmor's upstart team reached its first Stanley Cup final in 1981, losing to the powerful New York Islanders.

In 1991, Smith and Neal Broten, a member of the 1981 playoff team, were again contributors as the Bob Gainey-coached squad surprisingly made the final, after finishing in sixteenth place overall in regular-season play. The North Stars fell in the final to the mighty Pittsburgh Penguins.

The North Stars' tremendous playoff run also temporarily revived lagging fan interest in Minneapolis but in 1993 Norm Green, who had become the team owner three years earlier, moved the franchise to Dallas. Dropping the North from their nickname, the Stars were the first NHL club in Texas and the sixth in the United States 'Sun Belt'.

Stoically handling a family tragedy—his wife Cathy's brain cancer that would later claim her life—Bob Gainey guided the freshly transplanted franchise to a 97-point regular-season, best in its history.

Lone Star Star: In Mike Modano, the Dallas Stars have a capstone player; what both the Stars and Modano need is a supporting cast.

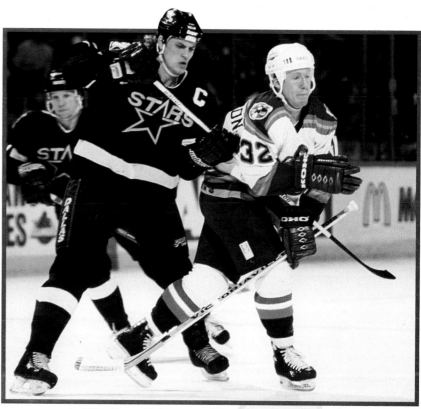

Wheelhorse Defenseman: When Dallas general manager Bob Gainey looks at hulking defenseman, Kevin Hatcher, he must see quite a bit of Larry Robinson, Gainey's Hall of Fame teammate in Montreal.

Promising flashes

Gainey, once described by Russian coach Anatoli Tarasov as the best technical player in the game, remained in the dual role of coach and general manager until last January 8, when he stepped aside as coach in favor of Ken Hitchcock. A successful junior coach, Hitchcock also had a winning record at Kalamazoo, a Stars minor league affiliate.

Despite showing early signs of improvement under Hitchcock, the Stars, who lost both goaltenders Andy Moog and Darcy Wakaluk to injuries at one point, failed to qualify for post-season play. They did, however, see center Mike Modano return to form, scoring 30-plus goals for the fourth time in his seven-year career.

Finnish right winger Jere Lehtinen, a fourth-round choice from the 1992 draft, showed flashes of being a great two-way player, as Gainey was during his career. And the hulking Hatcher brothers—Derian and Kevin—made their 225-pound presence felt on the Dallas defense. "My focus has been to get the excitement and energy back into the hockey club," said Hitchcock. "It's an ongoing process and it's been difficult, but we're starting to see some of the fruits of that."

Detroit is an NHL powerhouse again, much as it was in the first half of the 1950s, when the Red Wings won four Stanley Cups in six years. That was the era of the Production Line of Gordie Howe, Ted Lindsay and Sid Abel, defensive stalwarts Red Kelly and Bob Goldham, icy-veined Terry Sawchuk in goal and Jolly Jack Adams at the managerial helm.

The modern-day Red Wings may not enjoy such dominance but under pizza-company honcho Mike Ilitch, who purchased the stale, struggling NHL franchise in 1982, no one is sarcastically calling them the Dead Things anymore.

Red hot past

The late 1990s Red Wings are an exquisite blend of smooth-skating Russians, with names such as Sergei Fedorov, Igor Larionov and Vyacheslav Kozlov, home-grown products such as Steve Yzerman and Keith Primeau and key trade additions such as defenseman Paul Coffey and forward Dino Ciccarelli.

It's enough to send an old-timer's mind spinning back to the good old days of a franchise that started its NHL existence in 1926 as the Cougars before changing its name to Falcons in 1930 and, finally, Red Wings in 1932, after American industrialist James Norris bought the franchise. He named it Red Wings after the Winged Wheelers, a team he had played for in the Montreal Athletic Association.

The Red Wings carved a winning reputation under Adams and Norris in the 1930s and really found their niche between 1948-55, when they won an NHL-record seven consecutive regular-season titles.

The key number, however, was 9, which belonged to Howe, a shy man from the Canadian prairies who had dynamite in his wrists and—as opponents discovered—his elbows. Until Wayne Gretzky came along a few decades later, Howe was the NHL's leading career goal-scorer with 801, all but 15 of them coming with Detroit.

While Howe was a tough customer, his linemate Lindsay is regarded by many as the toughest of all time, and he had the imprint of countless errant sticks on a scarred face to prove it. Abel, who went on to coach the Red Wings, was the set-up man on the line.

Sawchuk was impenetrable in goal, recording 85 shutouts with Detroit and an NHL record 103 in his career.

Wings to fame

The numbers brought Sawchuk an election to the Hall of Fame, one of 46 people associated with the Red Wings who have earned such an honor. Red Wings head coach Scotty Bowman, who had six Stanley Cup titles—five with Montreal, one with Pittsburgh—before joining the Red Wings in 1993 was elected to the Hall in 1991.

Bowman has coached more games than anyone in NHL history, surpassing Al Arbour's mark of 1,607 last December.

"I thought I was finished coaching for good when I left

First Among Equals: The flashiest player in Detroit's five-man unit is undoubtedly Sergei Fedorov, a two-way superstar.

Buffalo in 1987," said Bowman. "But things change."

Around the same time Bowman reached his milestone, Coffey became the first NHL defenseman to record 1,000 assists.

The durable Coffey is only one cog in a well-oiled winged wheel. The Red Wings are blessed with depth, a factor that is likely to keep them among the NHL elite for several years to come.

Three Wings topped 30 goals last season—Yzerman, Fedorov and Kozlov, while Chris Osgood made strides toward becoming one of the league's top goaltenders, a position that has been troublesome for the Wings in past years.

It all added up to an NHL-record 62 regular-season victories in 1995-96.

Stevie Y: For years the lone bright spot on middling Detroit teams, Yzerman is now an elder statesman on a superb Red Wings club.

⭐ ROLL OF HONOR ⭐

Conference/Division	**Western/Central**
First season	**1926-27 (Cougars); 1930-31 (Falcons); 1932-33 (Red Wings)**
Honor roll	**Seven straight regular-season titles (1948-49 to 1954-55)**
Home rink/Capacity	**Joe Louis Arena/19,275**
Stanley Cups	**7 (1936, 1937, 1943, 1950, 1952, 1954, 1955)**

Playing Record

	W	L	T	Pts
Regular Season	1990	1949	725	4705
Playoffs	180	188		

★ ROLL OF HONOR ★

Conference/Division	**Western/Pacific**
First season	**1979-80**
Honor roll	**5 Cups in first 11 seasons**
Home rink/Capacity	**Edmonton Coliseum/17,111**
Stanley Cups	**5 (1984, 1985, 1987, 1988, 1990)**

Playing Record

	W	L	T	Pts
Regular Season	655	515	168	1478
Playoffs	120	60		

EDMONTON OILERS

They didn't join the NHL until 1979—one of four World Hockey Association franchises to do so—but the Edmonton Oilers surely made up for lost time. In five years, the Oilers built a powerhouse that produced five Stanley Cups in seven years, between 1983-84 and 1989-90. They might have bagged five consecutive Cups but for a twist of fate in the division final of the 1985-86 series.

In the seventh and deciding game against bitter-rival Calgary, a young defenseman named Steve Smith mishandled the puck and inadvertently had it bounce off the leg of Oilers goaltender Grant Fuhr, handing the game-winning goal to the Flames.

If the Oilers had got beyond that series, they would have been heavy favorites to win the Cup, which was surprisingly captured by the Montreal Canadiens that year. Ironically, it was Montreal's record of five Stanley Cups in the late 1950s that the Oilers were trying to match.

Knights of Camelot

What made the Oilers successful? A superb nucleus of players that came of age together and a coach and general manager in Glen Sather who had a green thumb in developing the vast talent on hand.

"In the 1980s it was Camelot," recalls Oilers owner Peter Pocklington. "It was almost surreal. We were always on a roll."

The supporting cast sometimes changed but the main actors did not. There was Wayne Gretzky, arguably the finest player to lace on skates, menacing Mark Messier, crafty Jari Kurri, multi-dimensional Glenn Anderson, the steady Kevin Lowe on defense and the unflappable Grant Fuhr in goal.

After the fourth Stanley Cup in five years in 1988, Pocklington stunned the hockey world by trading Gretzky to the Los Angeles Kings, an August 9 deal that was likened to the Boston Red Sox trading Babe Ruth to the New York Yankees in 1920.

The Gretzky trade brought Pocklington between $12-15 million in cash, along with center Jimmy Carson, forward Martin Gelinas and three first-round draft choices. And while it signalled the impending demise of Camelot, it wasn't the end of the Oilers' spring skate with the Stanley Cup. Messier, Anderson, Kurri, Fuhr and Lowe were around for one last hurrah, in 1989-90.

Young for old

The old gang has subsequently been sold or dealt to other clubs in restructuring moves by Pocklington. But Sather is still a fixture as general manager and, slowly but surely he is restoring the Oilers to respectability.

A shrewd trader, Sather packaged Esa Tikkanen, a remnant from the glory years, to the New Rangers for promising Doug Weight, who has developed into Edmonton's top point-getter. For Bernie Nicholls Sather acquired Zdeno Ciger, who seems poised to become a perennial 30-goal man.

At the draft table, Sather selected rangy center Jason Arnott in 1993. He was an instant fixture in the Oilers' lineup and, after struggling in 1994-95, he now appears ready to deliver on his enormous potential.

The same might be true for Polish-born winger Mariusz Czerkawski, a heralded Boston prospect whom Sather obtained last year when he dealt goaltender Bill Ranford to the Bruins.

Working with a small budget, Sather has built a young squad—the average age is just over 23—that toils tirelessly, often outhustling opponents that take them too lightly.

Edmontonians, who staged an aggressive season-ticket campaign last spring in an effort to quell rumors the team might be moving, are feeling good about their hockey club again.

Oiler on the Rise: After dazzling people in his rookie year, Jason Arnott has struggled to realize his enormous potential.

Carrying his Weight: On the post-dynasty Oilers, Doug Weight is the scoring star.

★ ROLL OF HONOR ★

Conference/Division	**Eastern/Atlantic**
First season	**1993-94**
Honor roll	**Most points (83) by first-year team (1993-94)**
Home rink/Capacity	**Miami Arena/14,703**
Stanley Cups	**0**

Playing Record

	W	L	T	Pts
Regular Season	94	87	33	221
Playoffs	12	9		

FLORIDA PANTHERS

Third-year Panthers have scratched surprised opponents, parlaying brilliant defense and timely scoring into a playoff run.

What could be more fitting than an NHL team owned by Wayne Huizenga of the Blockbuster Video empire hiring a man nicknamed Captain Video as its first head coach?

It seemed like a marriage made in heaven when renowned hockey tactician Roger Neilson got the job in 1993, shortly after the Panthers were granted a franchise, joining Tampa Bay as NHL entries from the Sunshine State.

Regarded as the first NHL coach to use the video as a teaching tool, Neilson implemented the neutral-zone trap and his fledgling charges executed his system almost to perfection. The trap, while boring, is designed to keep play between the two bluelines, smothering any offensive thrusts and slowing down the pace of the game.

Open to success

With a proven goaltender in former New York Ranger John Vanbiesbrouck, the club's first pick in the 1993 expansion draft, the defensive-minded Panthers became the most successful first-year NHL team, collecting 83 points and narrowly missing a spot in the Stanley Cup playoffs.

The Panthers came achingly close to a playoff berth in the lockout-shortened 1994-95 season, adhering to the same smothering style. But Panthers mangement, headed by Bill Torrey, who shaped the New York Islanders' dynasty in the early 1980s, decided a newer, more exciting video was in order. Neilson was replaced by Doug MacLean, a product of the Detroit Red Wings system.

MacLean modified the neutral-zone trap last season, favoring a mix of offense and defense and the combination vaulted the Panthers into the playoffs. A team that had a scarcity of sharpshooters suddenly had a handful—Scott Mellanby, first-round 1993 entry-draft pick Rob Niedermayer and late-season acquisition Ray Sheppard.

Ed Jovanovski, the first selection overall in the 1994 Entry Draft, returned from an early-season broken hand to anchor the Florida defense, something he will be doing for many years to come.

"In the past we've been afraid to open the game up," explained Vanbiesbrouck. "Now that we're opening it up, it's kind of like we're broadening our horizons."

Rat pack

While the broader horizons can be linked to MacLean's approach to the game, it might also have something to do with a rat. Just before the Panthers took to the ice for their home opener last October, a rat scooted toward the team's locker room. Some players jumped out of the way but Mellanby, practicing his slap shot, scored a direct hit on the rat.

Mellanby's straight shooting continued when the game started. He scored two goals which, combined with his one-timer on the rat prompted Vanbiesbrouck to proclaim he had scored a "rat-trick."

The Stopper: Great goaltending from John Vanbiesbrouck helped the Florida Panthers play respectable hockey from Year 1.

Powerful Panther: Big Ed Jovanovski delivers punishing body checks and plays big minutes in Miami.

Ever since, Florida fans throw toy rats onto the ice after Panther goals, which are now more plentiful than the first two years of the team's existence. The panther, or felis coryi, after which the Florida franchise is named, was placed on the United States' first-ever Endangered Species Act in 1973. Amid negotiations for a new arena in Broward County there have been rumblings that the hockey Panthers may indeed be an endangered species in Florida. But a vote by County commissioners to move ahead with a project for a new building appears to have solidified the club's future in the state.

The future also seems bright on the ice. Backed by Vanbiesbrouck's stellar goaltending, and with strong contributions from virtually all team members, the Panthers advanced to the Stanley Cup finals, beating the Philadelphia Flyers and Pittsburgh Penguins along the way, before being stopped by the Colorado Avalanche.

Compuware hockey man Jim Rutherford is slowly but surely building a respectable club out of the sad-sack Whalers.

Life has seldom been easy for the Hartford Whalers since joining the NHL ranks in 1979 as one of the four transplanted former World Hockey Association teams. Two years before they became an NHL member the roof of the Hartford Civic Center collapsed under the weight of ice and snow. An enlarged, repaired building wasn't ready until February, 1980, which meant the Whalers operated out of Springfield for the first half of their inaugural NHL season.

Apathy in Hartford

Later, it was the collapse of the Hartford economy that had a bearing on the Whalers, cutting into attendance and creating a cloud of uncertainty about the future of the franchise in the New England city.

The Whalers' lack of a winning tradition has contributed to fan apathy. The club has finished first in its division only once—in 1986-87—and, that season aside, has never ended higher than fourth place. The Whalers have missed the Stanley Cup playoffs in nine of their 16 seasons and even when they qualified they advanced only once beyond the first round.

Hartford's first NHL season featured the Howe family—the legendary Gordie and sons Mark and Marty—whom the Whalers had signed to a WHA contract two years earlier. Gordie, a 50-year-old grandfather, played in all 80 games in 1979-80, scoring 15 goals and collecting 41 points, inspiring his young teammates to a playoff berth before retiring at the end of the season.

But the player who has most marked the Whalers' history is center Ron Francis. He spent all of the 1980s with the club and remains the leader in most of the franchise's offensive categories. Francis collected 821 points and 264 goals in 714 games as a Whaler.

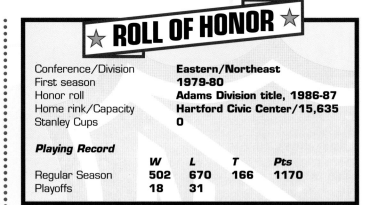

Head Whaler: A prototypical power forward, Brendan Shanahan combines physical toughness with spectacular offensive skill.

Learning to win

Despite finishing under the .500 mark for a seventh consecutive season in 1995-96, the Whalers and their new Compuware ownership group seem poised to turn things around in the near future. The Peter Karmanos-run Compuware group had a successful formula with their youth and junior hockey operations and it is using the same blueprint with the Whalers. General manager Jim Rutherford and head coach Paul Maurice were both members of that Compuware program.

Maurice became the youngest head coach in professional sports when he was named last November, at the age of 28, to replace Paul Holmgren behind the Hartford bench. Highly successful with the Detroit Junior Red Wings, where he compiled an 86-38-8 record in two years, Maurice kept the Whalers in the playoff hunt until the final few weeks.

"I think it's an ideal situation for me," Maurice said, playing down the notion he's too green for the job. "In a lot of ways we have nothing to lose because we don't have the tradition of winning in Hartford, so there's a lot to improve on."

Supported by the rock-solid Sean Burke in goal, the Whalers are making strides toward respectability. They have a pair of top-notch scorers in Brendan Shanahan and Geoff Sanderson, a good playmaker in Andrew Cassels, and center Nelson Emerson, a former 33-goal man in Winnipeg, seems to be undergoing a career rebirth.

"This team needed a vocal leader like Brendan Shanahan," said Burke. "You get a guy of his caliber and it makes everyone else better."

Center Jeff O'Neill, the club's top pick in the 1994 entry draft, is already fitting comfortably into the Whalers' system. That's encouraging, especially since, in a daring move, Rutherford last year traded three future first-round picks to obtain defenseman Glen Wesley from the Boston Bruins.

Rock of Stability: Sean Burke carried most of the goaltending load for Hartford last season, playing 66 games.

LOS ANGELES KINGS

Wayne Gretzky-less Kings are hoping that LA fans will be patient as the California club rebuilds with youth.

They are still Kings without a crown, almost 30 years after Canadian-born entrepreneur Jack Kent Cooke engineered the NHL's West Coast expansion by establishing a franchise in Los Angeles.

The crown almost materialized in 1993, when the Kings imbued their fans with a fever reminiscent of the California gold rush by reaching the Stanley Cup final for the first time. Alas, they fell in five games to the Montreal Canadiens, a setback from which the Kings and their supporters are still reeling.

Mixed ownership

The Kings' cupboard may be bare of Stanley Cups but the franchise has had its share of jewels. One of them was Marcel Dionne, a diminutive but Houdini-like center who was acquired in a trade with Detroit after the 1974-75 season.

Dionne skated his way into the Hall of Fame, scoring 550 of his 731 career goals—third-best in NHL history—as a member of the Kings. Along the way, Dionne inherited Charlie Simmer and Dave Taylor as linemates and the Triple Crown Line, as they were dubbed, were the scourge of the league for several seasons.

They were new heroes to cheer at the Great Western Forum, which by then belonged to Dr. Jerry Buss, who bought the Kings, the Lakers of the National Basketball Association and the sports facility from Cooke in 1979 for a whopping $67.5 million.

The Dionne era ended in 1987, when he was dealt to the New York Rangers. But in true Hollywood fashion another superstar arrived on the set just over a year later. Fellow by the name of Wayne Gretzky. The NHL's marquee player arrived from Edmonton in a blockbuster trade between Oilers owner Peter Pocklington and the Kings' Bruce McNall, a collector of coins and various trinkets who had bought the Kings from Dr. Buss.

While Gretzky revived sagging hockey interest in Los Angeles, the Kings got no closer to their first Stanley Cup triumph until the 1992-93 final against Montreal. They won the first game of the series and led in the second game until Montreal coach Jacques Demers requested a late-game measurement of Marty McSorley's stick. A check by officials showed it was beyond the legal curvature and McSorley was penalized. Montreal tied the score with McSorley in the penalty box, won it in overtime and swept the next three games.

Turning it around

Another stunning development came after the series, when McNall, encountering financial and legal problems, sold the Kings to television executive Joseph Cohen.

In a rebuilding mode in 1995-96, the Kings hired Larry Robinson, a Hall of Famer for his stellar play on the great Montreal Canadiens teams of the 1970s, as the head coach. They also dealt Gretzky to the St. Louis Blues prior to the trade deadline last March, obtaining three prospects and a first-round pick in the 1997 entry draft.

The Kings are already cashing in on the 1995 draft,

Man of the Future: Finnish defenseman Aki-Petteri Berg has the kind of talent teams build winning franchises around.

where they made Finnish defenseman Aki-Petteri Berg the No. 3 selection overall. Under Robinson's tutelage, the 6-foot-3, 205-pound Berg fit nicely into the Kings' lineup last year. He joins veteran Rob Blake, who reminds people of Robinson in his heyday, to give Los Angeles strength at that position.

"I think we're on the right track," says Robinson. "We have a lot of young players who are going to progress well. It's a matter of being patient and learning on the job."

On the Rebound: Injuries have stifled the development of Kings' defenseman Rob Blake, a 20-goal scorer two seasons ago.

★ ROLL OF HONOR ★

Conference/Division   **Western/Pacific**
First season   **1967-68**
Honor roll   **Reached Stanley Cup final**
     1992-93
Home rink/Capacity   **Great Western Forum/16,005**
Stanley Cups   **0**

Playing Record

	W	L	T	Pts
Regular Season	885	1052	339	2109
Playoffs	55	87		

☆ ROLL OF HONOR ☆

Conference/Division	**Eastern/Northeast**
First season	**1917-18**
Honor Roll	**Record for most consecutive Stanley Cup titles (5) Home**
Home rink/Capacity	**Molson Centre/21,361**
Stanley Cups	**24 (1916, 1924, 1930, 1931, 1944, 1946, 1953,1956, 1957, 1958, 1959, 1960, 1965, 1966, 1968, 1969,1971, 1973, 1976, 1977, 1978, 1979, 1986, 1993)**

Playing Record

	W	L	T	Pts
Regular Season	**2579**	**1557**	**754**	**5912**
Playoffs	**376**	**239**		

MONTREAL CANADIENS

The Canadiens hope former players Rejean Houle and Mario Tremblay can entrust the torch to a crop of talented, young players.

Jacques Lemaire wasn't really struck by the Montreal Canadiens' tradition of excellence until former members of the team gathered last spring for ceremonies marking the closing of the venerable Forum.

"I looked around the dressing room and then I realized why we have won so many Stanley Cups," said Lemaire, who is one of 40 Canadiens elected to the Hockey Hall of Fame.

As sports dynasties go, the team with the CH—for Club de Hockey Canadien—on its chest is the creme de la creme, with 24 Stanley Cups. That tops the New York Yankees and their 22 World Series triumphs and beats the Boston Celtics, who have 16 National Basketball Association crowns. It is also 11 more Cups than the Toronto Maple Leafs, who rank No. 2 on the NHL list.

Torch of glory

Little did J. Ambrose O'Brien realize when he founded the team on December 4, 1909 and dressed it in a navy blue uniform that it would gain world-wide renown for its hockey prowess. In fact, O'Brien sold the club to George Kennedy a year later and by 1924, when the $1.5 million Forum was erected, it was the Maroons, rather than the Canadiens who were the darling of Montreal hockey fans.

That started to change in 1926, when the Canadiens became permanent tenants at the Forum and players such as Newsy Lalonde, Aurel Joliat, Joe Malone, Georges Vezina and Howie Morenz became star attractions.

The late 1950s produced an unmatched five consecutive Stanley Cups, as the team responded to an excerpt from the John McRae poem In Flanders Fields—"To you from failing hands we throw the torch. Be Yours to Hold it High"—which has been a fixture in the dressing room since 1952.

No one grabbed the torch with as much gusto as Maurice (Rocket) Richard, the team's career goal-scoring leader with 544, many of them coming after spectacular bursts from inside the blue line, when Richard's smouldering eyes lit up like a pinball machine.

An icon in Quebec, where he was the source of French-Canadian pride, Richard's suspension by NHL president Clarence Campbell for striking a linesman, touched off a riot by fans at the Forum on March 17, 1955.

The string of Stanley Cups started the following year as Jean Beliveau, Dickie Moore, Boom Boom Geoffrion, Doug Harvey, Jacques Plante and Maurice's kid brother Henri led a star-

Leading Man: A native Montrealer, Vincent Damphousse is the on-ice leader for the young, improving Canadiens.

studded cast coached by Toe Blake, who would win eight Cups in 13 seasons behind the bench.

Big changes

With Scotty Bowman at the helm and such performers as Lemaire, Guy Lafleur, Larry Robinson and Ken Dryden, the Canadiens added four straight Stanley Cups between 1975-76 and 1978-79.

The memories and banners from the Stanley Cup years have all been transported from the Forum to the $230 million Cdn. Molson Centre, which the Canadiens opened last March 13. The move capped a tumultuous year, which included the firing of coach Jacques Demers and long-time general manager Serge Savard after the team lost its first five games of the season.

Mario Tremblay and Rejean Houle, members of the great teams of the 1970s, were brought in as coach and general manager respectively.

"When you play for the Montreal Canadiens, expectations are always high," says Tremblay.

The torch has been passed to a new generation which includes center Pierre Turgeon, smooth Saku Koivu of Finland, forward Vincent Damphousse and 21-year-old goaltender Jocelyn Thibault, whose fine play comforted fans outraged by the trading of the popular Patrick Roy. He was dealt early last season after a tiff with Tremblay.

Little Big Man: As a rookie, Saku Koivu scored 20 goals and won a strong following with the Canadiens.

NEW JERSEY DEVILS

EASTERN NHL CONFERENCE

Most people have probably forgotten that the New Jersey Devils were once the Kansas City Scouts. Others may vaguely remember them as the Colorado Rockies, a club that John McMullen and his group purchased in 1982 and moved to the New Jersey Meadowlands.

Some might recall that the Devils were almost as dreadful as the Scouts and Rockies in their early years in New Jersey. In fact, after a 1983 game in which Edmonton routed New Jersey 11-4, Oilers superstar Wayne Gretzky likened the Devils to Mickey Mouse, a comment that Devils supporters have never let Gretzky forget when he visits the Meadowlands.

The long wait

Until 1988, the Rockies-Scouts-Devils had qualified for a playoff berth only once in 13 seasons and had one playoff-game victory—by Colorado in 1977-78. But the first taste of post-season play as the Devils was memorable, both on and off the ice.

The Devils reached the Wales Conference championship

Franchise Defenseman: Scott Stevens anchors a rock-solid defense in New Jersey.

before losing to Boston in seven games. The series was marked by fireworks, ignited by New Jersey coach Jim Schoenfeld who, enraged at referee Don Koharski, confronted the official following the third game, made a reference to his weight and suggested he "have another doughnut." Schoenfeld was suspended, but when the Devils got a restraining order, the officiating crew walked out prior to Game 4 and amateur officials had to fill in.

Despite the presence of exciting young talent such as Kirk Muller, Brendan Shanahan and John MacLean, and the signing of well-regarded Russian defenseman Viacheslav Fetisov and Alexei Kasatonov, the Devils would not reach the conference final again until 1994. That ended in heartbreak, when Stephane Matteau's overtime goal in the seventh game sent the New York Rangers, rather than New Jersey, to the Stanley Cup final.

Strength regained

But the Devils, under coach Jacques Lemaire, part of eight Stanley Cup championships as a player with Montreal, learned from such adversity. In 1994-95, the club embarked on a playoff run in which it lost only four of 20 games, culminating in a four-game sweep of the favored Detroit Red Wings for the first Stanley Cup in the history of the franchise.

Goaltender Martin Brodeur, the Devils' No. 1 pick in the 1990 entry draft, was instrumental in the victory, as was playoff MVP Claude Lemieux, combining pesky play with a deft scoring touch, and defenseman Scott Stevens, a pillar in front of Brodeur. But it was Lemaire's successful implementation of a system that turned the Devils into a winner. Lemaire, who left coaching in Montreal because he wasn't comfortable under the constant scrutiny of fans and the media, stressed a methodical brand of hockey predicated on strong defense and patiently waiting for the opposition to make a mistake.

The Devils ran into numerous potholes in 1995-96 as they attempted to defend the Cup, not the least of which was Lemieux joining the Colorado Avalanche and high-scoring Stephane Richer battling a season-long slump.

The upshot was that the Devils missed the playoffs, the first team since the Montreal Canadiens in 1969-70 to win the Cup one year and miss the playoffs the next.

Strength down the center seems to be in the Devils' future. The club is starting to reap the benefits of previous entry-draft picks, as Petr Sykora, a former sensation in the Czech League, settled in nicely last season and Steve Sullivan showed promise.

Goalie Prodigy: Martin Brodeur has won the Calder Trophy as top rookie and backstopped his team to a Stanley Cup. He's only 24.

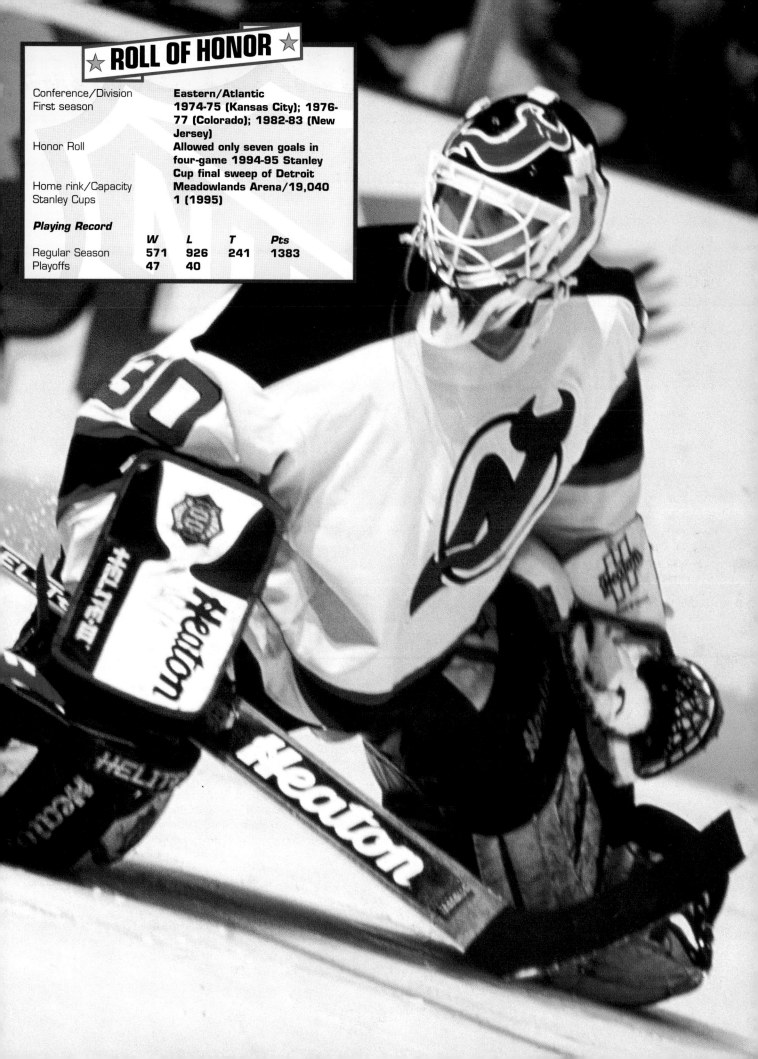

★ ROLL OF HONOR ★

Conference/Division	Eastern/Atlantic
First season	1974-75 (Kansas City); 1976-77 (Colorado); 1982-83 (New Jersey)
Honor Roll	Allowed only seven goals in four-game 1994-95 Stanley Cup final sweep of Detroit
Home rink/Capacity	Meadowlands Arena/19,040
Stanley Cups	1 (1995)

Playing Record

	W	L	T	Pts
Regular Season	571	926	241	1383
Playoffs	47	40		

★ ROLL OF HONOR ★

Conference/Division	**Eastern/Atlantic**
First season	**1972-73**
Honor roll	**Four straight Stanley Cups, 1979-80 to 1982-83**
Home rink/Capacity	**Nassau Veterans Memorial Coliseum/16,297**
Stanley Cups	**4 (1980, 1981, 1982, 1983)**

Playing Record

	W	L	T	Pts
Regular Season	869	757	268	2006
Playoffs	128	90		

Blessed with a cluster of impressive youngsters, the Islanders are a promising work-in-progress.

Just as mighty oaks grow from tiny acorns, Stanley Cup champions spring from blue-chip draft selections. The New York Islanders are a case in point. They had a humble start to their NHL existence as the product of expansion, joining the Atlanta Flames as a new league member that began play in the 1972-73 season.

The Islanders managed only 12 victories and 30 points in their fledgling season but they improved dramatically from then on, as astute general manager Bill Torrey, who'd been an executive with the expansion California Seals, started weaving his magic.

Built to win

Torrey hired Al Arbour as head coach following the 1972-73 season. One week later, he drafted Denis Potvin, a gifted young junior defenseman. At the draft table the following year, Torrey grabbed a bruising forward named Clark Gillies and a shifty center named Bryan Trottier.

The combative Billy Smith, a little-known goaltender that Torrey had selected in the 1972 expansion draft, suddenly became a key component in the building process. In the 1977 draft, Torrey plucked a wiry, high-scoring forward named Mike Bossy from the Quebec Major Junior League and the last building block was virtually in place.

By the 1979-80 season, these five players led an Islanders charge that displaced the Montreal Canadiens as the dominant NHL force. The Canadiens were seeking a fifth straight Cup when the upstart Islanders breezed through four series, including a six-game victory over Philadelphia in the final, for the first of four consecutive Stanley Cup championships.

Following the fourth Stanley Cup, the Islanders were invited to the White House by U.S. President Ronald Reagan, who was handed a hockey stick by Smith with the inscription: "The puck stops here."

The Islanders narrowly missed matching the Canadiens' record five straight Cups. They reached the final in 1983-84, only to lose to the Edmonton Oilers, who were about to replace the Islanders as the NHL's powerhouse.

It was a wonderful run while it lasted. Trottier became new York's all-time points leader with 1,353 and Bossy, forced into premature retirement because of an aching back, topped the goal-scoring list with 573. Fittingly, he was followed, in order, by Trottier, Potvin and Gillies. Smith, meanwhile, had the most career victories (304) among Islanders goaltenders.

Hope renewed

The Islanders have fallen on lean times since the halcyon days of the franchise. They missed the playoffs last year for the second straight season. But under general manager Mike Milbury, there are signs of a brighter future. Slovakian Zigmund Palffy, a second-round choice in the 1991 entry draft, has blossomed into the club's top scorer.

A trade with Toronto that sent Wendell Clark back to the Leafs gave the Islanders an injection of young blood, including that belonging to defenseman Kenny Jonsson, who is about to fulfill the promise that prompted the Leafs to tab him as their No. 1 pick in the 1993 draft.

Johnsson joins Bryan McCabe, another bright prospect, as a fine work-in-progress on the Islanders' defense. McCabe was selected second by the Islanders in the 1993 draft, behind right winger Todd Bertuzzi, whose play has been likened to that of Gillies in the glory years. Bertuzzi has fast become one of the club's cornerstones.

"Both players are a big part of our future," says Milbury, referring to Bertuzzi and McCabe. "Both of them have the ability to become very, very special, and I see that happening. They have unlimited potential."

Scoring Whiz: In Zigmund Palffy, the Islanders have a bona fide NHL sniper.

On the Move: A smooth skater and a gifted offensive player, Kenny Jonsson is one of a cluster of talented young defensemen on the Island.

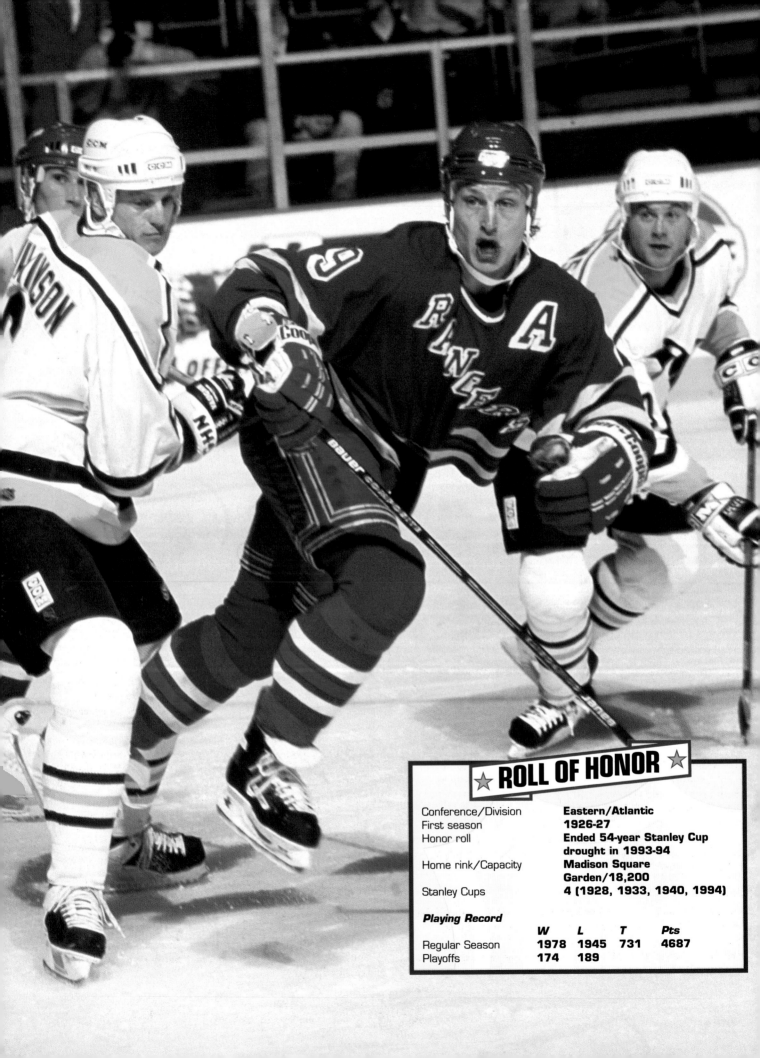

⭐ ROLL OF HONOR ⭐

Conference/Division	**Eastern/Atlantic**
First season	**1926-27**
Honor roll	**Ended 54-year Stanley Cup drought in 1993-94**
Home rink/Capacity	**Madison Square Garden/18,200**
Stanley Cups	**4 (1928, 1933, 1940, 1994)**

Playing Record

	W	L	T	Pts
Regular Season	1978	1945	731	4687
Playoffs	174	189		

NEW YORK RANGERS

One year after joining the NHL in 1926-27, the New York Rangers won their first Stanley Cup. No team since has matched the Rangers for such quick success. But no NHL team has gone without a Stanley Cup for 54 years, as the Rangers did before striking paydirt in 1993-94, finally silencing the chants of the rival fans, who seldom let the Rangers forget their lengthy stretch of futility.

Cup drought

In the early years, Madison Square Garden echoed with exhortations for scoring star Frank Boucher, brothers Bill and Bun Cook and Lester Patrick, the club's first coach and general manager. In the second game of the 1928 Stanley Cup finals, the 44-year-old Patrick was pressed into service as the team's goaltender. He allowed only one goal, the Rangers won in overtime and Patrick was forever etched in the club's history.

Another brother combination—Mac and Alex Shibicky— joined with future Hall of Famer Neil Colville to lead the Rangers to their 1940 Cup triumph. That team included fiery Phil Watson, who would go on to coach the Rangers in the late 1950s, a roster that featured such stalwarts as Andy Bathgate, defenseman Harry Howell and goaltender Lorne (Gump) Worsley.

While the Rangers' Cup drought continued, the club made the playoffs nine straight years, starting in 1966-67. That era was marked by the explosive line of Rod Gilbert, Jean Ratelle and Vic Hadfield. Gilbert and Ratelle remain the team's all-time top goal-scorers with 406 and 336 respectively, while Hadfield was the club's first 50-goal scorer.

The Garden also reverberated with chants of "Eddie! Eddie!" in appreciation for the work of colorful netminder Eddie Giacomin.

The Rangers, with yet another brother duo—Dave and Don Maloney—flirted with a championship in 1979, losing to Montreal in the final. They wouldn't get another chance until 1994, when Stephane Matteau's goal in double overtime against New Jersey sent the Rangers to the final against Vancouver.

The Cup-clinching goal in Game 7 of the final came from Mark Messier, a five-time Cup winner with Edmonton and one of several acquisitions made by Rangers general manager Neil Smith in building his championship squad.

As the Rangers and the city of New York basked in the glow of a long-awaited Stanley Cup triumph, head coach Mike Keenan dropped a bombshell by announcing after the series that he was leaving the Rangers to join the St. Louis Blues. He was replaced by Colin Campbell.

Keeping it up

Smith has been an architectural wizard since taking command of the Rangers in 1989. Twice in his tenure the team has finished first

Little Mess: Rugged and skilful, Adam Graves has learned his NHL lessons well from his mentor, Messier.

New York's Moose: He's regarded as the best leader in all of hockey and Mark Messier has the Stanley Cup rings to prove it.

overall in the regular-season standings. He's been an active trader and signer of free agents. Among his free-agent acquisitions is left winger Adam Graves, whose 52 goals in 1993-94 is a single-season team record, breaking Hadfield's mark. But it is Graves's leadership qualities that have endeared him to fans and teammates alike.

Smith's splashiest free-agent signing came during the off-season when he signed Wayne Gretzky, reuniting him with former Edmonton Oilers teammates Messier, Jeff Beukeboom, and Marty McSorley. Gretzky could well be reunited on a line with sniper Luc Robitaille, his former Los Angeles Kings linemate, but he will not be feathering passes to free agent Pat Verbeek, a 41-goal scorer in 1995-96, who signed with the Dallas Stars during the summer, rather than remain with the Rangers.

Brian Leetch, who is closing in on Ron Greschner's 610-points total as the club's career leader among defensemen, shows no signs of succumbing to the wear and tear of eight hard-hitting NHL seasons.

OTTAWA SENATORS

Under seasoned hockey man Pierre Gauthier the Senators hope their fortunes improve.

The Ottawa Senators are no strangers to the Stanley Cup. Not the modern-day Senators, who joined the NHL in 1992 as an expansion entry along with Tampa Bay, but their predecessors, an original member when the NHL was formed in 1917.

The old Senators won five Stanley Cups prior to the NHL assuming control of the silverware in 1927. They were the first winners of the Cup under the NHL banner and remained a league member until the franchise was transferred to St. Louis in 1934.

It was almost 60 years before the NHL returned to Ottawa. The new Senators have some distance to go before they can begin to approach the success of their ancestors. While 18 victories and 41 points in 1995-96 represent their best season, they were still 50 points from earning their first playoff berth.

The Senators' final victory, however, was over New Jersey, knocking the defending Stanley Cup-champion Devils from the playoffs.

Stormy weather

It was a ray of sunshine for a franchise with plenty of stormy moments in its four-year existence. Mel Bridgman, the club's first general manager was fired immediately after the Senators' maiden season of 24 points—second-lowest in NHL history for a minimum 70-game schedule. The first-year Senators also tied an NHL record with only one road victory.

The abysmal record gave Ottawa the first draft choice in 1993 and the Senators grabbed Quebec Junior League scoring whiz Alexandre Daigle. But another controversy developed when the Senators signed Daigle to a five-year, $12 million deal, with the club gaining exclusive marketing rights to its prospective star. The enormity of the contract for an unproven talent rankled many NHL general managers.

Daigle struggled his first two seasons and was just starting to show flashes of his potential in the 1995-96 season when he broke his arm and missed the last several weeks.

The Daigle contract still dogged the Senators in 1995-96 as 1992 first-round selection Alexei Yashin, the team scoring leader for the previous two seasons, staged a long and bitter holdout in a contract dispute with Ottawa general manager Randy Sexton.

It was three months before a settlement was reached. In the interim, the popular Rick Bowness—Ottawa's head coach from Day One—was fired and key administrative personnel such as former NHL tough guy John Ferguson left the organization in frustration.

Sexton, too, eventually walked the plank, replaced by Pierre Gauthier, a rising executive with the Anaheim Mighty Ducks, whose first move was to sign Yashin to a five-year deal. In late January, after six weeks of assessing a club that had two victories in its previous 36 games, Gauthier dumped interim coach Dave Allison for the seasoned Jacques Martin. Gauthier also swung a

Swedish Sharpshooter: Daniel Alfredsson's multi-talented game helps give Ottawa fans hope for a promising future.

trade that brought goaltender Damien Rhodes from Toronto and promising young defenseman Wade Redden, the No. 2 overall draft pick in 1995, from the New York Islanders.

A new stability

The arrival of Martin and Rhodes, in particular, seem to provide the franchise with some much-needed stability. Rhodes compiled a goals-against average of well under 3.00 on a team that was in the league's lower echelon defensively. "Everybody respects Jacques—everybody has confidence in him," says veteran defenseman Steve Duchesne.

Gilt-edged rookie Daniel Alfredsson, a fifth-round draft pick in 1994, led the team in scoring, joining a rejuvenated Yashin and Radek Bonk, the club's No. 1 pick in 1994, to raise the hopes of Senators' supporters who, at mid-season settled into the franchise's new headquarters, the $217 million Cdn. Coral Centre.

Big Shoulders: The Ottawa Senators are hoping talented center Alexei Yashin can carry their franchise closer towards the playoffs.

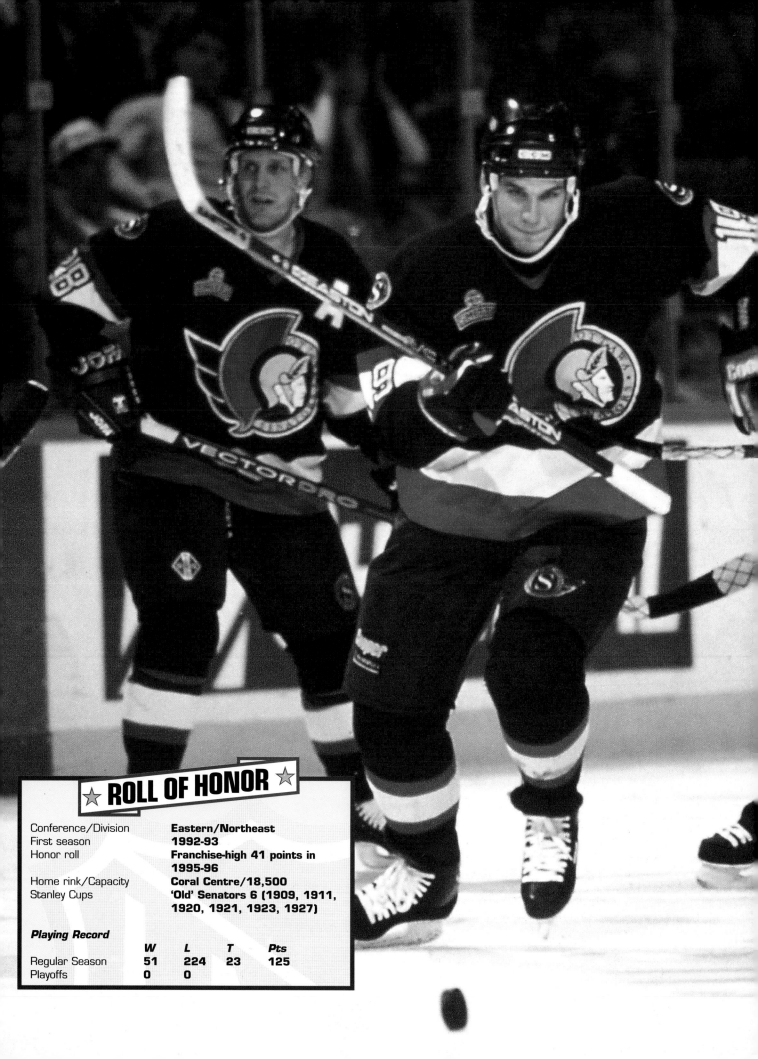

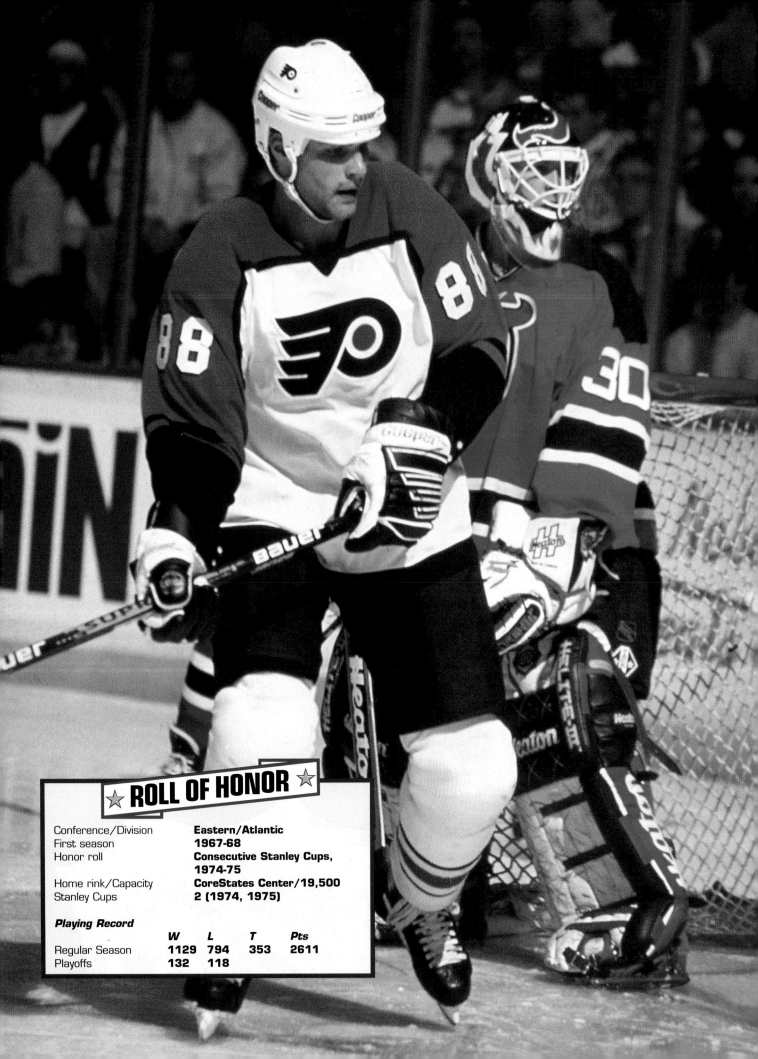

★ ROLL OF HONOR ★

Conference/Division	**Eastern/Atlantic**
First season	**1967-68**
Honor roll	**Consecutive Stanley Cups, 1974-75**
Home rink/Capacity	**CoreStates Center/19,500**
Stanley Cups	**2 (1974, 1975)**

Playing Record

	W	L	T	Pts
Regular Season	1129	794	353	2611
Playoffs	132	118		

PHILADELPHIA FLYERS

Former captain Bob Clarke has restored the Flyers to a place among the NHL's elite organizations.

There's always been something special about the Philadelphia Flyers. The first year they joined the NHL as one of six expansion teams in 1967-68, the roof blew off the Spectrum, forcing the Flyers to play the final month of the regular schedule on the road. Undaunted, the Flyers still went on to finish first in the West Division.

The next year, the Flyers selected a tough, enormously determined teenager from Flin Flon, Manitoba, named Bobby Clarke and he became the heart and soul of the franchise, of which he continues to be a big part as the president and general manager.

The Bullies

Clarke was the team captain at the age of 23. He won the Hart Trophy as the NHL's most valuable player in three of four seasons between 1972-73 and 1975-76. He led the Flyers in scoring eight times in his 15-year career.

While Clarke was the acknowledged leader, the supporting cast was a wonderful complement as Philadelphia became the first expansion team to win the Stanley Cup, doing so in 1973-74 and repeating the exploit the following year. The Flyers were denied a third consecutive championship when the fast-skating, finesse-oriented Montreal Canadiens toppled the budding dynasty in 1976.

Dubbed the Broad Street Bullies, the Flyers of that era were an intimidating force, with Dave (The Hammer) Schultz, Bob (Hound Dog) Kelly and Don Saleski doing plenty of body-thumping. It got no better for opponents when they crossed the Flyers' blueline, where a bruising defense corps of Andre (Moose) Dupont, the Watson brothers—Joe and Jim—and Ed Van Impe dished out more bitter medicine.

But the Flyers, under the coaching of mastermind Fred Shero, were much more than mere brawn. They had a 50-goal man in Rick MacLeish, another in Reggie Leach, who in 1975-76 notched 61 goals, only the second NHLer to reach that mark. And they had the consistent Bill Barber, whose 420 goals in 903 games as a Flyer remains the career best on the club.

In goal, Bernie Parent, traded to Toronto in 1971 and re-acquired from the Leafs two years later, was a fortress. He won the Conn Smythe Trophy as the most valuable performer in the Stanley Cup playoffs in both 1974 and 1975, the only player in NHL history to accomplish the feat.

God bless Kate

And then there was the inspirational force of Kate Smith, whose stirring rendition of God Bless America was played at the Spectrum whenever the Flyers had a must-win game. More often than not, Smith was a good-luck charm—prior to the 1995-96 season, the

Flyers had a 63-15-3 record in games preceded by Smith's recording.

Amid the triumphs, the franchise has also experienced tragedy. Barry Ashbee, one of the Flyers' best defensemen, had his career ended in 1974 after being struck in the eye by a puck. Vezina Trophy winner Pelle Lindbergh was killed in an automobile accident at the height of his goaltending career.

Out of the playoffs for five straight years between 1989-90 and 1993-94, the Flyers are back among the NHL elite. Clarke, who returned to the organization in 1994 after a three-year absence, has seen to that by acquiring Eric Lindros in a trade with Quebec and John LeClair from Montreal. They have joined 1990 draft pick Mikael Renberg to form one of the NHL's most productive—and physical—lines, an asset they will bring to the CoreStates Center, the Flyers' new home as of the 1996-97 season.

Big Man on Campus: Eric Lindros has re-kindled Stanley Cup fever in Philadelphia with his power game.

Legionaire of Doom: Teamed with Lindros and John Leclair, Swedish star Mikael Renberg is an offensive force in Philadelphia.

PHOENIX COYOTES

The Jets left a proud legacy in Winnipeg; the Coyotes hope to build one in Phoenix.

Like the legendary bird of Greek mythology, the Winnipeg Jets will be rising from the ashes to start a new NHL life in 1996-97 as the Phoenix Coyotes. The Jets entered the NHL in 1979, along with three other former World Hockey Association franchises. At the time, Winnipeg was the most successful of the four, having won three straight Avco Cups, the symbol of WHA supremacy.

Winnipeg wasn't nearly as proficient in the NHL. The club managed a pair of second-place finishes in its division and only twice was it able to advance beyond the first round of the Stanley Cup playoffs.

But the Jets were instrumental in the evolution of European players in the NHL and, consequently, they had much to do with shaping the style and substance of the game.

Shifty Coyote: Alexei Zhamnov's skills were often overshadowed with the Winnipeg Jets by his former teammate, Teemu Selanne.

Foreign strength

While Swedish stars Ulf and Kent Nilsson and Anders Hedberg from the WHA years didn't accompany the Jets to the NHL, Europeans such as Willy Lindstrom and Lars-Erik Sjoberg carried the torch. The Jets also had NHL scoring great Bobby Hull for 18 games that first season, before trading him to Hartford.

As the 1980s unfolded, two players emerged as the cornerstones of the franchise. Dale Hawerchuk, a skillful center who was the No. 1 overall pick in the 1981 NHL draft, was the team's leading scorer for the next nine years, a remarkable stretch that helped him become the team's all-time leader in goals (379) and points (929).

Thomas Steen, of Sweden, wasn't a prolific scorer. But he combined toughness, speed and grace for 14 seasons with the Jets, making him the club's longest-serving player. There wasn't a dry eye in the Winnipeg Arena when the Jets retired Steen's No. 25 in a ceremony following the 1995 season.

While Steen and his teammates worked feverishly on the ice, there were equally fervent efforts on the sidelines to save the Jets, long-rumored to be on their way out of Winnipeg because of financial problems.

Following the 1995 season, a movement called Operation Grassroots was launched, seeking pledges of public money to keep the Jets in Winnipeg. Kids emptied their piggy banks, groups held raffles and bake sales, Jets' supporters from as far away as Japan and Australia called with offers of support. In the end, $13.5 million was raised but it was well short of what was required to preserve the Jets.

Reluctantly, Barry Shenkarow, a Winnipeg native who had owned the club since its WHA days, announced the sale of the Jets to BG Hockey Ventures LP, a group headed by Richard Burke and Steven Gluckstern. The NHL governors approved the sale last January and the Coyotes will play at America West Arena in Phoenix.

Jetting to Arizona

The transplanted Jets still have a strong European flavor, despite the trading to Anaheim last mid-season of fan favorite and perennial all-star Teemu Selanne. The deal brought Oleg Tverdovsky, a highly regarded defenseman, and center Chad Kilger who, like Tverdovsky, is a former No. 1 draft pick of the Mighty Ducks.

Center Alexei Zhamnov and forward Igor Korolev provide offensive support for budding superstar Keith Tkachuk, who topped the 50-goal mark in 1995-96, and veteran Craig Janney, who landed in Winnipeg last March for Darren Turcotte, two weeks after he'd been traded to San Jose by St. Louis.

The Coyotes also have the makings of a solid defense corps, with Tverdovsky joined by Deron Quint, Norm Maciver and rugged Dave Manson.

Leader of the Pack: Keith Tkachuk , a 50-goal scorer in 1995-96, is the on-ice leader Coyotes in their first year in Phoenix.

⭐ ROLL OF HONOR ⭐

Conference/Division	**Western/Central**
First season	**1979 (Winnipeg); 1996 (Phoenix)**
Honor roll	**Club record 43 wins and 96 points in 1984-85**
Home rink/Capacity	**America West Arena/17,500**
Stanley Cups	**0**

Playing Record

	W	L	T	Pts
Regular Season	506	660	172	1184
Playoffs	19	43		

PITTSBURGH PENGUINS

Mario Lemieux rescued the Penguins franchise, which has emerged as one of the NHL's best.

One-On-One Dazzler: A swift skater and one of the strongest on his skates in hockey, Jaromir Jagr is probably the best one-on-one player in the NHL.

T he history of the Pittsburgh Penguins did not start on June 9, 1984, the day the club selected Mario Lemieux as the top pick in the NHL entry draft. But there's no doubt the fortunes of the franchise improved dramatically as of that date.

The team still finished out of the playoffs in five of the next six years in the fiercely competitive Patrick Division but the seed was planted. With a little nurturing and a few additives, there was luscious fruit for the franchise in the form of consecutive Stanley Cup triumphs in 1991 and 1992, the first such silverware for an organization that was one of six NHL expansion entries in 1967-68.

Offensive for success

It was a franchise that struggled initially but seemed destined for better times after climbing to second place in 1969-70, a season that featured a 44-point performance by center Michel Briere, one of the brightest prospects on the club. Briere was killed in a car crash following the season and it was some time before the pall lifted.

In the ensuing years, the Penguins became a strong offensive threat, led by the Century Line of Syl Apps Jr., Jean Pronovost and Lowell McDonald. In 1973-74, the trio combined for 107 goals, the second highest-scoring line in the NHL.

Later, there was help from No. 1 draft pick Pierre Larouche and Rick Kehoe, whose 55 goals in 1980-81 was a franchise record until Lemieux came along.

Lemieux started a string of six straight 100-plus-points seasons in 1984-85, the year he was drafted. In 1988-89, his 85 goals were the third-highest in NHL history for a single season.

Gradually, Penguins general manager Craig Patrick assembled a strong supporting cast for Lemieux. Jaromir Jagr, a gifted Czechoslovakian was grabbed in the 1990 entry draft, two-way center Ron Francis was obtained in a trade with Hartford and rangy Larry Murphy was added to the defense corps to clear the goal crease for netminder Tom Barrasso.

Two outstanding hockey minds joined the Penguins for the 1990-91 season—(Badger) Bob Johnson as coach and Scotty Bowman as the director of player development. Together, the former Stanley Cup-winning duo pieced together the puzzle, and the Penguins, out of the playoffs in seven of the previous eight seasons, were suddenly a champion.

Stable strength

Bowman made it two straight Cups when he relieved Johnson as coach at the start of the next season. Johnson died of cancer several weeks later and fans honored his memory in a moving candlelight ceremony at the Civic Arena.

Johnson was a profile in courage and Lemieux emulated him in returning from a back injury and then winning a battle against life-threatening Hodgkin's disease that caused him to sit out the 1994-95 season.

"I thank God for Mario every day," says Pittsburgh coach Ed Johnston, who has a bird's-eye view of Lemieux's awesome skills and the wonderful chemistry between Lemieux and linemate Jagr. The pair routinely account for more than one-third of the Penguins' goal production

Francis, a former winner of the Frank Selke Trophy as the top defensive forward, is equally proficient offensively—he was the third Penguin to surpass the 100-point plateau in 1995-96.

Patrick, an active trader, has moved out older players and replenished the roster with young talent such as defenseman Sergei Zubov and center Petr Nedved, who flourished in 1995-96. Patrick acquired both players from the New York Rangers for Luc Robitaille and Ulf Samuelsson.

Simply the Best: Sublime may be the most appropriate word to describe Mario Lemieux's extraordinary talent.

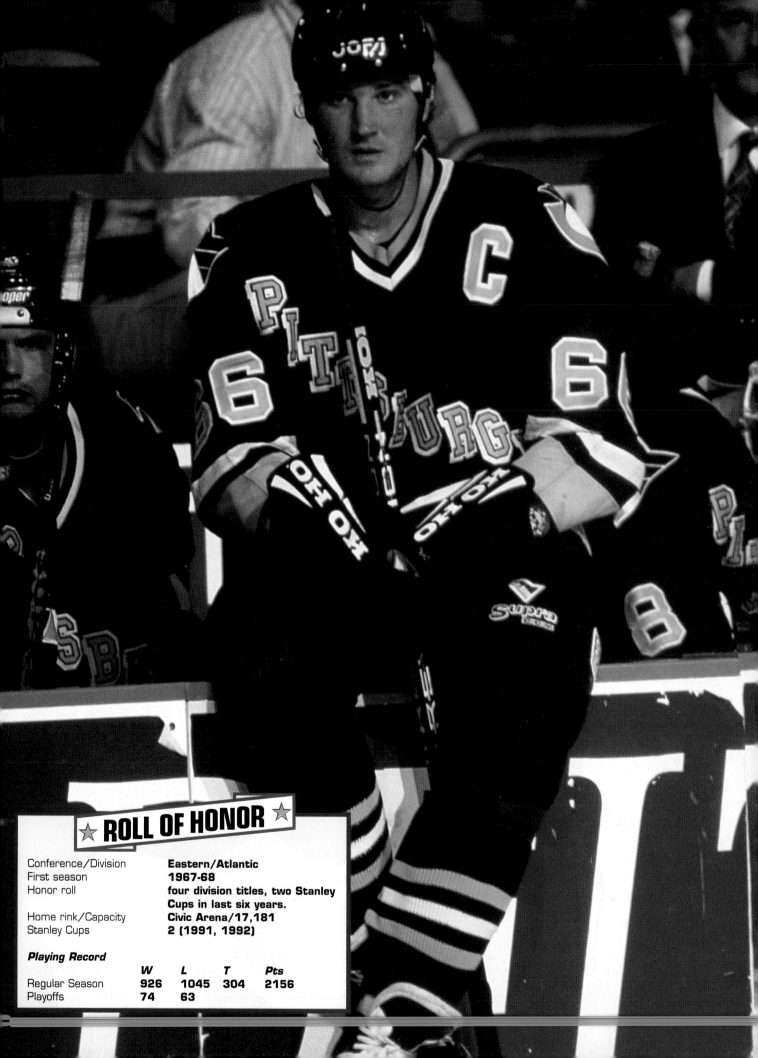

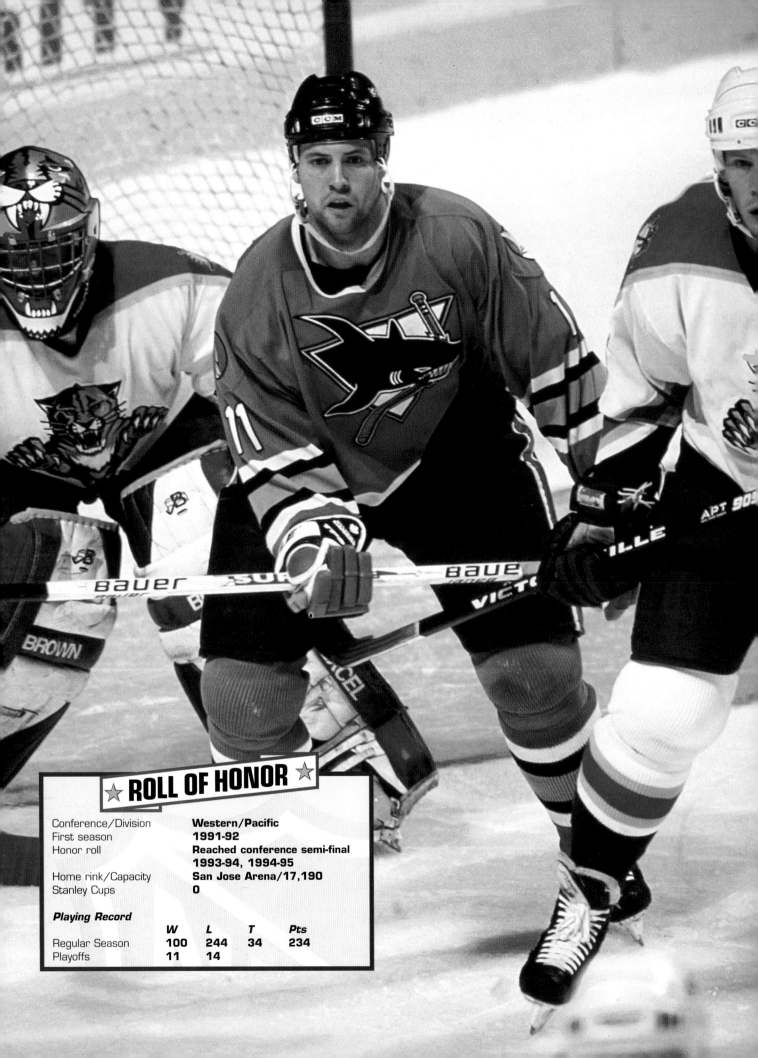

⭐ ROLL OF HONOR ⭐

Conference/Division	Western/Pacific			
First season	1991-92			
Honor roll	Reached conference semi-final 1993-94, 1994-95			
Home rink/Capacity	San Jose Arena/17,190			
Stanley Cups	0			

Playing Record

	W	L	T	Pts
Regular Season	100	244	34	234
Playoffs	11	14		

A young franchise, the Sharks have put the bite on more than one NHL opponent in their short history.

Shortly after George and Gordon Gund sold the Minnesota North Stars in 1990 in return for the rights to an NHL expansion team in San Jose, they needed a nickname for their new club.

A contest was devised and suggestions poured in from as far away as Italy. Popular submissions included Fog, Gold, Icebreakers, Redwoods. But Sharks finally won out and the nickname is fitting for a franchise that has frequently struck without warning and shattered the Stanley Cup aspirations of the old guard.

Killer instinct

Ask the Detroit Red Wings, a strong Cup contender in 1993-94, who were stunningly ripped by the Sharks in the first round, losing in an emotion-charged seventh game. San Jose was in only its third season and had managed only 11 victories in an 84-game schedule the previous year.

But under the tutelage of Kevin Constantine, a former U.S. national team coach, the Sharks improved by a league-record 58 points in the space of one year. They carried the momentum into the playoff round, eventually losing in seven games to Toronto after their upset of Detroit.

The Sharks, whose team colors of Pacific teal, gray, black and white were an instant merchandising hit, pulled another major surprise in 1994-95, eliminating the second-seeded Calgary Flames in seven games in the opening round of the Western Conference playoffs.

San Jose's opponents didn't have to fear a similar fate in last spring's playoffs because the Sharks, in a transition phase, didn't qualify for post-season play. Several of the heroes of the Sharks' previous conquests are gone, including Constantine, who was surprisingly fired at mid-season, a few months after signing a three-year contract extension. He was replaced by Jim Wiley, a coach from the San Jose farm system.

Right winger Pat Falloon, the Sharks' first-ever pick in the entry draft, was packaged to Philadelphia. Rushing defenseman and power-play linchpin Sandis Ozolinsh was dealt to Colorado for tough, high-scoring Owen Nolan. Aging veterans Sergei

Deadly Shark: The Sharks pried Owen Nolan from the Colorado Avalanche last season and he led San Jose in scoring.

Makarov and Igor Larionov were moved out, as was former first-round selection, defenseman Mike Rathje.

Ray Whitney, selected by San Jose just after Falloon in the 1991 draft, remains, as does goaltender Arturs Irbe, although he yielded first-string goaltending duties to Chris Terreri last season.

Sharks' Finns

The Sharks, who own the distinction of being the first NHL team to set up a Web site on the Internet, spent much of the 1995-96 season integrating young talent into the NHL. At the head of that list is Jeff Friesen, the club's No. 1 pick in the 1994 draft who finished among the Sharks' top point-getters.

Marcus Ragnarsson, a 1992 draft choice from Sweden, and former Czechoslovakian League standout Michal Sykora got in full seasons on the San Jose defense and they figure to provide a much-needed boost at the position.

The Sharks are still awaiting the emergence of left winger Viktor Kozlov, whose flashy play with the Russian junior squad and later the Moscow Dynamo prompted San Jose to tab him as its top draft pick in 1993.

European players are likely to figure heavily in the Sharks' future, since they have tabbed that source extensively at the draft table in recent years. At the 1995 entry draft, six of San Jose's 12 selections were from Finland's junior ranks, including No. 1 pick right winger Teemu Riihijarvi.

Sleeping Giant: Injuries and orientation problems have slowed the development of Viktor Kozlov, a gifted and sizeable center from Russia.

ST. LOUIS BLUES

The retooling continues for the Blues as Wayne Gretzky passes through St. Louis on his way to Broadway and the Rangers.

You didn't have to be a music lover to get hooked on the St. Louis Blues in the early years of their existence, which sprang from NHL expansion in 1967-68. The Blues provided every hockey fan with a trip down memory lane, drafting or signing many of the heroes of their youth—Glenn Hall and Jacques Plante in goal, Doug Harvey, Al Arbour and Jean-Guy Talbot on defense, center Phil Goyette and diminutive forward Camille Henry. The first year, the Blues even coaxed former Montreal Canadiens great Dickie Moore and his aching knees out of retirement.

They were the almost-over-the-hill gang, tugging at the heartstrings of fans as much as they pulled at the paraphernalia of opposing skaters.

Sentimental favorites

Teaming up with young snipers such as Red Berenson, Gary Sabourin and Frank St. Marseille, the old-timers were sprightly enough to get the Blues into the Stanley Cup final in each of the club's first three seasons.

In two of the three seasons the Blues won the West Division regular-season title. They were sentimental favorites in each of the Stanley Cup finals but, despite a gritty effort, the Blues were swept two straight years by Montreal and by Boston in 1969-70. Scotty Bowman, launching a Hall-of-Fame coaching career, was behind the Blues' bench for the latter two seasons.

The euphoria of those early years hasn't been matched, but

support for the Blues hasn't diminished, as fans routinely fill the Kiel Center beyond its capacity, cheering on a club that has not won a Stanley Cup but has failed to qualify for the playoffs only three times in its 29-year existence.

The Blues have hit several high notes in that span, especially in the goal-scoring department. In the early years there was Berenson, who tied a modern-day NHL record with six goals in a November 7, 1968 game at Philadelphia. Joe Malone's seven goals for the Quebec Bulldogs in 1920 is the NHL record.

For several years, the trio of Bernie Federko, Brian Sutter and Wayne Babych, along with Doug Gilmour made the Blues a powerful offensive force. On defense, one name—Plager—was synonmous with the Blues, as brothers Bob, Barclay and Bill Plager all wore the jersey with the Bluenote.

Winning dimensions

In 1988, the Blues traded defenseman Rob Ramage and goaltender Rick Wamsley to Calgary for a youngster of rich hockey bloodlines but undetermined potential. The kid—Brett Hull—has become the team's career goal-scoring leader, with just under 500 in eight seasons, including 86 in 1990-91, a single-season output topped only by Wayne Gretzky.

Hull and Gretzky were teammates down the stretch in 1995-96, after the Blues, ever aggressive on the trade market, dealt three prospects and their first-round draft choice in 1997 to the Los Angeles Kings in February for Gretzky, the NHL's all-time leading scoring leader. Despite being sidelined by a back injury shortly after joining the Blues, he crashed the 100-point barrier for the 15th time in his 17-year career. But if he reaches that plateau again, it will be as a member of the New York Rangers, with whom he signed a two-year contract during the off-season.

The Blues made a free-agent signing of their own, bagging winger Joe Murphy, a 22-goal scorer for Chicago in 1995-96. Murphy's 51 points represent precisely half of Gretzky's output. The Blues also are hoping goaltender Grant Fuhr, who set an NHL record by making 76 straight starts in goal, returns from a blown-out knee he suffered in the playoffs against the Toronto Maple Leafs.

The Great One: Wayne Gretzky's portfolio includes a slew of scoring records as well as being the best marketing device the league has ever known.

He Shoots, He Scores: Brett Hull's blazing slap shot and unobtrusive style make him a stealthy sniper.

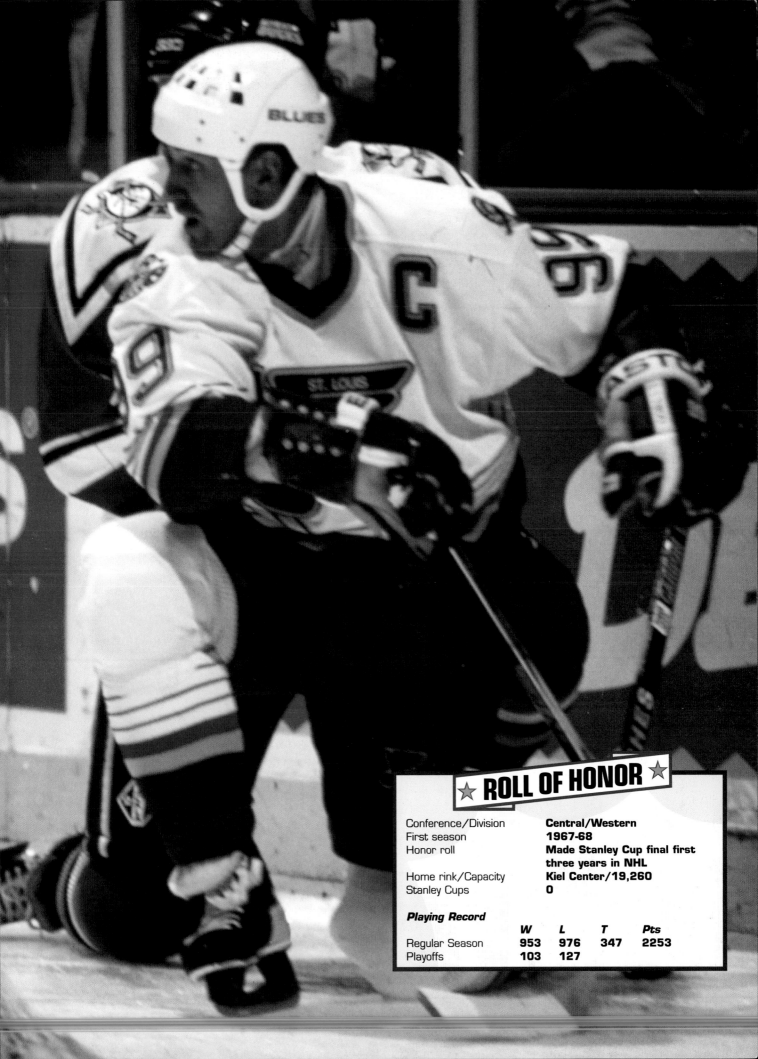

★ ROLL OF HONOR ★

Conference/Division	**Central/Western**
First season	**1967-68**
Honor roll	**Made Stanley Cup final first three years in NHL**
Home rink/Capacity	**Kiel Center/19,260**
Stanley Cups	**0**

Playing Record

	W	L	T	Pts
Regular Season	953	976	347	2253
Playoffs	103	127		

After making the playoffs for the first time in 1995-96, Tampa is looking to build on that first brush with playoff success.

Not many NHL teams can claim to have a faithful following in both North America and Japan. But that's easy for the Tampa Bay Lightning to say. The outcome of the team's games is big news on Florida's West Coast and in the Tokyo office of Takashi Okubo, the Japanese businessman who is the majority owner and chairman of the Lightning, an entry along with the Ottawa Senators when the NHL expanded in 1992-93.

With the Japanese financial backing, the Lightning became the first major professional North American sports franchise to have its majority ownership outside the continent.

Box office records

From day one, Okubo has entrusted hockey matters to the brother duo of Phil and Tony Esposito, both former NHL stars who are respectively the general manager and director of hockey operations for the Lightning. They, in turn, selected the glib Terry Crisp as their head coach and, four years later, he's still in that position, making him the longest-serving current NHL coach.

With Crisp coaxing and cajoling, the Lightning qualified for the Stanley Cup playoffs in 1995-96 for the first time in its history. The club finished eighth in the Eastern Conference and pushed the Philadelphia Flyers to six games before losing their first ever playoff series.

"It's a team of hard workers," said Crisp. "We're capable of accomplishing a lot."

While the four seasons have produced ups and downs in the standings, the Lightning has been a record-setter at the box office. Because it moved in its second season into the ThunderDome, with the largest seating capacity in the league, the team has drawn more than 23,000 fans several times, including an NHL record 27,227 for its 1993-94 home opener against state-rival Florida Panthers.

The Lightning left the Dome after the 1995-96 season and will settle into the new, 19,500-seat Ice Palace in downtown Tampa.

One player who won't be accompanying the Lightning to the new building is goaltender Manon Rheaume. But she remains a part of the club's early history, as the first woman to play one of the four professional major sports in North America. Rheaume was signed by Phil Esposito and invited to training camp in 1992. She made one appearance in an exhibition game, making seven saves in a 20-minute period before joining a Tampa Bay minor league affiliate.

Phil's choices

The first Lightning player to score a goal—23 seconds into the team's first exhibition game—is one of its most consistent performers. Center Brian Bradley has been Tampa Bay's leading scorer in all four seasons, notching more than 20 goals in three of the four seasons.

Peter Klima and Russian forward Alexander Selivanov, both

Future Star: Rugged winger Chris Gratton gives the Lightning size, strength and scoring.

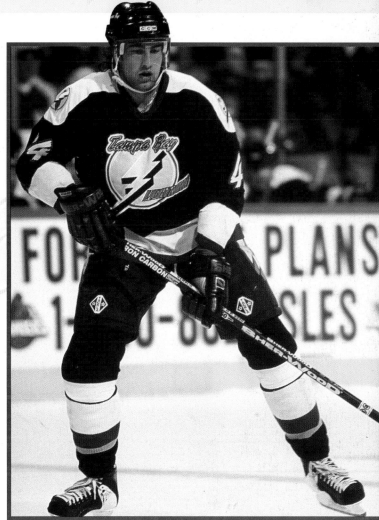

Blueline Stalwart: Defenseman Roman Hamrlik is a budding star and the linchpin of Tampa's defensive corps.

acquired by Esposito for lower-round draft picks, are strong contributors offensively.

Esposito has never been one to remain idle on the trade or free-agent market. Hours after the Lightning participated in the 1992 expansion draft to begin stocking the franchise, Esposito swapped goaltender Frederick Chabot, whom he grabbed from Montreal, for another Canadiens netminder, Jean-Claude Bergeron.

An even better goaltender deal was tabbing Darren Puppa from Florida in the 1993 phase of the expansion draft. Puppa has compiled a sub-3.00 goals-against average for three straight seasons.

Tampa Bay is also reaping the benefits of smart choices in the entry draft of amateur players. Defenseman Roman Hamrlik, the 1992 top pick, is a franchise gem. Center Chris Gratton and left winger Jason Wiemer, No. 1 picks in 1993 and 1994 respectively, are both delivering on their promise.

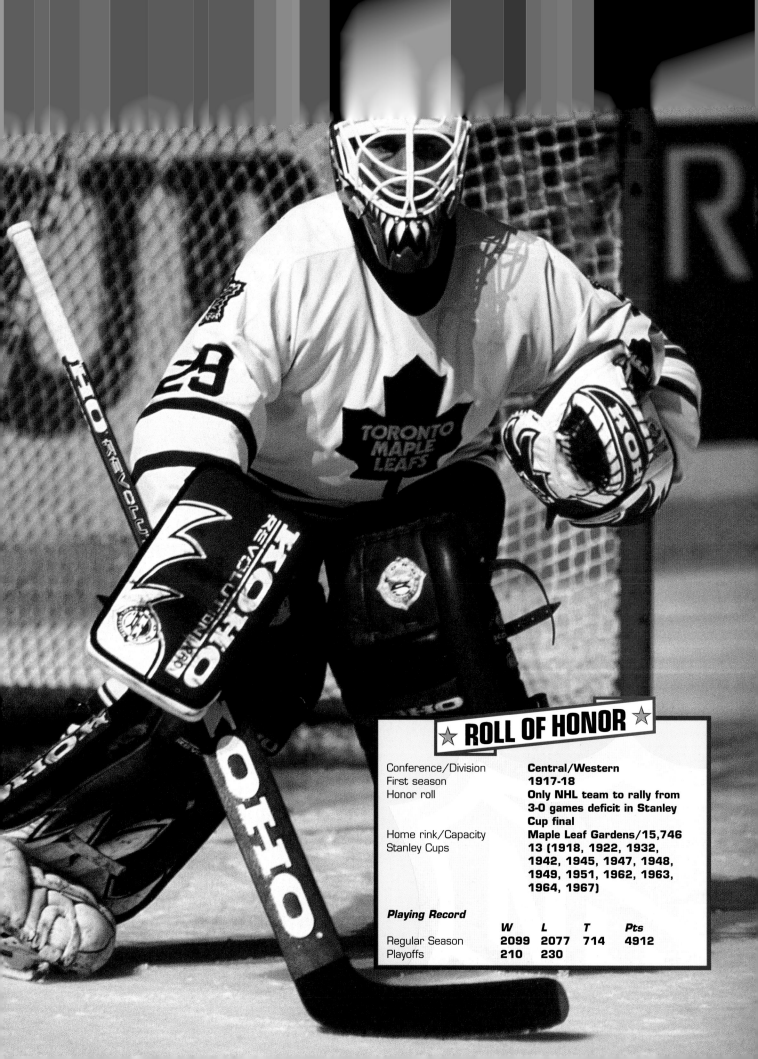

★ ROLL OF HONOR ★

Conference/Division	**Central/Western**
First season	**1917-18**
Honor roll	**Only NHL team to rally from 3-0 games deficit in Stanley Cup final**
Home rink/Capacity	**Maple Leaf Gardens/15,746**
Stanley Cups	**13 (1918, 1922, 1932, 1942, 1945, 1947, 1948, 1949, 1951, 1962, 1963, 1964, 1967)**

Playing Record

	W	L	T	Pts
Regular Season	**2099**	**2077**	**714**	**4912**
Playoffs	**210**	**230**		

TORONTO MAPLE LEAFS

As a legacy of success recedes into history, the Leafs blend young and old to build a winner.

Many of the names are as colorful as the history of the Toronto Maple Leafs: (Happy) Day; (King) Clancy; (Turk) Broda; (Busher) Jackson; (Teeder) Kennedy; (Punch) Imlach; 'The Big M'. Long before the Maple Leaf made its way on to the Canadian flag it was on the chests of the NHL's representative from Toronto, which entered the league in 1927.

So many have sported it with pride. Clancy, for example, was with the organization as a player, coach and executive for 50 years. And well he should have been, since it cost Leafs owner Conn Smythe $30,000 to get him from Ottawa in 1930—$10,000 of which Smythe raised by winning at the horse track.

A string of cups

The Leafs have won 13 Stanley Cups—second to the 24 hoisted by the Montreal Canadiens. No Cup was more satisfying than the one in 1942, when the Leafs became the only NHL club to overcome a 3-0 deficit in games in a Stanley Cup final. The Leafs roared back after Detroit won the first three games.

The Leafs were the first team to win three straight Cups, between 1947-49, with Day behind the bench and Broda, Kennedy, Syl Apps and a new kid named Howie Meeker in starring roles. In Meeker's rookie season of 1947, he scored five goals in one game, still an NHL mark for a rookie.

Toronto also won three consecutive times between 1962-64, a golden era that featured a defense corps of Tim Horton, Bobby Baun, Allan Stanley and Red Kelly, ageless Johnny Bower in goal, with Dave Keon and (Big M) Frank Mahovlich doing the scoring and Eddie (The Entertainer) Shack clearing the track.

In the 1964 Cup triumph, it was Baun's sixth-game overtime goal, scored while he had a broken ankle, that got the Leafs over the hump. Baun was among the graying group that got another sip of champagne in 1967, the last year the Leafs won the Cup.

Between cups

The Cup-less interval has not been without great Leafs performers, notably Darryl Sittler, who on February 7, 1976, scored six goals and added four assists in Toronto's 11-4 rout of Boston. Sittler's 10 points are still a single-game NHL record.

Skilled Swedish defenseman Borje Salming arrived for a 15-year career and became the club's all-time leading scorer at that position. Wendel Clark arrived, combining a brawn-and-scoring brio that pleased both the Maple Leaf Gardens crowd and the Leafs so much that Clark was reacquired by the team in 1995-96, less than two years after he'd been dealt to Quebec.

In obtaining Clark and defenseman Mathieu Schneider from the New York Islanders, the Leafs had to sacrifice blossoming Swedish defenseman Kenny Jonsson.

Nimble as a Cat: Goaltender Felix Potvin led the Maple Leafs to the Stanley Cup semifinals in 1993.

Luxury Swede: Mats Sundin's size, speed and scoring prowess have made him a prized commodity in the NHL.

It was one of several moves made by Leafs general manager Cliff Fletcher, who dismissed four-year head coach Pat Burns in early March after the Leafs were 3-16-3 after the mid-January all-star break. Former Los Angeles Kings GM Nick Beverley replaced Burns.

On paper, the Leafs have a solid lineup, with top-scorer Mats Sundin and veterans such as Clark, Doug Gilmour, Mike Gartner and Kirk Muller contributing. Gartner, in fact, has had an NHL-record 16 seasons of 30 or more goals.

Center Brandon Convery, the club's top pick in the 1992 entry draft, is working his way toward regular NHL status. Smooth Larry Murphy anchors the defense and Felix Potvin is among the NHL's top goaltenders.

Canucks' architect Pat Quinn hopes injuries won't ruin the Bure-Mogilny reunion two years in a row.

King Richard. Steamer Smyl. The Russian Rocket. They are more commonly known as Richard Brodeur, Stan Smyl and Pavel Bure. All three have, at various times, played a lead role in the story of the Vancouver Canucks. But the guy whose name keeps turning up as the franchise torch-bearer is Pat Quinn.

He's an original Canuck, a burly defenseman selected in the 1970 expansion draft, when Vancouver, a new entry that year along with Buffalo, started to stock its franchise. As a player, Quinn left Vancouver after two seasons but he returned as the team's general manager in 1987 and later added coaching duties.

Hiring Quinn in 1987 was a bit costly for the Canucks, since then-NHL president John Ziegler ruled that Quinn and the Canucks had negotiated while Quinn was under contract as the Los Angeles Kings coach. Ziegler temporarily suspended Quinn and issued fines of $310,000 and $130,000 Cdn. to the Canucks and Kings respectively.

Once Quinn returned behind the bench he became the most successful skipper in team history, fashioning a .554 winning percentage between 1992-95. After winning a division title in 1992-93, Vancouver advanced to the Stanley Cup final for only the second time in its history the following year.

The only other time was in 1981-82, when Brodeur and Smyl were instrumental in a stunning upset of Chicago in the Conference championship.

Out of the shadows

The Canucks spent many of their early years in the shadow of the Sabres, their expansion cousin who, on the spin of a carnival wheel, got the first choice in the NHL entry and selected center Gilbert Perreault. That left Vancouver with defenseman Dale Tallon, who would not be quite the impact player as Perreault was in a Hall-of-Fame career with Buffalo.

But Vancouver, with Andre Boudrias leading the team in scoring for the second straight year, won its first Smythe Division title in 1974-75, the same year Buffalo was first in the Adams Division.

The signature phrase of Frank Griffiths, the patriarch of the family who formed and still run the Canucks, was "2 points", the number awarded to a team for each victory. The two points were

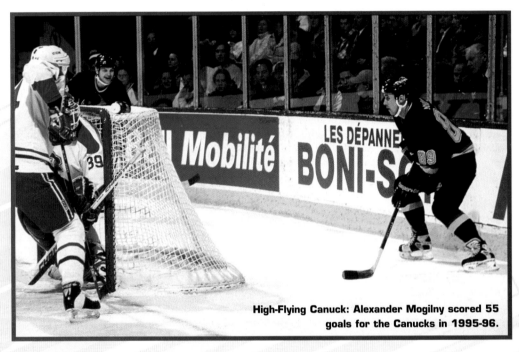

High-Flying Canuck: Alexander Mogilny scored 55 goals for the Canucks in 1995-96.

easier to come by once Quinn arrived as the GM in 1987.

He engineered an aggressive rebuilding plan, starting with the selection of right winger Trevor Linden in the 1988 entry draft and adding another cornerstone—the Soviet League star Bure—in the 1989 draft.

Quinn pulled off another coup at the draft table in 1995, trading Mike Peca, Mike Wilson and his first-round draft pick to Buffalo for Alexander Mogilny, a one-time 76-goal man with the Sabres who was Bure's linemate in the Soviet League.

Tailspin

The reunion hit a snag one month into the 1995-96 season when Bure tore knee ligaments, prematurely ending his season.

Even without Bure, Mogilny topped the 100-point mark but the Canucks, after struggling early and then catching fire for about two months, went into a late-season tailspin. The slump spurred Quinn into reluctantly firing coach Rick Ley and taking the reins himself. "Pat's an excellent teacher," said Linden. "He's a very patient man and he can sometimes get the most out of people."

It was the second time that Quinn had fired and personally replaced a Canucks coach. He took over from Bob McCammon and finished out the 1990-91 season before staying on for the next three years, during which he fashioned the club's winningest coaching record.

Captain Canuck: Veteran center Trevor Linden brings grit and skill to the Vancouver lineup.

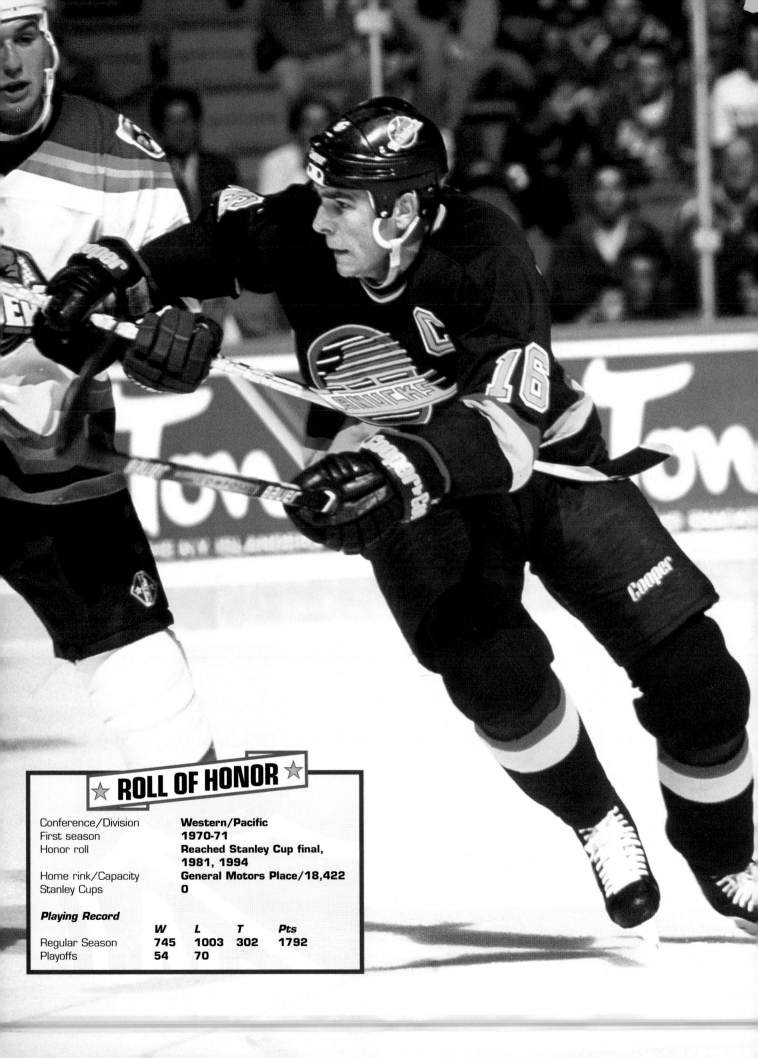

☆ ROLL OF HONOR ☆

Conference/Division	**Western/Pacific**			
First season	**1970-71**			
Honor roll	**Reached Stanley Cup final, 1981, 1994**			
Home rink/Capacity	**General Motors Place/18,422**			
Stanley Cups	**0**			

Playing Record

	W	L	T	Pts
Regular Season	745	1003	302	1792
Playoffs	54	70		

WASHINGTON CAPITALS

Once the prototype for NHL failure, the Capitals have been a consistent winner under David Poile.

The Mask: Goaltender Jim Carey gives the Capitals the championship goaltending they have lacked in recent years.

R ight from the start, the only way was up for the Washington Capitals. It could not have gotten any lower for a team that joined the NHL as an expansion franchise in 1974-75 and proceeded to set all kinds of modern-day league records for futility.

Most of the records are still in the book, more than two decades after the Capitals have become a model of consistency under the regime of general manager David Poile, qualifying for 14 straight Stanley Cup playoff appearances.

But that first year? "It was demoralizing and depressing but you tried not to have a defeatist attitude," remembers Doug Mohns, an NHL veteran who was on that club.

Out of the pit

The 1974-75 Capitals established a record for the fewest points—21—in a 70-game season. Their .131 winning percentage remains the lowest in NHL history. They managed only one victory on the road. In one stretch they lost 17 games in a row, still a record.

The team went through three coaches, allowed an all-time record 446 goals and one of its goaltenders—Michel Belhumeur (which translated from French means good humor) appeared in 35 games and was the winning goaltender in none.

Indeed, the only way was up and climb the Capitals did—incrementally at first as Guy Charron arrived as a bonafide scorer and, finally, beyond the .500 mark and into the playoffs for the first time in 1982-83.

That coincided with the arrival of David Poile, whose father, Bud, was a well-respected NHL player and executive. Fourteen years later, the Capitals have had only one season under .500 and one Patrick Division title, in 1988-89.

Key draft picks such as sparkplugs Mike Gartner, Bobby Carpenter and Ryan Walter joined with defensemen Scott Stevens, Larry Murphy and Rod Langway—the latter pair coming after big trades with Los Angeles and Montreal—to continue Washington's rise from rags to respectability.

Gartner remains the Capitals' career leader in every major offensive category, despite being traded to Minnesota for Dino Ciccarelli and Bob Rouse in 1989. Gartner had nine seasons of 35 or more goals with Washington.

Contending stability

The Capitals also had stability behind the bench through the 1980s, an era that saw Bryan Murray compile a .574 winning percentage before he stepped aside as coach and was replaced on January 15, 1990, by his brother Terry. That move left a Murray in the job until the 1993-94 season, when Jim Schoenfeld was hired.

Two hidden jewels that Poile plucked from recent entry drafts are playing big roles in maintaining the club's contending status.

Goaltender Jim Carey, grabbed out of collegiate hockey in Wisconsin in the second round of the 1992 draft, followed up a team-record 2.13 goals-against average in 1994-95 with a league-high nine shutouts last season.

Unsung Peter Bondra, a native of Luck, Ukraine and the 156th player taken in the 1990 draft, topped 50 goals in 1995-96, after his 34 goals in the strike-shortened previous season led the NHL. "He has a hunger to score goals," says Schoenfeld of Bondra. "He is an exciting player who brings people to the edge of their seats."

Bondra has developed a special chemistry with veteran Michal Pivonka, another Capitals draft pick who is on the team's top line. Along with play-maker Joe Juneau they give the Capitals plenty of soul to go with the heart of Dale Hunter, who exemplifies the team's strong work ethic.

Capital Gain: Peter Bondra had his best season in his fine, young career in 1995-96, scoring 52 goals

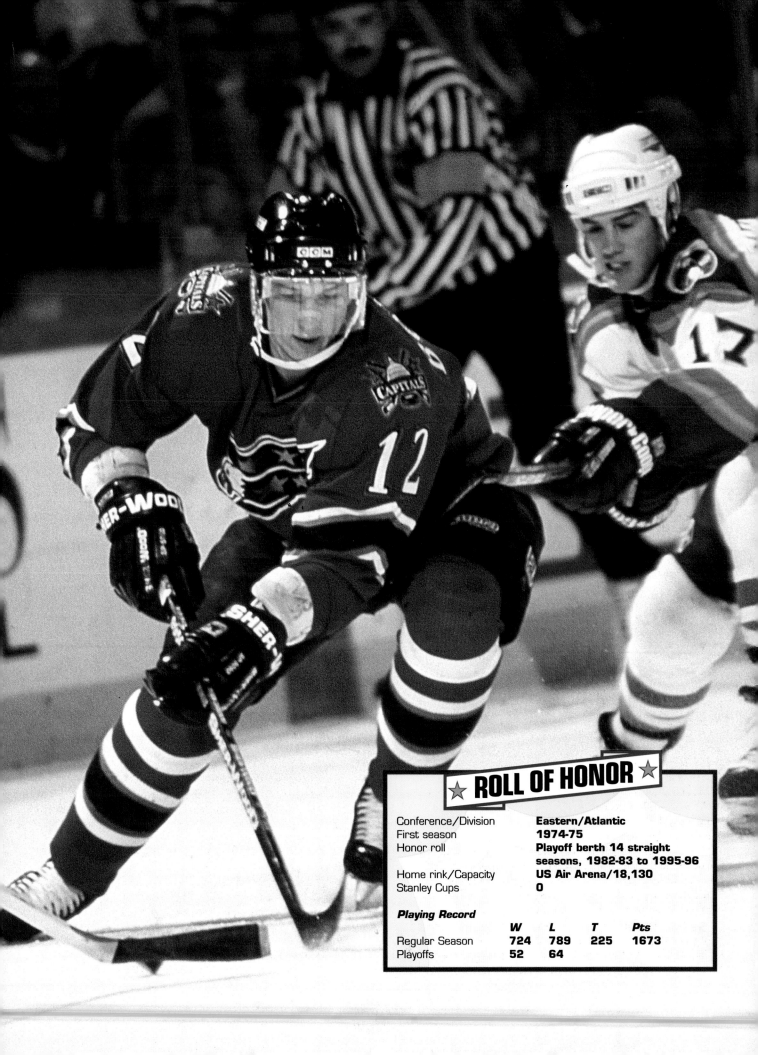

☆ ROLL OF HONOR ☆

Conference/Division	**Eastern/Atlantic**
First season	**1974-75**
Honor roll	**Playoff berth 14 straight seasons, 1982-83 to 1995-96**
Home rink/Capacity	**US Air Arena/18,130**
Stanley Cups	**0**

Playing Record

	W	L	T	Pts
Regular Season	724	789	225	1673
Playoffs	52	64		

HOCKEY HEROES

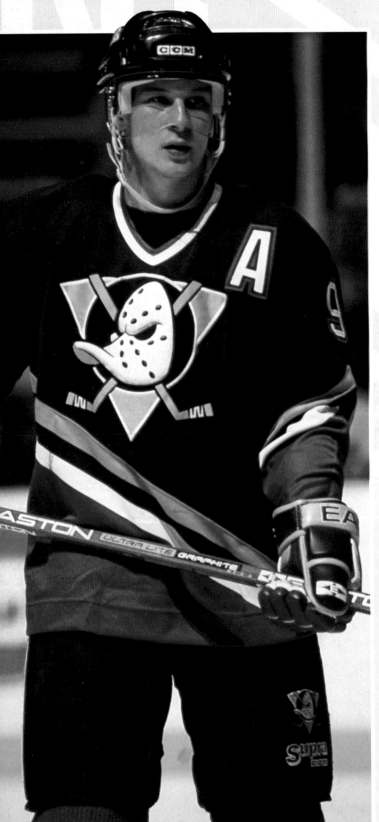

It's a truism in professional team sports that collective play wins championships. It's no less true that fans come out to watch the stars of the game, to marvel at their virtuosity, as much as to root for a winner.

Across its 79-year history the National Hockey League has produced and continues to produce as richly varied a cast of sporting legends as any professional league in the world.

Each generation of fans, it turns out, has its Golden Age; each new wave of player talent leaves behind indelible memories of sporting brilliance that resonate forever in the collective imagination.

Some of the memories are passed down, like the legend of One-Eyed Frank McGee, who once scored 14 goals—eight of them consecutively—in a Stanley Cup game, a 23-2 drubbing of Dawson City by the Ottawa Silver Seven. McGee's nickname was no joke—he lost an eye when he was struck there by the butt end of a hockey stick.

Keen hockey fans, even the young ones, know of Frank Nighbor, who perfected the poke check, of Fred (Cyclone) Taylor, said to have scored a key Stanley Cup goal while skating full speed backwards, of Joe Malone, who once scored 44 goals in a 20-game season.

They certainly know the story of Lester Patrick, the coach of the New York Rangers, who in a 1928 Stanley Cup game, shed his jacket, shirt and tie and put on the goalie pads, and replaced the injured Lorne Chabot. The Rangers won the game and, later, the Cup.

Patrick was surely one of many stars of his era. The NHL of the 1920s and 1930s boasted names like Syl Apps, Ace Bailey, King Clancy, Clint Benedict, the first goalie to wear a mask, and Howie Morenz, known as the Stratford Streak, and the most electrifying player of his time.

What's my line?

The 1930s, 1940s and 1950s were famous for the marvelous forward lines that made hockey magic. The Toronto Maple Leafs had the Kid Line, with Gentleman Joe Primeau flanked by Harvey (Busher) Jackson and Charlie Conacher. The Boston Bruins featured the Kraut Line—Milt Schmidt, Bobby Bauer and Woody Dumart.

The Montreal Canadiens delivered the Punch Line, with 'Elegant' Elmer Lach centering for Maurice (Rocket) Richard and Hector (Toe) Blake, The Old Lamplighter. Richard was the first to score 50 goals in 50 games, the first to reach 500 goals.

And Detroit, the automobile center of America, assembled the Production Line, with Sid Abel centering for Gordie Howe and Terrible Ted Lindsay, as tough and mean a player as he was skilled.

Stars like Rocket Richard, Henri (Pocket Rocket) Richard, Jean Beliveau, Jacques Plante, Doug Harvey, Dickie Moore and Bernard (Boom Boom) Geoffrion took the Montreal Canadiens

Anaheim's Paul Kariya. A star in the making? And his best is yet to come.

Detroit's five-man Russian Unit - Fedorov, Larionov, Kozlov, Fetisov and Konstantiov - a feature of the 1990's NHL international galaxy of stars

to the Stanley Cup finals for ten straight years in the 1950s. They won six Cups, including a record five in a row.

In the early 1960s, goaltender Glenn Hall, defenseman Pierre Pilotte, and fowards Stan Mikita and Bobby Hull, The Golden Jet, made the Chicago Blackhawks a feared opponent.

Stars on ice

The Toronto Maple Leafs, blending the talents of aging stars such as Bob Baun, Tim Horton and Johnny Bower with the emerging brilliance of Frank (The Big M) Mahovlich and Davey Keon, won three straight Stanley Cups.

Sublime individual feats remained a constant as the NHL expanded, first from six to 12 teams in 1968, then to 14 and 18, on up to its current 26-team membership.

Guy Lafleur's six straight 50-goal, 100-point seasons with the Montreal Canadiens in the 1970s; Mike Bossy saying he would match Richard's 50 goals in 50 games, then going out and doing it in 1981; Denis Potvin breaking the legendary

Bobby Orr's goal-scoring and points records. The stars, indeed, keep on coming.

In the 1980s, sprightly Wayne Gretzky kept coming and coming, like a bad dream, his opponents thought. Here was Gretzky, scoring 92 goals, bagging 212 points, both records in 1982, winning the scoring championship by 65-point margin. There was Greztky, winning seven straight scoring titles, breaking the all-time scoring marks of Gordie Howe, leading the Edmonton Oilers to four Stanley Cups in five years.

And suddenly, The Great One had a rival—Mario Lemieux, The Magnificent One, who scored 85 goals and added 114 assists for 199 points in 1989.

As the NHL entered the 1990s, the league's galaxy of stars had become truly international, with names like Jaromir Jagr, Sergei Fedorov, Pavel Bure, Alexander Mogilny, Peter Forsberg and Teemu Selanne taking their place in the pantheon.

As spectacular as the NHL's stars have been for close to 80 years, the best, it seems reasonable to suggest, is yet to come.

Hard work, practice and quick wits gave Bossy the scorer's edge.

MIKE BOSSY

You've heard of the scorer's touch? Mike Bossy personified it. Bossy's feel for a hockey stick was so precise that he'd send the sticks he ordered back to the manufacturer if they were a fraction of an ounce heavier than they should have been. Bossy could determine this merely by hefting the sticks.

When a stick met Bossy's exacting specifications, there was little he could not accomplish with one.

Bossy tore up the Quebec Major Junior Hockey League with the Laval Titan, but many critics dismissed him as a gunner with no grasp of defense at all.

His defensive shortcomings mattered little to the New York Islanders, who were assembling a championship team around defenseman Denis Potvin. In Bossy's rookie NHL season, he scored 53 goals and had 91 points. The following season he set a record for right wingers with 69 goals.

With offensive talent like that, Bossy could learn defense on the job, the Islanders figured.

Practice makes perfect

A swift skater, who knew how to find the gaps in the defense, he often accelerated into a defensive seam just as he received a pass from center Bryan Trottier. With his quick release and pinpoint accuracy, a step on an opponent was all he needed.

He scored in bunches, too. In ten seasons with the Islanders, Bossy scored three or more goals in a game 39 times (30 three-goal games, nine four-goal games), second in league history behind Wayne Gretzky.

He scored 50 or more goals in a season nine times, an NHL record. In five of those seasons, he scored 60 goals or more.

"Mike's asset is that he never waits," former NHL goaltender Dan Bouchard once said. "And he hits the net with 95 per cent of his shots."

Bossy practiced hard at his craft.

"When I shoot, I don't try to think of what I'm doing," Bossy would say. But hours and hours of muscle memory went into his deadly shot.

Jackpot

Bossy was not a diffident shooting star. For about a month before the 1980-81 season, Bossy spoke openly about gunning for Maurice (Rocket) Richard's record of scoring 50 goals in 50 games, a feat that had not been duplicated. Bossy did it with one minute 29 seconds to spare in a game against the Quebec Nordiques (now Colorado Avalanche) on Jan 24, 1981, when he beat goaltender Ron Grahame from the left faceoff circle for the record-tying goal.

Bossy scored 573 goals in ten seasons, averaging a shade under 60 goals a season. He should have been in his prime when he retired, but chronic back pain forced him from the game.

CAREER RECORD

Personal

Birthplace/Date	Montreal, Quebec/1-22-57
Height/Weight	6-0/185

Awards

Calder Memorial Trophy	1978
Lady Byng Trophy	1983-84, 1986
Conn Smythe Trophy	1982
First All-Star Team	1981-84, 1986
Hall of Fame Inductee	1991

NHL Career — 10 seasons New York Islanders

NHL Record

	Games	Goals	Assists	Points	PIM
Regular Season	752	573	553	1126	210
Playoffs	129	85	75	160	38

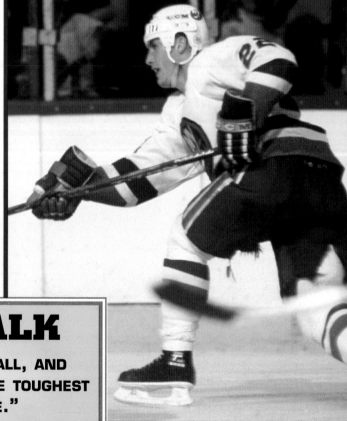

Fast Hands: One of the keys to Mike Bossy's success was his lightning-quick release.

ICE TALK

"I FACED THEM ALL, AND MIKE'S SHOT IS THE TOUGHEST TO HANDLE."

BILLY SMITH, FORMER ISLANDERS GOALTENDER

His skill has led
talent-thin Boston to
the Stanley Cup finals.

The Bruins' Workhorse
RAY BOURQUE

Bobby Orr was the ultimate Bruin of the late 1960s and 70s, and Ray Bourque has been Mr Bruin in the 1980s and 90s. Like Orr, Bourque is a defenseman with sublime offensive skills, capable of changing the tempo of a game on his own. Like Orr, Bourque arrived in the NHL as an elite player who made an immediate impact.

ICE TALK

*"THERE'S NO WAY I'LL
LET PEOPLE DOWN BY
NOT GIVING EVERYTHING
I'VE GOT OR NOT
SHOWING UP AND
PLAYING HARD.
I FEEL EVERYONE
SHOULD FEEL THAT WAY.
THAT'S JUST MY
MAKEUP."*

RAY BOURQUE

Bruins' Big Shooter: A perennial All-Star, Bourque thrilled Boston fans at the 1996 game when he scored the winning goal.

A prod to success

In 1995-96, on a Bruins team bothered by injuries to stars like Cam Neely and others, and struggling under a rookie coach, Bourque found himself speaking up in the dressing room more than he normally wants to. Fearful of hurting the feelings of his teammates, Bourque had to force himself to prod the Bruins to perform better.

"It's not something that was easy for me to do," Bourque says. "I had to grow into that role off the ice. On the ice, it's (leading by example) always been easy."

The prodding obviously helped. In danger of missing the playoffs, the Bruins lost just six of their final 19 games to qualify for the Stanley Cup tournament for the 29th straight season.

Bourque, 35, walked his prodding talk too, posting his ninth 20-goal season and leading all NHL defensemen in scoring with 80 points).

Since Bourque joined the Bruins, they have twice advanced to the Stanley Cup finals and twice made it to the Eastern Conference finals (semifinals). His 139 points, including 33 goals, in 157 playoff games through 1994-95, demonstrate that his level of play doesn't diminish any in the post-season. the absence of a Stanley Cup championship on his impossibly packed resume is hardly through any fault of his own.

In his rookie season, Bourque scored 17 goals and added 48 goals for 65 points, a National Hockey League record (since broken) for points by a rookie defenseman.

Not surprisingly, Bourque was named rookie-of-the-year in the NHL and was named a first-team NHL all-star, establishing a nearly annual NHL tradition. He has been the best defenseman of his era, winning the James Norris Trophy five times in his career.

Boston centerpiece

In an era of unprecedented player movement—Wayne Gretzky has played for three NHL teams—Bourque has been a fixture in Boston, where he has been the centerpiece player for 17 seasons. He's also been a workhorse on talent-thin Bruins teams that win through the brilliance of Bourque and a handful of others, and the relentless hard work of the supporting cast. None works harder than Bourque, though. He routinely plays 25-30 minutes a game.

Bourque has scored more than 20 goals in a season nine times, including a 31-goal performance in 1983-84, when he totaled 96 points, the most in his career. He also posted a plus-minus record that season of plus 51. That means Bourque was on the ice for 51 more goals by his own team at even strength than the Bruins' opponents scored, a barometer of his effectiveness at both ends of the ice.

A quiet leader who prefers to let his on-ice performance speak for itself, Bourque was named co-captain (with Rick Middleton) of the Bruins at the beginning of the 1985-86 season. He has been the lone captain there since 1988.

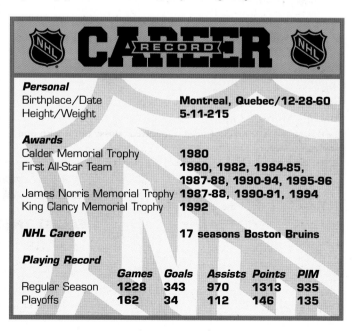

CAREER RECORD

Personal				
Birthplace/Date	Montreal, Quebec/12-28-60			
Height/Weight	5-11-215			

Awards				
Calder Memorial Trophy	1980			
First All-Star Team	1980, 1982, 1984-85, 1987-88, 1990-94, 1995-96			
James Norris Memorial Trophy	1987-88, 1990-91, 1994			
King Clancy Memorial Trophy	1992			

NHL Career   **17 seasons Boston Bruins**

Playing Record

	Games	Goals	Assists	Points	PIM
Regular Season	1228	343	970	1313	935
Playoffs	162	34	112	146	135

From minor-league goalie to NHL-best claimant in just two years—that's brilliance.

MARTIN BRODEUR

F ate helped goaltender Martin Brodeur get a skate in the door as the No. 1 goaltender with the New Jersey Devils, but his stellar play and nothing but has kept him there.

Circus Save: Brodeur's spectacular goaltending carried the Devils to the 1995 Stanley Cup. At 24, his best years are ahead of him.

The year before Brodeur emerged as one of the best young goalies in the National Hockey League, the Devils' goaltending combination consisted of Chris Terreri and Craig Billington, both solid veteran goaltenders.

But Billington was shipped to Ottawa in a trade that brought Peter Sidorkiewicz to New Jersey. Sidorkiewicz, it turned out, had not recovered from a severe shoulder separation and was not ready for the 1993-94 training camp. Enter Brodeur, a promising minor-league goalie at the time.

Brodeur's play was so good as a rookie that he eased Terreri out of the No. 1 job. Brodeur played in 47 games, posted a won-lost-tied record of 27-11-8 and a regular-season goals-against average of 2.40.

As impressive as his regular-season performance chart was, Brodeur was even more brilliant in the playoffs. He posted an 8-9 won-lost mark in the Stanley Cup tournament, with a sparkling goals-against average of 1.95 as he backstopped the Devils to the Eastern Conference Finals.

Devils' Cup

By this time, Brodeur had not only supplanted Terreri as the top goalie in the Devils organization, he had staked a claim as the best goaltender in the NHL—period.

Brodeur played 40 of the 48 games for New Jersey in the lockout-shortened 1994-95 season, going 19-11-6 with a 2.45 goals-against average in regular-season play.

His playoff performance was spookily brilliant. He played in all 20 of the Devils' playoff games, winning 16, three of them by shutout. All three shutouts came in the Devils' first-round victory over the Boston Bruins, and produced this unlikely linescore for Brodeur: a 4-1 won-lost record; an 0.97 GAA and a .962 save percentage.

The wonder is that the Bruins won a game at all, facing goaltending that stingy.

Brodeur's brilliance carried the Devils' to their first-ever Stanley Cup victory, but it was winger Claude Lemieux who won the Conn Smythe Trophy as the top playoff performer, as he scored 13 goals in New Jersey's playoff run.

Rink rat

There was a certain resonance about Brodeur playing so well and winning a Stanley Cup on a team coached by Jacques Lemaire, a brilliant center with the great Montreal Canadiens teams of the 1960s and 70s. Lots of Canadian kids are rink rats, but Brodeur grew up hanging around the Montreal Forum, where his father, Denis, was the team photographer for the Canadiens. Brodeur had been just 14 when Devils teammates Stephane Richer and Claude Lemieux had helped the Canadiens win the Stanley Cup in 1986.

In 1994-95, Brodeur was indisputably The Goalie in New Jersey. The Devils traded Terreri and handed the backup role to Corey Schwab. That role was a bit part, really, since Brodeur played in 77 of the team's 82 regular-season games, including 44 straight starts, as the Devils fought for inclusion in the Stanley Cup playoffs the entire second half of the season.

CAREER RECORD

Personal

Birthplace/Date	Montreal, Quebec/ 5-6-72
Height/Weight	6-1/205

Awards

NHL All-Rookie Team	1994
Calder Memorial Trophy	1994

NHL Career 3 seasons New Jersey Devils

Playing Record

	Games	Wins	Losses	Ties	GAG
Regular Season	168	82	53	26	2.40
Playoffs	38	24	14	0	1.86

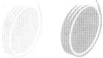
Back after a traumatic injury, he looks set to continue his high-scoring career with the Canucks.

After Pavel Bure's first game with the Vancouver Canucks, the media nicknamed him the 'Russian Rocket' and his brilliant rookie season touched off Pavelmania among the long-suffering Canucks fans.

In Bure, the Canucks finally had landed a superstar to build a true contender around.

The 5-foot-10, 187-pound right winger certainly arrived in Vancouver with pedigree. He first dazzled North American hockey people at the World Junior Championships in Anchorage, Alaska in 1989-90. Playing on a line with Sergei Fedorov and Alexander Mogilny, Bure scored eight goals and added six assists for 14 points to help the USSR win the gold medal in that tournament. He was named the tournament's top forward.

The following year, he helped the Soviets win gold at the World Hockey Championships. He starred for both the junior and senior men's teams in 1990-91 also, helping the juniors win a silver medal and the senior men win the bronze.

Bure frenzy

The Canucks had drafted Bure in the sixth round of the 1989 entry draft, only to have then-NHL president John Ziegler rule him ineligible. The decision was reversed more than a year later, clearing the way for Bure to join the Canucks.

Three years after Bure was named rookie-of-the-year in the Soviet National League, he scored 34 goals for the Canucks and won the Calder Trophy as the top freshman in the NHL—and

CAREER RECORD					
Personal					
Birthplace/Date	Moscow, USSR/3-31-71				
Height/Weight	5-10/187				
Awards					
Calder Memorial Trophy	**1992**				
First All-Star Team	**1994**				
NHL Career	**5 seasons Vancouver Canucks**				
Playing Record					
	Games	**Goals**	**Assists**	**Points**	**PIM**
Regular Season	**283**	**180**	**153**	**333**	**240**
Playoffs	**60**	**34**	**32**	**66**	**72**

created a frenzy among Vancouver hockey supporters.

In 1992-93, Bure scored 60 goals and added 50 assists for 110 points, becoming the first Canuck ever to score as many as 50 goals and reach 100 points in a season.

Bure snapped off another 60-goal season in 1993-94, slipping to 47 assists and 107 points. He then led all playoff goalscorers with 16, leading the Canucks to the Stanley Cup final, which they lost in a seven-game thriller to the New York Rangers.

Bure negotiated a rich new contract in the midst of the playoff run, which pushed some noses out of joint. Bure obviously had learned that leverage matters in the free enterprise system, another indicator that he was a quick study in adapting to North American life and the NHL.

Some thought the swift, creative Bure too slight to withstand the inevitable physical pounding NHL forwards are subjected to. Owing to his total commitment to his sport, Bure spent his first summers in North America adhering to a severe fitness regimen overseen by his father, Vladimir, a former swimmer and three-time Olympian for the Soviet Union.

Temporary stall

Fitness regimens are little protection from traumatic injury, though. Off to a slow start in 1995-96, with seven goals and 13 points in his first 15 games, Bure's season ended early after he was checked by Chicago Blackhawks defenseman Steve Smith. Bure caught his skate in a rut and suffered a torn anterior cruciate ligament in his right knee.

Since the Canucks had acquired Bure's former junior linemate, Alexander Mogilny, in the off-season, the injury deprived Vancouver fans of seeing one of the most explosive duos in the NHL

There were early fears that the injury would cut short his pro career, but those worries eased as the season—and his rehabilitation—progressed. By season's end, Bure was skating again, elevating the hopes of the fans he won over in the very first NHL game he ever played, back in November 1991.

Pavelmania!: The charismatic Bure touched off a fan frenzy in his rookie season and continues to improve.

PAUL COFFEY

One great shining moment illustrates Paul Coffey's arrival as a world-class defenseman. It was in the 1984 Canada Cup (now World Cup) tournament final—in overtime. Coffey was the only defenseman back on a two-on-one break by Russian forwards Vladimir Kovin and Mikhail Varnakov.

Just inside the Canadian blue line, Coffey went to one knee, used his stick to intercept a pass and, in one motion, swept to his feet and launched a Canadian rush into the Soviet zone. Mike Bossy scored on the play, deflecting a Coffey shot.

It was pure hockey brilliance—thwarting the opposition at one end and scoring on them at the other. It also answered some of the critics who pigeon-holed the swift, impossibly smooth-skating Coffey as a one-way points machine, but a disaster in his own end.

That tournament appearance came after Coffey's fourth National Hockey League season with the talent-laden Edmonton Oilers, in which he scored 40 goals and added 86 assists. His 126 points led not only all NHL defensemen, they placed Coffey second overall in league scoring, an eye-popping 79 points behind teammate Wayne Gretzky's 205 points. Gretzky's brilliance overshadowed Coffey's achievement.

Nonetheless, Coffey's explosive scoring ability, and his seemingly effortless skating skills prompted comparisons with legendary Bobby Orr, the prototypical 'offenseman.' Coffey enhanced his extraordinary skating skills by wearing skate boots several sizes too small and by using an elongated blade, to increase his ability to glide. But it's his ability to make plays at high speed that sets him apart, not merely his speed.

Goal maker

In 1985-86, Coffey scored 48 goals, breaking Orr's NHL record for goals by a defenseman, and added 90 assists for 138 points, the most by a defenseman since Orr totaled 139 in 1970-71. That achievement earned Coffey his second straight James Norris Trophy as the best defenseman in the NHL, but did not cement his future with the Oilers, the NHL's dynasty of the mid-80s.

Just one season later, Coffey was traded to the Pittsburgh Penguins in a multi-player deal. Edmonton's coach and general manager, was beginning the process of turning over the club's assets—trading those the club no longer could afford for younger, less expensive talent.

The developing Penguins missed the playoffs in Coffey's first year in Pittsburgh, but he was an important part of the first of two straight Stanley Cup victories in 1990-91. He scored 24 goals that season and added 69 assists for 93 points.

A great-offense-no-defense tag continued to dog Coffey, though, and shortly after the mid-point of his fifth season, he was off to Los Angeles, to be reunited with old teammate Gretzky. Just 60 games later, Coffey was off to Detroit in another multi-player deal that rankled Gretzky.

Creative discipline

In Detroit, despite some friction with defensive-minded head coach Scotty Bowman, Coffey seems to have found as permanent a home as one finds in the NHL. His skating skills and creativity mesh smoothly with the skills of players like Steve Yzerman,

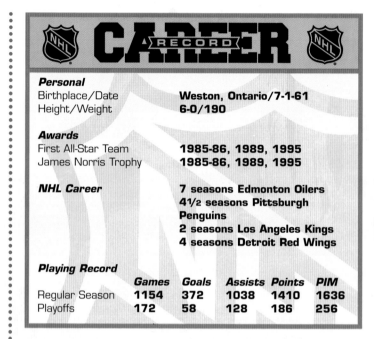

CAREER RECORD

Personal

Birthplace/Date	Weston, Ontario/7-1-61
Height/Weight	6-0/190

Awards

First All-Star Team	1985-86, 1989, 1995
James Norris Trophy	1985-86, 1989, 1995

NHL Career

7 seasons Edmonton Oilers
4½ seasons Pittsburgh Penguins
2 seasons Los Angeles Kings
4 seasons Detroit Red Wings

Playing Record

	Games	Goals	Assists	Points	PIM
Regular Season	1154	372	1038	1410	1636
Playoffs	172	58	128	186	256

Sergei Fedorov and Vyacheslav Kozlov.

All the Red Wings have had to learn to express their creativity within a disciplined, defensive style, and Coffey is no exception. His offensive numbers are not as gaudy as they once were.

Still, he scored 11 goals and added 58 assists for 69 points in 1995-96. His 58 assists were second on the Red Wings to Fedorov.

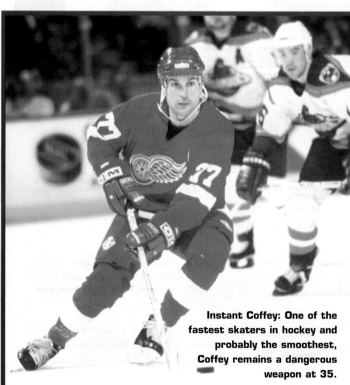

Instant Coffey: One of the fastest skaters in hockey and probably the smoothest, Coffey remains a dangerous weapon at 35.

MARCEL DIONNE

Small of stature but big on talent, he was a player who sadly missed out on his fair share of awards.

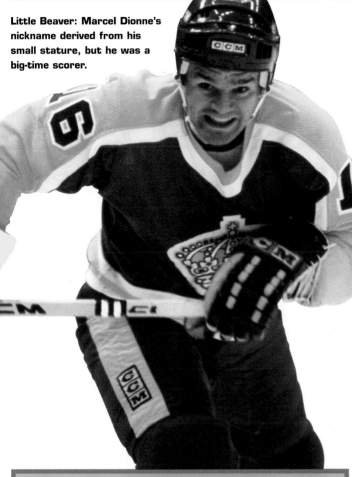

Little Beaver: Marcel Dionne's nickname derived from his small stature, but he was a big-time scorer.

D ionne grew up in Drummondville, Que., but his springboard to the NHL was St. Catharines, Ont., where he starred for the St. Catharine's Blackhawks of the Ontario Hockey Association.

Playing in the same arena where Bobby Hull and Stan Mikita had served their hockey apprenticeship, Dionne was the dominant star in the OHA in his era, despite his size. He also was a huge star in St. Catharine's, running his own hockey school as a teenager, a little Big Man on the junior hockey campus.

Dionne stood just 5-foot-7, but made up for his small stature by being a fast, shifty skater with a vast repertoire of moves. In the NHL, he remained the scoring wizard he had been in junior, but he played most of his pro career for mediocre teams.

Selected second in the 1971 Entry Draft, right behind Guy Lafleur, Dionne joined the woeful Detroit Red Wings, an organization in disarray at the time.

Dionne produced 366 points through his first four seasons—more than any NHL player had ever generated in a four-year period. But the Red Wings were unsuccessful in building a team around their sensational young star and at the end of the 1974-75 season, they shipped their prized asset to the Los Angeles Kings.

Triple Crown Line

The Kings, owned by the flamboyant Jack Kent Cooke, wore royal purple uniforms at the time and played at an arena known as the Fabulous Forum.

Dionne was the King of the Kings, and centered the Triple Crown Line with wingers Dave Taylor and Charlie Simmer.

Simmer, a laborious skater but a big, strong presence, was the finisher, planting himself near the goal crease for tip-ins and rebounds. Taylor, a fitness freak, was an excellent corner man and skilful with the puck, although far from a flashy player.

Dionne was the puck carrier, a juking waterbug of a skater, he mesmerized the defense before passing to one of his linemates or drilling a shot on net himself.

The line was deadly.

In 1979-80, Dionne won the Art Ross Trophy as the league's leading scorer. Both he and Wayne Gretzky, an NHL rookie that year, amassed 137 points. Dionne was awarded the scoring title because his 53 goals were two more than Gretzky scored.

But the Triple Crown Line's best season was 1980-81, when Dionne produced 135 points, including 58 goals, Taylor had 112 points (47 goals) and Simmer connected for 56 goals and 105 points-352 points by a single line.

A true gentleman

Along with his one scoring championship, Dionne won two Lady Byng Trophies as the league's most sportsmanlike player.

It was his misfortune never to get close to any post-season awards—personal or team. In his entire 18-year career, Dionne played in just 49 playoff games, compared to 128 playoff games for his contemporary, Lafleur, for example.

Dionne played his final two seasons as a power-play specialist with the New York Rangers. He remained in the New York area following his retirement and built a dry-cleaning business.

CAREER RECORD

Personal

Birthplace/Date	Drummondville, Quebec/9-03-51
Height/Weight	5-8/190

Awards:

First All-Star Team	1977, 1980
Art Ross Trophy	1980
Lester B. Pearson Award	1979-80
Lady Byng Trophy	1975, 1977
Hall of Fame Inductee	1992

NHL Career

4 seasons Detroit Red Wings
12 seasons Los Angeles Kings
2 seasons New York Rangers

Playing Record

	Games	Goals	Assists	Points	PIM
Regular Season	1348	731	1040	1771	600
Playoffs	49	21	24	45	17

The Canadiens' Intellectual Athlete

He was an instant success, and his effective goalkeeping helped Montreal to the top.

KEN DRYDEN

The term 'raw rookie' never described Ken Dryden. An Ivy League scholar from Cornell University, Dryden was in first year law school at McGill University in 1971 when he joined the Canadiens and backstopped them to an improbable Stanley Cup victory.

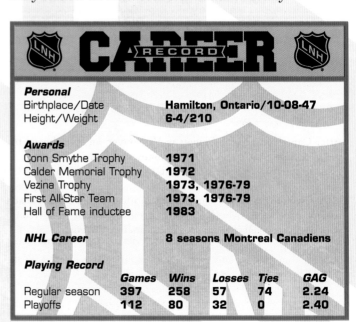

Dryden, 23 at the time, played only home games that year for the Montreal Voyageurs, the Canadiens' farm club. That way, he didn't have to cut classes. He played just six regular-season games for the Canadiens—all at home and none against the Boston Bruins, Montreal's first-round opponents that spring.

Not confident with regulars Rogatien Vachon and Phil Myre, Montreal management inserted the little-known Dryden against the first-place Bruins, who set an NHL record by scoring 399 goals and were led by Bobby Orr and Phil Esposito, whose 76 goals and 152 points both were league records. No one gave Montreal much chance.

Against all odds

In the opening game, Dryden was brilliant and the Canadiens played a solid game, but still lost 3-1, which seemed to confirm conventional wisdom.

In Game 2, the Bruins skated to a 5-1 second-period lead before Henri Richard scored a late-period goal to reduce the margin to three goals.

"Don't worry," Canadiens coach Al McNeil told his players, "the Bruins are too loose, your chances will come", all the usual platitudes. But the Canadiens scored five unanswered goals in the third period to win the game 7-5. Suddenly, the best team in hockey was in a competitive series.

The Canadiens had many stars that spring: Frank Mahovlich, who set a playoff scoring record with 14 goals and 27 points; Jacques Lemaire, who scored some key goals; Henri Richard, who netted the Cup winner. But the team that had been inconsistent during the season in front of Vachon and Myre, was exceptional with Dryden in goal. He was the difference. "He has arms like a giraffe," said Boston's Esposito, frustrated by Dryden often that series.

During play stoppages, the lanky, 6-foot-4 Dryden stood with his arms folded, leaning on the knob of his goalie stick, pensively surveying the scene.

Skate Save: Ken Dryden backstopped the Canadiens to six Stanley Cups in eight Hall of Fame seasons in the NHL.

Dryden's was an uncommon NHL presence: an intellectual-athlete who joined the Canadiens precisely when they needed a special player to lift them.

Only the best

Dryden won the Conn Smythe Trophy as the most valuable player in the playoffs in 1971, then won the Calder Trophy as the NHL's rookie of the year the following season. He's the only player in league history to win a major NHL individual award before winning the rookie award.

Dryden played just eight seasons for the Canadiens, helping Montreal win six Stanley Cups in that span.

He took a 'sabattical' in 1973-74 and 'articled' with a Toronto law firm, a requirement in the Canadian legal system. He also was effectively holding out for more money. Having established himself as the league's best goalie, Dryden expected to be paid 'the going rate' for being the best.

He rejoined the club for the 1974-75 season and helped the Canadiens win four straight Stanley Cups from 1976-79, when he retired. He never lost more than ten games in a season and won five Vezina Trophies.

In retirement, Dryden continued to make a special mark on hockey, first with the publication in 1983, of *The Game*, which many consider the finest book ever written on hockey.

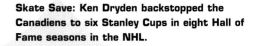

CAREER RECORD

Personal

Birthplace/Date	Hamilton, Ontario/10-08-47
Height/Weight	6-4/210

Awards

Conn Smythe Trophy	1971
Calder Memorial Trophy	1972
Vezina Trophy	1973, 1976-79
First All-Star Team	1973, 1976-79
Hall of Fame inductee	1983

NHL Career — 8 seasons Montreal Canadiens

Playing Record

	Games	Wins	Losses	Ties	GAG
Regular season	397	258	57	74	2.24
Playoffs	112	80	32	0	2.40

PHIL ESPOSITO

For a guy who began his NHL career as a second banana, Phil Esposito developed a boffo act. Esposito didn't begin skating until he was in his teens, and perhaps because of the late start, the native of Sault Ste. Marie didn't take the NHL by storm.

He was a second-line center his first four years in the league, playing in the shadow of Chicago Blackhawks teammates Stan Mikita, Bobby Hull and Kenny Wharram.

In his fourth year, Esposito cracked the Top 10 list in NHL scoring, finishing seventh overall with 21 goals and 40 assists, hinting at his capabilities. The Blackhawks management was not sufficiently impressed. In 1967, they traded Esposito, Ken Hodge and Fred Stanfield to the Boston Bruins.

Esposito won the Art Ross Trophy as the NHL's leading scorer five of the next seven years. More than that, he raised the standard of scoring excellence in the NHL.

The 50-goal plateau had been magic, hockey's analog to Babe Ruth's 60 home runs. Bobby Hull, the Golden Jet, had unleashed his rocket blast of a slap shot sufficiently to score 58 goals in 1968-69, but he was an acknowledged superstar.

Questioned success

When Esposito scored 76 goals and added 76 assists in 1970-71, he broke the equivalent of hockey's scoring sound barrier. Seventy-six goals? A record 152 points? By a guy who couldn't skate?

He was dismissed as a garbage collector. "Jesus Saves, but Espo puts in the rebound", read a Boston bumper sticker. Esposito, conventional wisdom had it, was cashing in on the brilliance of Bobby Orr.

More likely, the two fed off each other's skills: Orr, the swift-skating defenseman who distributed the puck to his teammates; Esposito, the immovable object in front of the opposition's net, the guy with the lightning-quick release.

The Bruins were a scoring machine during the Orr-Esposito years, and set a league record in 1970-71 by scoring 399 goals in 78 games—more than five goals a game.

Esposito and Orr led the Bruins to Stanley Cup victories in 1969 and 1972, but it was Esposito's performance in the 1972 Canada-Soviet Summit Series that really established him as a hockey legend.

Triumph and savvy

After Canada lost to the Soviets in Vancouver, and was booed by the fans, Esposito, made an impassioned speech on TV, telling Canada the team was doing its best, that it needed support to carry on and defeat the Soviets.

He won the fans over and his play in Moscow led Team Canada to a narrow victory over the Soviets on a goal by Paul Henderson with 34 seconds left in Game 8. Esposito set up the goal.

Esposito closed his playing career with the New York Rangers, six years during which he never duplicated his glory years with the Bruins when he was hockey's dominant scorer and personality.

In the mid-1980s, Esposito became the Rangers' general manager, wheeling and dealing players so aggressively, he earned the nickname, Trader Phil.

When Tampa, Fla., won an expansion franchise in 1991, there was Esposito, fronting for a group of Japanese businessmen. He had lost none of his flamboyance.

He invited Manon Rheaume, a female goaltender, to the club's training camp as a publicity stunt, and even let her play part of an exhibition game.

Esposito knows how to make an impact.

In the Slot: Phil Esposito in his office during his years as the deadliest scorer in the NHL.

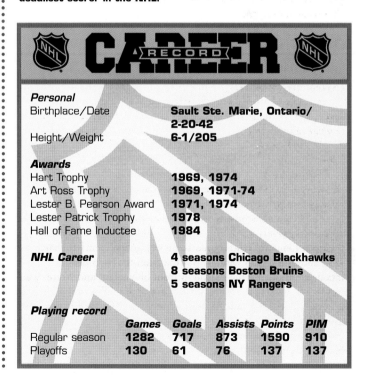

CAREER RECORD

Personal

Birthplace/Date	Sault Ste. Marie, Ontario/ 2-20-42
Height/Weight	6-1/205

Awards

Hart Trophy	1969, 1974
Art Ross Trophy	1969, 1971-74
Lester B. Pearson Award	1971, 1974
Lester Patrick Trophy	1978
Hall of Fame Inductee	1984

NHL Career

4 seasons Chicago Blackhawks
8 seasons Boston Bruins
5 seasons NY Rangers

Playing record

	Games	Goals	Assists	Points	PIM
Regular season	1282	717	873	1590	910
Playoffs	130	61	76	137	137

SERGEI FEDOROV

As part of the Red Wings' Russian unit this poster-boy hockey powerhouse has made a fine team great.

ICE TALK

"FEDOROV IS AS GOOD AS ANYBODY IN ANY ERA SKILLWISE. FEDOROV IS ONE OF A KIND."

AN NHL SCOUT

Squeeze Play: Opponents rarely contain Red Wings star Sergei Fedorov, whom many consider the best all-around player in the NHL.

When Sergei Fedorov arrived in Detroit, the Red Wings already had a No. 1 center — veteran Steve Yzerman. So Fedorov, brilliantly talented offensively, was asked to handle a big part of the defensive load. That would seem a waste. Except Fedorov applied himself to the task and, in his second season in the NHL, he was named runner-up to Guy Carbonneau for the Frank J. Selke Trophy as the league's best defensive forward.

Two years later, in 1994, he won the trophy.

He also won the Hart Trophy that year as the league's most valuable player, was named to the first all-star team and won the Lester B. Pearson Award, voted on by his peers and awarded to the league's outstanding player.

It wouldn't be a stretch to suggest that not only is Fedorov the best all-around player in hockey, but everyone in hockey knows it.

Russian might

He came to the league with impeccable credentials. As a junior in Russia, he centered a line with wingers Pavel Bure and Alexander Mogilny — one of the most electrifying trios ever assembled.

Fedorov played four years with Central Red Army, and helped the Soviet National team win gold medals at the World Championships in 1989 and 1990.

With his speed, improvisational moves executed at full speed, and all-around game, Fedorov made an immediate impact on the NHL, leading all rookies in goals (31), assists (48) and points (79) in 1990-91. He finished runner-up to Ed Belfour in the voting for the Calder Trophy.

As exciting as his skills are, Fedorov always has understood that even star players perform best as part of an ensemble.

Luckily, his Detroit coach, Scotty Bowman, understands this also. It was Bowman who acquired veteran Russian Igor Larionov and assembled a five-man unit with Fedorov, Vyacheslav Kozlov, Vlyacheslav Fetisov and Vladimir Konstantinov.

The unit, used selectively by Bowman, a master strategist, performed brilliantly for the Red Wings in 1995-96. Fedorov, ever the team man, moved to right wing on the unit, ceding the center position on the line to Larionov, who centered the famous KLM (Vladimir Krutov, Larionov and Sergei Makarov) for the Soviet National team in the 1980s.

Like the five-man units in the Russian national teams, Detroit's unit stressed puck control and patience, preferring to circle back in the neutral zone, and to hold on to the puck in the offensive zone rather than try a low percentage play.

Russian light

A crackdown on obstruction penalties by NHL officials enhanced the unit's effectiveness also. Its play, which turned an already fine Detroit team into a special one, was one of the best stories of the 1995-96 season.

Fedorov's spectacular play, sly sense of humor and good looks convinced Nike to make him their poster boy for their hockey equipment. He showcased Nike's new line of skates at the mid-season All-Star Game in Boston.

That might be the ultimate signal of Fedorov's utter assimilation into North American hockey and the NHL. He not only skates circles around his peers on the ice, he outdistances them in the arena of commercial Capitalism, also.

Talk about your Russian Revolution.

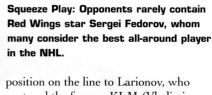

CAREER RECORD

Personal	
Birthplace/Date	**Pskov, USSR/ 12-13-69**
Height/Weight	**6-1/200**

Awards	
All-Rookie Team	**1991**
First All-Star Team	**1994**
Frank J. SelkeTrophy	**1994, 1996**
Lester B. Pearson Award	**1994**
Hart Trophy	**1994**

NHL Career — **6 seasons Detroit Red Wings**

Playing Record

	Games	Goals	Assists	Points	PIM
Regular season	432	212	317	529	316
Playoffs	68	19	58	77	57

The Great One goes Broadway
WAYNE GRETZKY

This talented player has helped open up warm-weather United States to NHL action.

Almost a decade before he reached the NHL, Wayne Gretzky let the hockey world know he was on his way by scoring 378 goals as a 10-year-old. In his one full year of major junior hockey, Gretzky scored 70 goals and added 112 assists with the Sault Ste. Marie Greyhounds. Then, at 17, he turned pro, racking up 110 points as a rookie in the World Hockey Association, playing for the Edmonton Oilers.

In 1979-80, his first season in the NHL, Gretzky scored 51 goals and had 86 assists for 137 points, the same as Art Ross Trophy-winner Marcel Dionne, who won the title on the basis of two more goals scored. Gretzky would win the scoring title the next seven years, play runner-up to Mario Lemieux for two seasons (1987-88 and 1988-89), then win two more. Gretzky has been the league's top pointgetter ten times and holds countless NHL scoring records.

His dominance is not a function of an imposing physical presence. Gretzky is listed at six feet tall, 180 pounds.

Studied foresight

A deceptively fast skater, preternaturally able to anticipate the game's patterns, Gretzky rarely absorbed punishing body checks. And phenomenal energy enables Gretzky to play at a high level even in a game's late stages.

Gretzky shares with Bobby Orr the gift of redefining the game, making it his own. One skill he brought to the NHL involved setting up behind the opposition's net, where he could see the entire pattern of play in the attacking zone and feed passes to onrushing teammates. His Oilers teammates called this space Gretzky's 'launching pad.'

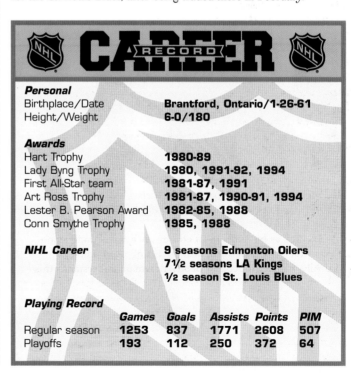

The Great One: Wayne Gretzky may have slowed down with advancing years, but he still collected more than 100 points in 1995-96.

ICE TALK

"He's one of the few players who knows where all 12 men are on the ice, and what they're going to do."

Gordie Howe

---

profession by instinct; yet in my own way I've spent almost as much time studying hockey as a med student puts in studying medicine."

Gretzky became a hockey demigod in Edmonton. When Oilers owner Peter Pocklington, viewing him merely as a depreciating asset, traded Gretzky to the Los Angeles Kings in 1989, an entire country felt betrayed.

Sunny revival

But Gretzky became something more than a hockey deity in Los Angeles, he was a marketer's dream. His high-profile presence made it hip to attend Kings games and re-established hockey in Southern California. That, in turn, helped sell the game to warm-weather markets such as South Florida, where the NHL had long yearned to penetrate.

Gretzky could well finish his storied career in North American sport's largest market after signing a two-year deal as a free agent with the New York Rangers in the off-season, after just half a season for the St. Louis Blues, after being traded there in February.

Gretzky led the Oilers to four Stanley Cups in five years. The talent-rich Oilers sandwiched a pair of Stanley Cups around a surprise cup victory by the Montreal Canadiens in 1986.

"Nine out of ten people think what I do is instinct," Gretzky once said. "It isn't. Nobody would ever say a doctor had learned his

---

CAREER RECORD

Personal

Birthplace/Date	Brantford, Ontario/1-26-61
Height/Weight	6-0/180

Awards

Hart Trophy	1980-89
Lady Byng Trophy	1980, 1991-92, 1994
First All-Star team	1981-87, 1991
Art Ross Trophy	1981-87, 1990-91, 1994
Lester B. Pearson Award	1982-85, 1988
Conn Smythe Trophy	1985, 1988

NHL Career

	9 seasons Edmonton Oilers
	7½ seasons LA Kings
	½ season St. Louis Blues

Playing Record

	Games	Goals	Assists	Points	PIM
Regular season	1253	837	1771	2608	507
Playoffs	193	112	250	372	64

The son of a star has made his own goal-scoring way to the top in St. Louis.

When Bobby Hull was on the ice, all eyes were on him. Brett Hull plays a different game from his dad. A labored skater, the younger Hull moves quietly around the ice, particularly in the offensive zone, circling into spaces others have left, positioning himself to accept a setup pass. He tries to draw as little attention to himself as possible, laying in the weeds, as the hockey players say. Until, that is, he unleashes The Shot.

By the time the defenders realize it is Hull who is shooting, it often is too late. Possessed of one of the fastest, hardest slap shots in hockey, Hull is a prolific but mostly unflashy scorer. He has been called the NHL's Stealth Bomber.

Quietly to the top

Similarly, Hull insinuated himself into the NHL elite quietly. Because of his name, the NHL saw Hull coming up through the junior and college ranks, but he was not regarded as a rising star.

The Calgary Flames selected Hull in the sixth round of the 1984 entry draft, an unheralded 117th overall out of the University of Minnesota-Duluth.

In his full first NHL season—1987-88—Hull scored 26 goals in 52 games for the Flames, who traded him before season's end to St. Louis.

With the Blues, Hull was paired with Adam Oates, one of the league's

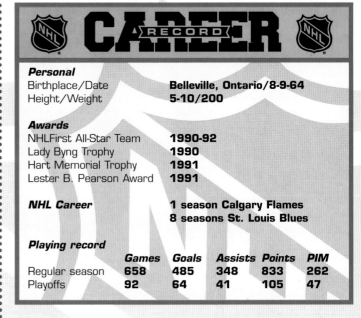

CAREER RECORD

Personal	
Birthplace/Date	Belleville, Ontario/8-9-64
Height/Weight	5-10/200

Awards	
NHL First All-Star Team	1990-92
Lady Byng Trophy	1990
Hart Memorial Trophy	1991
Lester B. Pearson Award	1991

NHL Career	
	1 season Calgary Flames
	8 seasons St. Louis Blues

Playing record	Games	Goals	Assists	Points	PIM
Regular season	658	485	348	833	262
Playoffs	92	64	41	105	47

top playmakers. Hull and Oates quickly became a hit.

Hull scored 41 goals and added 43 assists for 84 points in his first full season with the Blues, but that was merely the warm-up.

In 1989-90, Hull scored 72 goals to lead the NHL in goal-scoring for the first of three straight seasons. The following year his quick-release shot found the net 86 times and another 70 times in 1991-92.

Along with the goal-scoring blitz came official recognition. Hull was a first-team all-star three straight times, won the Lady Byng as the league's most sportsmanlike player and the Hart Trophy as the most valuable player.

Ups and downs

He was named captain of the Blues, but he had made himself something more important to St. Louis—its franchise player.

The Blues traded Oates, the set-up man, to the Bruins in February 1992, but replaced him with Craig Janney, another able playmaker. Still, some of his fans were disappointed when Hull 'slumped' to 54 goals in 1992-93 and managed 'only' 57 goals in 1993-94. In the lockout-shortened 1994-95 season, Hull delivered 29 goals in 48 games, which pro-rates to 49 goals over an 82-game schedule. Strictly routine for the Golden Brett, some would say.

Head coach Mike Keenan stripped Hull of the captaincy in 1995-96. Nothing personal, he assured people. "The heck it's not personal," Hull said. "It's a complete slap in the face."

Gone, too, was the playmaking Janney, who had been traded to San Jose during the 1994-95 season. But in March 1996, Keenan brought the ultimate playmaker—Wayne Gretzky—to the Blues, in a blockbuster trade.

Injuries and the normal adjustment to a new team inhibited the Gretzky-Hull duo from immediately clicking. But the pairing holds enticing promise.

Golden Brett: Hull has been The Franchise since he was traded to St. Louis.

He's young, he's an artist, he scores goals like no one else—and he is set to continue for a long time.

Jaromir Jagr is the closest thing the NHL has to a rock star. He's young (24), good-looking, and has long, unruly hair, much too long for his helmet to contain. Jagr loves to laugh, too, and who can blame him? There seems little the 6-foot-2, 208-pound forward cannot do.

"He's still so young," says former teammate Rick Tocchet. "He's going to be a force in this league for a long time."

He's already a force, has been since his rookie season in 1990-91. He made the all-rookie team that year, scoring 27 goals and adding 30 assists. He added 13 points in the Pittsburgh Cup-winning playoff run.

His points totals have increased every season since then, with the exception of 1994-95, when the lockout slashed the regular season to 48 games. But Jagr won the scoring title, with 32 goals and 38 assists for 70 points.

More important, he arrived as a mature player, having to step up and shoulder the burden of being the go-to guy for the Penguins. Teammate Mario Lemieux took the season off to recover from his bout with Hodgkin's Disease and chronic back problems.

Record breaker

Playing the star comes effortlessly for Jagr, who has a long, fluid, deceptively swift skating stride, and he's equally fluid handling the puck. He truly creates art on ice.

"He is a master of deception," said New York Rangers goaltender Mike Richter. "If you try to anticipate with him, you'll often guess wrong. And if you just try to react, he's too fast and you get beat."

In 1995-96, Jagr lifted his artistry to new heights. He and Lemieux became the first pair of teammates in NHL history to score more than 60 goals each in a single season.

On March 28, Jagr displaced Peter Stastny from the record books when he recorded his 140th point of the season, which was also his 60th goal.

The Maestro: Many consider Jaromir Jagr the best one-on-one player in the NHL.

In 1995-96, Jagr and Lemieux separated from the scoring pack early in the season, putting on their own personal scoring race.

But the two are friendly, complementary talents, not rivals. Jagr says he never has felt overlooked, never worried that he was playing in Lemieux's shadow.

"No, I never looked at it that way when we were winning the Stanley Cup," said Jagr. "As long as we were winning, nothing else mattered. It's still the same now. I don't need a lot of attention."

Defenders' nightmare

He certainly gets it. The Montreal Canadiens, for example, make sure they deploy defenseman Vladimir Malakhov whenever Jagr is on the ice.

The rangy Malakhov defends against Jagr's attacks as effectively as anyone, and more than most.

More often, teams have little idea how to contain an improvising on-ice young maestro, who is too fast for many defenders, too strong for others and more creative than most players.

He also is durable. Despite being a target for opposing players, Jagr has missed just 17 games owing to injury in his six NHL seasons.

Since leaving Czechoslovakia and joining the Penguins, Jagr has been that rare thing: an artist who produces like clockwork.

CAREER RECORD

Personal

Birthplace/Date	Kladno, Czechoslovakia/2-15-72
Height/Weight	6-2/205

Awards

Art Ross Trophy	1995
All-Rookie Team	1991
First All-Star Team	1995, 1996

NHL Career	**6 seasons Pittsburgh Penguins**

Playing Record

	Games	Goals	Assists	Points	PIM
Regular Season	441	219	319	538	331
Playoffs	93	42	48	80	75

GUY LAFLEUR

With virtuoso artistry this blond-maned No.10 led the Canadiens to Stanley Cup glory.

When Montreal Canadiens general manager Sam Pollock was asked for his selection—No.1 overall—in the 1971 NHL entry draft, he broke up a crowded Montreal hotel ballroom by uttering one word: "Time!" Everyone in the room knew which player Pollock would select: Guy Lafleur.

Lafleur had scored more than 200 goals in his final two seasons of junior hockey with the Quebec Remparts and was seen as the obvious successor to the just-retired Jean Beliveau as the Francophone torch-bearer for a franchise that had become a symbol of excellence.

Lafleur even wore No.4 with the Remparts, the same number Beliveau had worn for 18 seasons with the Canadiens. With Montreal, Lafleur made No.10 famous, even if it took a while for the man they call Flower to blossom. Following the line of excellence that led from Maurice Richard to Beliveau to himself, was fraught with pressure.

"I played center in my first game ever with the team," Lafleur said. "I was between Frank Mahovlich on my left and Yvan Cournoyer on my right. I was very, very nervous."

Freed to score

For three years, Lafleur showed his great speed and dazzling moves only in flashes, saving most of his virtuoso artistry for Canadiens practices.

In his fourth year, he shed his helmet and, blond mane flapping, he emerged from his shell and scored 53 goals, bagged 119 points.

It was the first of six straight 50-plus goal seasons for Lafleur, who won three straight scoring titles during that stretch.

He played on a line with left winger Steve Shutt and center Pete Mahovlich, then Jacques Lemaire after Mahovlich was traded. The line embodied the sports cliche, the best defense is a good offense. When Shutt, Lafleur and Lemaire were on the ice,

CAREER RECORD

Personal	
Birthplace/Date	Thurso, Quebec./9-20-51
Height/Weight	6-0/180

Awards:	
Art Ross Trophy	1976-78
Hart Trophy	1977-78
Conn Smythe Trophy	1977
Lester B. Pearson Award	1976-78
First All-Star Team	1975-80
Hall of Fame Inductee	1988

NHL Career	
	13 seasons Montreal Canadiens
	1 season New York Rangers
	2 seasons Quebec Nordiques

Playing record

	Games	Goals	Assists	Points	PIM
Regular Season	1126	560	793	1353	399
Playoffs	128	58	76	134	67

the opposition rarely touched the puck.

Lafleur led the Canadiens to five Stanley Cups in the 1970s, including four straight from 1976-79.

The last one was perhaps the most dramatic. In Game 7 of the semifinal series against the Bruins, Montreal was only minutes away from elimination when the Bruins were penalized for having too many men on the ice.

On the ensuing power play, Lafleur powered a deft drop pass from Lemaire past Bruins goaltender Gilles Gilbert to tie the game 3-3, sending it into overtime.

The Canadiens won the game, and the series, 4-3, and defeated the New York Rangers in the Stanley Cup final for their fourth straight Cup.

Canadiens fall

Lafleur scored his customary 50 goals in 1979-80, but was injured in the playoffs and the Canadiens were eliminated in the second round. In 1981, the upstart Edmonton Oilers eliminated Montreal in the first round of the playoffs.

The Canadiens—and Lafleur—were in decline. Unable to adjust to the defensive style implemented by head coach Lemaire, his former linemate, a frustrated Lafleur retired in mid-season in February 1985.

He emerged from retirement to play one year with the New York Rangers in 1988-89, and played, as a part-timer, for two more years with the Quebec Nordiques. But in the public imagination, Lafleur remains a Canadien.

Guy, Guy, Guy: Lafleur's legions of NHL fans regularly chanted his name during the years when he was the most electrifying player in hockey.

A compact package combining quick acceleration and excellent straightahead speed, playmaking brilliance, a hard accurate shot and sound defensive ability, Brian Leetch is a Renaissance player—a defenseman who can do it all. And with considerable flair, at that.

It was Leetch, lifting his game to new heights of virtuosity, who led the New York Rangers to a Stanley Cup championship in 1994, the club's first in 54 years. He led all playoff scorers with 34 points, including 11 goals. He scored five times in the seven-game final series against the Vancouver Canucks and fully earned the Conn Smythe Trophy as the most valuable performer in the post-season.

Texas hockey

In doing so, he became the first American-born player—and a Texan, at that—to capture the Conn Smythe.

He joined the Rangers in 1988-89, following a year with the U.S. National team and an Olympic appearance as captain of the U.S. team. The international experience, coupled with one year with the Boston College Eagles obviously had fine-tuned his explosive raw talent—Leetch was named rookie-of-the-year in his first NHL season.

His numbers dropped off the following season, scoring 11 times and adding 45 assists, before being knocked out of action by a fractured left ankle, the first of a string of injuries that have disrupted his career.

But in 1990-91, Leetch re-asserted his claim to being a franchise defenseman by scoring 16 goals and adding 72 assists for 88 points, breaking Hall of Famer Brad Park's team record for most points (82) in a season by a defenseman.

In 1991-92, Leetch totaled 102 points, including 22 goals and won the James Norris Memorial Trophy as the best defenseman in the league.

On the Move: Leetch's acceleration launches him on rinklength dashes that often result in goals—by the speedy defenseman or one of his teammates.

Undeterred by injury

Injuries hit Leetch in 1992-93, when he missed 34 games with a neck and shoulder injury. Then he slipped on some ice on a Manhattan street, fracturing his right ankle, and missed the final 13 games that season. Doctors used six screws to attach a metal plate to the ankle to repair it.

The injury was ominous for a player whose game is based on speed, but Leetch dispelled any such fears with a superb regular-season (23 goals, 56 assists) and sublime playoff performance.

He also turned a strong performance in the 1994-95 playoffs, generating 14 points (6 goals) in 10 games as the Rangers failed to advance beyond the second round.

Since the 1993-94 season, Leetch has not missed a game, an Ironman string of 214 straight regular-season games. His reliability and all-around excellence permitted the Rangers to trade the talented, but redundant, Sergei Zubov to the Pittsburgh Penguins in a move that brought Ulf Samuelsson to the Rangers.

Samuelsson, a stay-at-home-and-harass-all-intruders sort of defenseman, gives the Rangers the physical presence that Leetch, for one, does not supply.

Leetch supplies virtually everything else a defenseman could possibly offer, though, and then some.

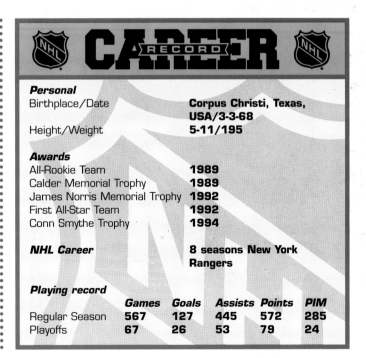

CAREER RECORD

Personal

Birthplace/Date	Corpus Christi, Texas, USA/3-3-68
Height/Weight	5-11/195

Awards

All-Rookie Team	1989
Calder Memorial Trophy	1989
James Norris Memorial Trophy	1992
First All-Star Team	1992
Conn Smythe Trophy	1994

NHL Career — 8 seasons New York Rangers

Playing record

	Games	Goals	Assists	Points	PIM
Regular Season	567	127	445	572	285
Playoffs	67	26	53	79	24

MARIO LEMIEUX

If ever proof was needed that the love of a sport is your life, Mario has provided it magnificently.

In an era of comebacks—Michael Jordan in basketball, Ryne Sandberg in baseball—no one has overcome what Mario Lemieux has and restored his game to a level all his own. Lemieux, a brilliant junior star who rewrote the scoring records in the Quebec Major Junior Hockey League, scored 100 points, including 43 goals, in his first NHL season.

Since then, the only seasons in which Lemieux scored fewer than 100 points (1990-91 and 1993-94), injuries and illness reduced him to participating in fewer than 30 games each season.

In the lockout-shortened 1994-95 season, Lemieux didn't play at all. He took time off to give his chronically aching back time to heal and get over the effects of radiation therapy to overcome Hodgkin's Disease, the treatable form of cancer that sidelined him in 1992-93.

Overcoming adversity

He had earned a sabattical. In his ten years in the NHL, Lemieux had won the Calder Memorial Trophy as rookie of the year, twice won the Hart Trophy as the league's most valuable player, won four scoring titles, two Conn Smythe Trophies as the most valuable player in the playoffs and led the Pittsburgh Penguins to two straight Stanley Cup championships.

His 1992-93 scoring title (69 goals, 91 assists, 160 points) was a courageous feat, considering he missed 20 games, while undergoing radiation treatment.

Lemieux, a commanding 6-foot-4, 220 pounds, with a graceful skating stride and magical puckhandling skills, dealt with personal adversity as elegantly as he skates.

CAREER RECORD

Personal

Birthplace/Date	Montreal, Quebec/10-5-65
Height/Weight	6-4/220

Awards:

Calder Memorial Trophy	1985
All-Rookie Team	1985
Lester B. Pearson Award	1986,1988,1992
Hart Trophy	1988, 1993, 1996
Art Ross Trophy	1988-89, 1992-93, 1996
First All-Star Team	1988-89, 1993, 1996
Conn Smythe Trophy	1991-92
Bill Masterton Trophy	1993

NHL Career	**11 seasons Pittsburgh Penguins**

Playing record

	Games	Goals	Assists	Points	PIM
Regular Season	669	563	809	1372	672
Playoffs	84	67	82	149	79

His return to mostly full-time play (he skipped the second of some back-to-back games) in 1995-96 was the story of the season. He didn't simply return; he dominated.

In a late-season encounter with the St. Louis Blues, and transplanted superstar Wayne Gretzky, Lemieux scored five goals and added two assists as the Penguins swamped the Blues 8-4.

The game is all

Lemieux has a flair for the dramatic.

When the NHL All-Star game was held in Pittsburgh in 1990, he made the mid-season exhibition his personal showcase, scoring four goals.

Lemieux's dramatic overtime winner—on a setup by Gretzky—lifted Canada to a Canada Cup victory over the Soviet Union in 1987. During Pittsburgh's successful Stanley Cup run in 1992, Lemieux led all players in points (34), goals (16), power-play goals (8) and game-winning goals (5), despite missing six games with injuries.

Beginning with the 1989-90 season, he has missed 178 games owing to injuries and illness—more than two seasons worth. Enough games and misery to send most players into a well-earned retirement. Not Lemieux.

"Every time you get away from something you love, it makes you appreciate it more," he said. "That's what I found out last season (1994-95). I'm just glad to have the chance to come back to the game."

The game was grateful to have Lemieux back.

"He could have said goodbye, but he wanted to come back," said teammate Ron Francis. "That's what makes the great players great—they absolutely love the game."

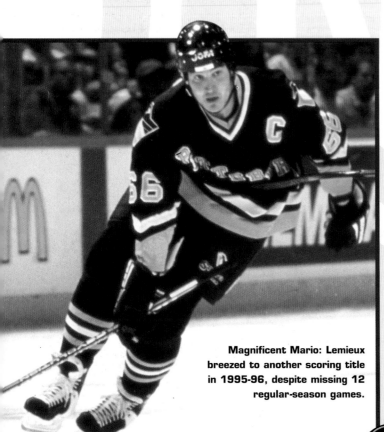

Magnificent Mario: Lemieux breezed to another scoring title in 1995-96, despite missing 12 regular-season games.

He combines the finesse of Gretzky, the size of Lemieux and the presence of Messier. Lindros' future is a no-brainer.

An astonishing blend of fearsome physical strength, speed, skill, rink savvy and unquenchable competitive desire, 6-foot-4, 229-pound center Eric Lindros moved with ridiculous ease up the hockey ladder—junior to international competition to the NHL.

ICE TALK

"HIS SOLE FOCUS IS GETTING HIS TEAM TO THE STANLEY CUP."

FORMER TEAMMATE CRAIG MACTAVISH

While still junior age, Lindros helped Canada win the gold medal at the Canada Cup. During that tournament, Lindros knocked rugged Ulf Samuelsson out of action with a devastating body check that was routinely easy for him.

Before he had played an NHL game he had served notice that he was going to be a force. He has lived up to his advance billing.

The Legion of Doom

Injuries reduced his effectiveness in his first two seasons—yet he still scored 85 goals and chipped in 87 assists in 126 games. Much of that production came while playing on a line with Mark Recchi and Brent Fedyk, both since traded. The line, called the Crazy Eights, was an instant hit in Philadelphia, where fans quickly warmed to Lindros.

But he really hit his NHL stride in 1995 when Flyers coach Terry Murray grouped him with 6-foot-2, 220-pound left winger John Leclair and 6-foot-1, 218-pound right winger Mikael Renberg. As talented as any trio in the league and certainly the best combination of skill and sheer physical power, the line was christened The Legion of Doom.

Lindros totaled 70 points, including 29 goals, in 46 games in 1994-95, tying Pittsburgh's Jaromir Jagr for the points lead, but losing the scoring title, on the final day of the shortened season, because Jagr scored three more goals.

Lindros and the Legion led the Flyers to the club's first division title since 1987 and first playoff berth since 1989. The Flyers lost in the conference final to the New Jersey Devils, the eventual Stanley Cup champions.

The strong performance by Lindros earned him the Hart Trophy as the most valuable player in the NHL, a mantle he assumed with a degree of unease.

The Big Guy: Lindros defines the team impact player—he can hurt opponents with his size, strength, speed, rink savvy and his considerable skill.

"The more people you have carry the game, the better the game's going to be," Lindros said. "When everybody carries it together, it makes it stronger... We've got some great people to carry this game."

Quebec's loss

Few would appear to have a greater upside potential than Lindros, whose leadership abilities were recognized early in Philadelphia, where he was named captain of the Flyers at 21.

In 1995-96, both Lindros and Leclair took serious runs at 50-goal seasons—Lindros finished with 47, Leclair with 51. The Flyers challenged the Penguins and the New York Rangers for first place overall in the Eastern Conference all season long.

At 23, Lindros has finally grown comfortable with the dominant role foreseen for him when the Quebec Nordiques drafted him first overall in 1991. He refused to report to the Nordiques, forcing a trade to the Flyers, who drained their organizational depth chart to land Lindros, sending eight players and $15 million to the Nordiques.

Nothing anyone could offer the Flyers could pry Lindros away now.

"He's a great player who's going to be greater," said Flyers general manager Bobby Clarke. "I think he started out terrific and he's progressing at the proper rate. He'll be better next year and even better the year after that."

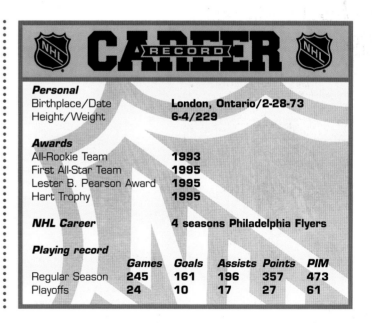

CAREER RECORD

Personal

Birthplace/Date	London, Ontario/2-28-73
Height/Weight	6-4/229

Awards

All-Rookie Team	1993
First All-Star Team	1995
Lester B. Pearson Award	1995
Hart Trophy	1995

NHL Career — 4 seasons Philadelphia Flyers

Playing record

	Games	Goals	Assists	Points	PIM
Regular Season	245	161	196	357	473
Playoffs	24	10	17	27	61

S peed defines some hockey players, strength others, still others personify skill. Mark Messier displays ample amounts of all three qualities, but to understand his essence, you start with the glare.

When Messier gets that look, his teammates get into formation behind him and opponents blanch just a little. The glare could translate into a game-breaking goal, a skilful passing play, a bone-rattling body check or even a well-timed, lethal elbow to an opponent's jaw.

Messier is the ultimate hockey player: big, fast, strong, skilful and junkyard-dog mean.

The captain of the New York Rangers is above all an incomparable on-ice leader, the capstone player on any team he has played for. He was a central player on five Edmonton Oilers teams that won the Stanley Cup, a leader on three Canadian teams that won the Canada Cup and indisputably the central force that carried the Rangers to the Stanley Cup in 1994, their first championship in 54 years.

Some consider him the fiercest, most inspirational leader in all of North American pro sports. He certainly has portfolio.

Trail of a giant

He has won two Hart Trophies as the league's most valuable player, one Conn Smythe Trophy as the best individual performer in the playoffs and two Lester B. Pearson Awards as the most outstanding player in the league, as voted on by his peers.

His individual performance chart reveals impressive statistics:

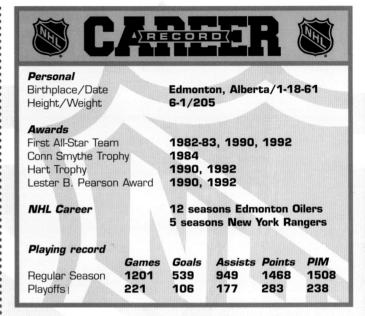

NHL CAREER RECORD

Personal	
Birthplace/Date	Edmonton, Alberta/1-18-61
Height/Weight	6-1/205

Awards	
First All-Star Team	1982-83, 1990, 1992
Conn Smythe Trophy	1984
Hart Trophy	1990, 1992
Lester B. Pearson Award	1990, 1992

NHL Career	12 seasons Edmonton Oilers
	5 seasons New York Rangers

Playing record	Games	Goals	Assists	Points	PIM
Regular Season	1201	539	949	1468	1508
Playoffs	221	106	177	283	238

one 50-goal season; six seasons of 100 points or more; more than 100 playoff goals and almost 300 post-season points; a record 13 playoff shorthanded goals.

But the true measure of Messier seems to be how teams he plays for perform. In 1990-91, Edmonton was 29-20-4 (won-lost-tied) with Messier in the lineup, just 8-17-2 without him.

In the 1991 Canada Cup, Team Canada coach Mike Keenan extended an eligibility deadline to make room on the team for Messier. Canada won the tournament that year.

In 1984, with the Wayne Gretzky Oilers, it was Messier who won the Conn Smythe Trophy as the most valuable player in the Stanley Cup playoffs as Edmonton won its first Cup in history.

No rash promise

The most celebrated illustration of Messier's leadership abilities came before Game 6 of the 1994 Stanley Cup semifinals against the New Jersey Devils.

The Devils held a 3-2 series lead, but Messier told a TV audience he guaranteed a victory by the Rangers in Game 6. He backed it up by scoring the hat trick as the Rangers won the game 4-2, sending the series to a seventh game in Madison Square which the Rangers won in double overtime, the third of three games decided in a second overtime period.

Not since New York Jets quarterback Joe Namath guaranteed a Super Bowl victory over the Baltimore Colts in 1969 had a New York sporting hero been so brash, then backed up his boast. Messier's guarantee had profound resonance for New York hockey fans.

The Rangers would need seven games to dispatch a determined and talented Vancouver Canucks team, but the most vivid Stanley Cup memory for many New Yorkers that year was Messier's Game 6 semifinal guarantee.

For the elite few unlucky enough to be around for the 54-year duration, it probably was worth the wait.

A Look that Chills: Messier is acknowledged as the best leader in the NHL. It doesn't pay to anger him.

Vancouver's Gifted Winger
ALEXANDER MOGILNY

Consistently brilliant this Russian is a dangerous Canuck.

Alex in Lotusland: When Mogilny was traded to Vancouver, he rejoined Pavel Bure, his linemate in Russia.

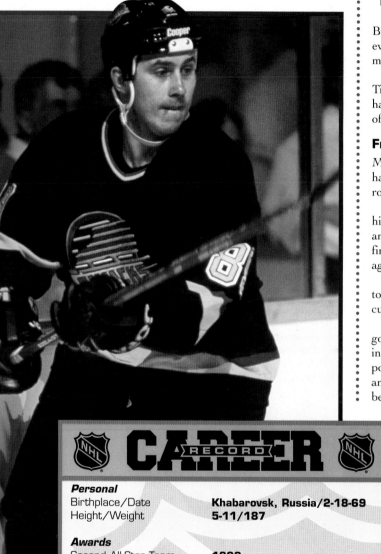

The pride of Khabarovsk, Russia, knew at an early age that he had a special talent for hockey. Alexander Mogilny joined Central Red Army and legendary head coach Viktor Tikhonov at age 17 for three years.

Tikhonov formed a line around Mogilny with wingers Pavel Bure and Sergei Fedorov, one of the most explosive forward trios ever seen. As an 18-year-old, Mogilny helped his country win a gold medal at the Calgary Olympics, the youngest player ever to do so.

There seems little doubt that playing under the demanding Tikhonov helped mould Mogilny into the swift, talented winger he has become. There also is no doubt that Mogilny wanted no part of the rigid Soviet system.

Fresh start

Mogilny defected in May 1989 and joined the Buffalo Sabres, who had drafted the 5-foot-11, 190-pound right winger in the fifth round (89th overall) of the 1989 entry draft.

Wearing No. 89—signifying his draft number and the year of his fresh start—Mogilny wasted no time proving he would make an impact on the NHL. He scored a goal for the Sabres on the first shift of his first game, 20 seconds into Buffalo's home opener against the Quebec Nordiques.

He scored 15 goals and had 28 assists in 1989-90, modest totals for a player of his talent, but understandable given the culture shock and language difficulty he was undergoing.

After back-to-back 30-goal seasons, Mogilny exploded for 76 goals in 1992-93, adding 51 assists and 127 points, seventh overall in the NHL. He scored 27 of those goals on the Sabres potent power play, one that included Pat LaFontaine, Dale Hawerchuk and Doug Bodger. In an ordinary season, Mogilny would have been a shoo-in for the first All-Star team, but in 1992-93 Teemu Selanne filled that position and Mogilny had to be content with a second All-Star team selection. In Game 3 of the Adams Division Finals against the Montreal Canadiens that spring, Mogilny suffered a fractured fibula in his right leg and ligament damage to his right ankle, a setback that seems to have slowed him little since.

New shores

Following the lockout-shortened 1994-95 season, the Sabres traded Mogilny to the Vancouver Canucks.

The Sabres were offloading some big salaries and the Canucks, on the verge of opening the new GM Place Arena, wanted to add some flash to an already talent-rich lineup to keep the new building full.

The deal reunited Mogilny with Bure, his Central Red Army linemate, but the reunion was postponed after Bure went down with a knee injury early in the 1995-96 season, finishing him for the year.

Luckily for the Canucks, Mogilny performed brilliantly, scoring 55 goals to lead his team in scoring and a place among the top ten in the NHL. He was one of few constants on the mercurial Canucks 1995-96. Canucks fans, no doubt, eagerly await the return of Bure, to see how the two Russian speed demons will perform in tandem over seasons to come.

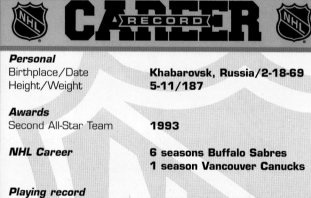

CAREER RECORD

Personal

Birthplace/Date	Khabarovsk, Russia/2-18-69
Height/Weight	5-11/187

Awards

Second All-Star Team	1993

NHL Career

6 seasons Buffalo Sabres
1 season Vancouver Canucks

Playing record

	Games	Goals	Assists	Points	PIM
Regular Season	460	266	285	551	219
Playoffs	37	15	24	39	26

The man who changed the role of defensemen and scored a legendary Stanley Cup winner.

BOBBY ORR

I n the Canadian hockey orthodoxy of the 1940s and 50s, the best skaters were forwards and the best qualifications for defensemen were size, strength and meanness. Bobby Orr changed all that. As a 14-year-old playing for the Oshawa Generals of the OHL, Orr was the best skater in the league, leading the offensive rush, often going end-to-end to score or set up a goal.

Amazingly, he was swift enough to recover and chase down an opponent if the attack failed. Quite simply, Orr changed the job description for defensemen, changed the way the game was played.

Instant domination

He burst into the NHL as an 18-year-old and began to dominate games almost immediately with his speed, on-ice vision, ability to turn on a dime, and seemingly instant acceleration.

He was named rookie of the year and named to the second All-Star team that first season, but that was merely prologue to further brilliance.

For the next eight seasons, Orr owned the James Norris Memorial Trophy as the NHL's top defenseman. He also won the Hart Trophy as the NHL's most valuable player three times, and twice he won the scoring championship, the only defenseman ever to lead the league in scoring.

Some have actually criticized Orr—not strong in his own zone, they claim. Brad Park, a contemporary of Orr, whose own excellent career was overshadowed by him, had an excellent answer for the critics: "You don't have to play defense if you've always got the puck."

When he joined the Bruins, they had not qualified for the playoffs since 1959. They missed the post-season tournament in Orr's rookie season, too—have not missed them since.

Turn-around star

He literally turned the fortunes of the franchise around. If he had only one great shining moment it would be May 10, 1970, when he scored the Stanley Cup winner against the St. Louis Blues. He was tripped as he scored the goal, and actually sent the puck into the net as he sailed through the air, his arms upstretched victoriously.

The goal—the photo that captured it for the ages—lives on in hockey legend.

Unfortunately, Orr's career was foreshortened by a pair of wonky knees. Knee injuries kept him from participating in the 1972 Summit Series between Canada and the Soviet Union, when Orr was only 24. He played—and superbly—for Canada in the 1976 Canada Cup, but by then his knees had slowed him noticably.

By the time Orr left the Bruins to play for the Chicago Blackhawks in 1978, his knees were virtually devoid of cartilage. Their damaged state makes it difficult for Orr to walk comfortably for any distance, a cruel irony for a man who literally skated circles around the best players in his prime.

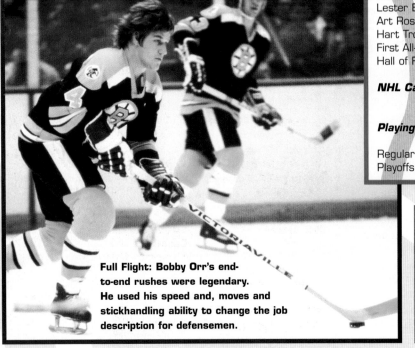

Full Flight: Bobby Orr's end-to-end rushes were legendary. He used his speed and, moves and stickhandling ability to change the job description for defensemen.

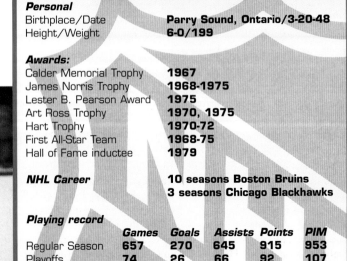

CAREER RECORD

Personal	
Birthplace/Date	Parry Sound, Ontario/3-20-48
Height/Weight	6-0/199

Awards:	
Calder Memorial Trophy	1967
James Norris Trophy	1968-1975
Lester B. Pearson Award	1975
Art Ross Trophy	1970, 1975
Hart Trophy	1970-72
First All-Star Team	1968-75
Hall of Fame inductee	1979

NHL Career	
	10 seasons Boston Bruins
	3 seasons Chicago Blackhawks

Playing record

	Games	Goals	Assists	Points	PIM
Regular Season	657	270	645	915	953
Playoffs	74	26	66	92	107

ICE TALK

"IF I WERE A HORSE, THEY'D PROBABLY SHOOT ME."

BOBBY ORR ON HIS PAINFULLY ARTHRITIC KNEES

Mile-High Goaltender
PATRICK ROY

Eccentric, miraculous and flawless, Montreal's ex-star must now prove his worth in Colorado.

St. Patrick: Patrick Roy, a demigod in Montreal, was traded to Colorado after delivering an ultimatum to the Canadiens owner last Fall.

During games, the rookie goaltender talked to his goalposts, and before each game started, he skated 40 feet in front of his net, turned and stared intently at his workplace, skated hard right at the crease, veered away at the last second, then settled into his work station for another night of brilliance.

Even among goaltenders, who are known for their eccentricity, Patrick Roy was a classic from his first NHL season in 1986.

Roy was magnificent during the playoffs as the Canadiens, with a rookie-laden club, won the Stanley Cup, surprising the hockey world.

Roy won the Conn Smythe Trophy, winning 15 and losing just five playoff games and posting a goals-against average of 1.92. He had staked his claim to the title of the best goalie in the NHL.

The next three seasons, he won the William Jennings Trophy, for the goalie whose team allows the fewest goals against. Three times (1989-90, 1992) Roy also won the Vezina Trophy, awarded to the league's best goalie, as voted on by the general managers.

Roy refined his goaltending technique the hard way. As a junior goalie, playing for the sad sack Granby Bisons of the Quebec Major Junior Hockey League, it was not uncommon for Roy to face 60- or 70-shot barrages.

Stellar start

When he arrived in the NHL as a regular, Roy was only 20, and had played one single, solitary game in minor pro hockey, but he was seasoned, which he quickly proved.

Roy has been at his best in pressure situations. His stellar play led the Canadiens to three Stanley Cup finals (1986, 1989, 1993), and two Cup championships.

Both those years, he won the Conn Smythe Trophy as the most valuable player in the playoffs. His performance in the 1993 Stanley Cup playoffs, when the Canadiens won ten of 11

overtime games, was just this side of miraculous.

It's not for nothing the Forum came to be known as St. Patrick's Cathedral during his glory years there.

In 1994, Roy was stricken with appendicitis after two games of the opening-round series against the Boston Bruins and had to be hospitalized. Antibiotics forestalled the need for surgery and Roy rose from his hospital bed to record two straight victories over the Bruins, one a 2-1 overtime thriller at the old Boston Garden in which he made 60 saves.

At his best, Roy is technically flawless, using a butterfly style in which he goes to his knees and splays his leg pads to cover the lower portion of the net, protecting the upper portion with his body and his cat-quick left hand.

Superstar shock

Roy was Montreal's franchise player, its superstar, and it was a shock on December 2 when the goaltender, embarrassed by an 11-1 pounding he had absorbed from the Detroit Red Wings, told club president Ronald Corey, on national TV, that he had played his last game with the Montreal Canadiens. Three days later, Roy was traded to the Colorado Avalanche. The unthinkable had happened. The Canadiens had shut St. Patrick from his own Cathedral.

In his first season as just a goaltender with a talented but certainly not exalted team in a city where hockey is far from the crucial sport, Roy performed solidly, though not brilliantly.

The pressure would be on in the playoffs, but even that pressure probably couldn't compare with what Roy had withstood, even thrived on in Montreal.

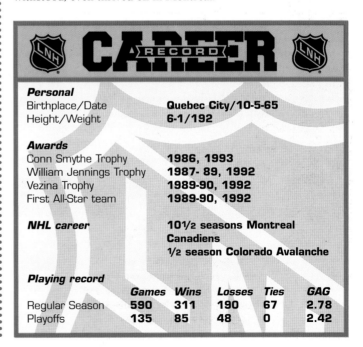

CAREER RECORD

Personal

Birthplace/Date	Quebec City/10-5-65
Height/Weight	6-1/192

Awards

Conn Smythe Trophy	1986, 1993
William Jennings Trophy	1987- 89, 1992
Vezina Trophy	1989-90, 1992
First All-Star team	1989-90, 1992

NHL career — 10½ seasons Montreal Canadiens / ½ season Colorado Avalanche

Playing record

	Games	Wins	Losses	Ties	GAG
Regular Season	590	311	190	67	2.78
Playoffs	135	85	48	0	2.42

Untouched by his club's changing fortunes this rising star can look forward to a brilliant new season.

He's not big, in fact, he's almost small by National Hockey League standards, but Joe Sakic is water-bug elusive, a slick, clever passer, an accurate shooter and perhaps the most unassuming superstar in hockey.

Sakic was a first-round draft pick by the then-Quebec Nordiques in 1987. He was taken 15th overall after a monster season (60 goals, 133 points) with the Swift Current Broncos of the Western Hockey League.

When he joined the once-mighty Nordiques, for the 1988-89 season, they had just finished last in the Adams Division and were about to embark on the darkest period in franchise history. They would finish last overall in the NHL the next three years in a row. Sakic's NHL apprenticeship did not come easy.

Nordique blues

Sakic was fortunate enough to have Nordiques' star center Peter Stastny around for most of his first two seasons as a role model. Sakic, it turned out, didn't need that much guidance.

He scored 23 goals and added 39 assists for 62 points in his first season, then recorded the first of four 100-plus point seasons the very next year, when he led the Nordiques with 39 goals and 63 assists.

When the Nordiques traded Stastny, their first real superstar, to the New Jersey Devils in 1990, the torch had been passed to the smallish, shifty Sakic. The Nordiques would soon surround Sakic with some of the best young talent in the game.

As the club improved, adding players like Owen Nolan, Mats Sundin, Curtis Leschyshyn, Stephane Fiset, Valeri Kamensky et al, expectations began to soar, also.

In 1992-93, the Nordiques made the playoffs for the first time in five years and drew provincial rival Montreal Canadiens as their first-round opponent. The talent-rich Nordiques won the first two games.

But Montreal goalie Patrick Roy stiffened and the Canadiens stunned the Nordiques, winning the next four games in a row. The critics howled, many of them at Sakic, but the quiet-spoken Sakic took the loss as a learning experience.

The following season, the Nordiques slumped as a team. They missed the playoffs again.

In the lockout-shortened 1994-95 season, Sakic's 19 goals and 43 assists put him fourth in league scoring and the Nordiques finished first overall in the Eastern Conference, then lost to the more experienced Rangers in the opening round of the Stanley Cup playoffs.

Colorado dawn

The lockout and uncertainty over the club's future clouded the Nordiques' season, but Sakic returned to his quietly consistent self in the team's new home in Denver, Colorado, during the 1995-96 season.

Sakic was among the league leaders in scoring all season long, easily surpassing the 100-point mark for the fifth time and recording his first-ever 50-goal season as the Avalanche cruised to the Pacific Division title.

Sakic is as close as it comes in the NHL to a sure bet to hit the century mark in points. And the Avalanche fans may be in for his best years yet.

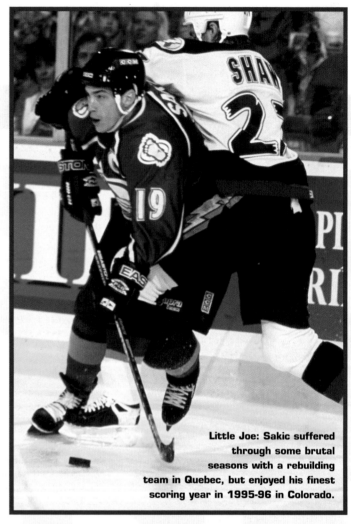

Little Joe: Sakic suffered through some brutal seasons with a rebuilding team in Quebec, but enjoyed his finest scoring year in 1995-96 in Colorado.

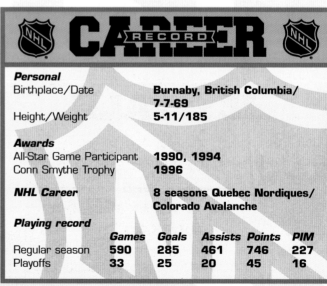

CAREER RECORD

Personal	
Birthplace/Date	Burnaby, British Columbia/ 7-7-69
Height/Weight	5-11/185

Awards	
All-Star Game Participant	1990, 1994
Conn Smythe Trophy	1996

NHL Career	8 seasons Quebec Nordiques/ Colorado Avalanche

Playing record

	Games	Goals	Assists	Points	PIM
Regular season	590	285	461	746	227
Playoffs	33	25	20	45	16

Surviving savage xenophobic tests, he became a Toronto star.

Borje Salming wasn't the first European to play in the National Hockey League, but he was the first one to become a star and in so doing, he became something of a target.

Ulf Sterner played a handful of games for the Rangers in the 1960s, and in 1972 Thommie Bergman, a defenseman for the Detroit Red Wings, became the first Swedish player to play a whole season in the NHL. But Europeans were decidedly a novelty in the league when Salming arrived in Toronto in 1973.

Test of fire

He joined the Maple Leafs precisely when the Philadelphia Flyers were emerging as the league's top team. The Broad Street Bullies also were the dirtiest club in the league, which, as a whole, was not exactly open-minded about a European influx.

Salming came to the Maple Leafs with winger Inge Hammerstrom, a skilled but gentle player whose dislike for the banging and crashing of NHL hockey provoked a disgusted Ballard to say: "He could skate into a corner with six eggs in his pocket and not break any of them."

Players 'tested' the newcomers, subjecting them to sometimes brutal attacks, under the guise of determining whether the stereotype 'chicken Swede' stood up to the factual evidence.

One of Salming's worst tests occurred in the Stanley Cup playoffs in 1976 between the Maple Leafs and Flyers. A stick-swinging incident escalated into a major brawl, during which Mel Bridgman badly beat up Salming. It was Salming's response that mattered, though.

Minutes later, center Darryl Sittler hit a streaking Salming

Slick Swede: Salming became a fan favorite at Maple Leaf Gardens as one of the first Europeans to cross the Atlantic and play in the NHL.

with a pass that sent him away on a breakaway. Salming, a smooth, swooping sort of skater, scored on Flyers' goalie Bernie Parent on the play, prompting a lengthy standing ovation from the Toronto fans at Maple Leaf Gardens.

"I felt sorry for him for everything the other teams did to him during the seventies," Maple Leafs' tough guy Dave (Tiger) Williams has said. "If they had done that stuff today to any player at all, they would be banned for life."

The tough get going

But Salming withstood often vicious attacks and became an elegant, creative presence on the Toronto blue line. Through his first nine seasons, he averaged more than 62 points.

Salming, Sittler and Lanny McDonald were the key cogs in Toronto's dangerous power play during those years, and the lanky defenseman was firmly established as a favorite of the Toronto fans.

Ironically, Salming's worst NHL injuries happened the way most do: accidentally.

On one occasion, Salming's face was literally sliced open, forehead to mouth, by the skate blade of Gerard Gallant, a winger with the Detroit Red Wings. That gruesome wound required 300 stitches and left Salming horrifically—but temporarily—disfigured.

Salming finished his 17-year NHL career by playing one season with Detroit, before returning to play in Sweden, where he still lives.

ICE TALK

"WE CALLED HIM KING BECAUSE HE WAS KING OF ALL THE EUROPEANS. ALL THE PLAYERS WHO CAME OVER LATER CAN THANK HIM FOR EVERYTHING."

DAVE (TIGER) WILLIAMS, FORMER MAPLE LEAFS TEAMMATE

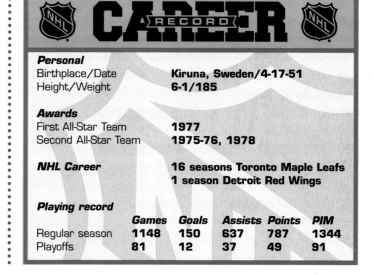

CAREER RECORD

Personal

Birthplace/Date	Kiruna, Sweden/4-17-51
Height/Weight	6-1/185

Awards

First All-Star Team	1977
Second All-Star Team	1975-76, 1978

NHL Career

16 seasons Toronto Maple Leafs
1 season Detroit Red Wings

Playing record

	Games	Goals	Assists	Points	PIM
Regular season	1148	150	637	787	1344
Playoffs	81	12	37	49	91

TEEMU SELANNE

After his surprise debut in the NHL as a fully-formed star with the Jets, the Finn is now set to score for Anaheim.

When you blend world-class skill and offensive creativity with eye-popping speed, you really discombobulate a defense. That description fits Teemu Selanne perfectly.

Selanne, The Finnish Flash, blazed through the National Hockey League in his first season with the Winnipeg Jets, scoring 76 goals and adding 56 assists to shatter the records for most goals.

Fully-grown rookie

The 6-foot, 200-pound Finnish speedster zoomed into the NHL in 1994 at 22, two or three years older than the average rookie. To say he made the adjustment from Jokerit in the Finnish Elite League with ease is to understate the magnitude of his achievement.

Selanne recorded his first three-goal hat trick in his fifth NHL game. In late February that season, Selanne scored four goals in a victory over the Minnesota (now Dallas) Stars.

He produced a string of scoring streaks that left Jets fans dizzy: an eight-game scoring streak (nine goals and 11 assists); a five-game goal-scoring streak in which he recorded 11 goals; a nine-game goal-scoring streak in which he scored 14 goals; a 17-game points streak that produced 20 goals and 14 assists. He rocketed through the Jets' final six games, scoring 13 goals and adding two assists.

In his first NHL playoff game, against the Vancouver Canucks, he not only scored a goal, he recorded another three-goal hat trick.

His Calder Memorial Trophy award as the top rookie in the league was expected. Astonishing was his arrival as a fully formed superstar, competing with both rookies *and* the best players.

His 76 goals tied for the league lead with Alexander Mogilny and he was selected as the right winger on the first All-Star team.

Kid start

Selanne was a mature player upon arrival in North America because he had not hurried his development in his native Finland.

He grew up in the minor hockey system in Helsinki, playing for KalPa-Espoo from the age of five. By nine, he was competing against players two years his senior, and at 16 he joined Jokerit,

one of the most successful of the teams in the Finnish Elite League for five seasons before he made the jump to the NHL.

"It is good to play there and get better and then come (to the NHL) later, when you are ready," he has said. "I had dreams to play in the World Championship and the Olympic Games before I came here and when I came here, I had done all that. I left with a clear conscience."

He left Winnipeg with a clear conscience, too, but not of his own accord. The Jets traded him to the Anaheim Mighty Ducks in 1996.

This gave Anaheim a one-two offensive punch of Selanne and Paul Kariya. Before the season was over, Selanne would record two hat tricks for the Mighty Ducks, 50 per cent of the organizational total.

The Ducks, no doubt, can look forward to plenty more scoring streaks from their Disney-fied Finnish Flash.

NHL CAREER RECORD

Personal

Birthplace/date	Helsinki, Finland/7-3-70
Height/Weight	6-0/200

Awards

Calder Memorial Trophy	1994
First All-Star Team	1994

NHL Career — 3½ seasons Winnipeg Jets, ½ season Anaheim Mighty Ducks

Playing record

	Games	Goals	Assists	Points	PIM
Regular Season	259	163	179	342	89
Playoffs	6	4	2	6	2

ICE TALK

"WHEN I WAS YOUNGER, THE NHL WAS JUST A DREAM BECAUSE I DID NOT KNOW HOW MUCH OF A SACRIFICE IT TOOK TO MAKE IT TO THIS LEVEL. BUT WHEN I WAS 18 OR 19, I STARTED HAVING MORE SUCCESS AND THEN MY GOAL WAS TO PLAY IN THE NHL."

Teemu Selanne

Finnish Flash: Selanne left Winnipeg reluctantly, but quickly warmed to life in California, particularly since he was paired with Paul Kariya, another talented speedster.

DARRYL SITTLER

Maple Leafs' scrappy center had some of the NHL's best-ever scoring performances.

What Guy Lafleur was to the Montreal Canadiens during the 1970s, Darryl Sittler was to the Toronto Maple Leafs. "Guy Lafleur is big in Quebec, but in Saskatchewan he can't compare to Darryl Sittler," Dave (Tiger) Williams, Sittler's Maple Leaf teammate once said.

Sittler joined a Maple Leafs club still rebuilding following the unlikely 1967 Stanley Cup with a collection of aging stars. The once-proud club rebuilt around Sittler, a talented center and a passionate team leader.

CAREER RECORD

Personal

Birthplace/Date	Kitchener, Ontario/9-18-50
Height/Weight	6-0/190

Awards

Second All-Star Team	1978
Canada Cup winning goal	1976
Hall of Fame Inductee	1989

NHL Career

12 seasons Toronto Maple Leafs
3 seasons Philadelphia Flyers
1 season Detroit Red Wings

Playing record

	Games	Goals	Assists	Points	PIM
Regular Season	1096	484	637	1121	948
Playoffs	76	29	45	74	137

With Sittler, winger Lanny McDonald, goaltender Mike Palmateer, tough guy Williams, and defenseman Ian Turnbull, the Maple Leafs had a nucleus of bright young stars. And if the team never regained its past glory, this was hardly Sittler's fault.

He shone brilliantly for the Maple Leafs, particularly in 1976. Sittler reached 100 points for the first time that season, scoring 41 goals and adding 59 assists.

Pure magic

His best night that year—his best night ever—came on Feb 7, 1976 against the Boston Bruins. He scored six goals and added four assists as the Maple Leafs administered an 11-4 drubbing to Boston.

"Every time I had the puck, something seemed to happen," Sittler remembers.

Good things happened one night in the playoffs that year against the Philadelphia Flyers, too. Sittler bagged five goals in a victory over Philadelphia, the first time anyone had done that since Maurice (Rocket) Richard scored all Montreal's goals in a 5-1 playoff victory over Toronto in 1944.

Sittler had more magic to display.

In September 1976, he played for Canada in the first Canada Cup hockey tournament. Sittler scored the tournament winner for Canada in overtime against Czechoslovakia, beating goaltender Vladimir Dzurilla on a partial breakaway in one of Canadian hockey's golden moments.

The game also was noteworthy for what happened after the Canada Cup was awarded. The players on both teams exchanged jerseys in an affecting moment of sportsmanship none who saw it will forget.

Maple Leaf Forever: Darryl Sittler, the Maple Leafs' captain through most of the 1970s, was the brightest light on a mediocre team.

ICE TALK

"GUY LAFLEUR IS BIG IN QUEBEC, BUT IN SASKATCHEWAN HE CAN'T COMPARE TO DARRYL SITTLER."

DAVE (TIGER) WILLIAMS

Rebellious and aggressive, innovative and quirky, this netminder changed NHL rules.

BILLY SMITH

It's a curiosity of the career of Battlin' Billy Smith that he only managed one first All-Star team selection. One would expect a handful of selections for the dominant goalie on the dominant National Hockey League team of the early 1980s. But then, the regular-season wasn't the crucial time for Smith. The Stanley Cup playoffs were his hockey stage.

"He may be the all-time money player," Bill Torrey, the Islanders general manager once said.

Smith backstopped four straight Stanley Cup championships for the Islanders. He shared the first one with Glenn (Chico) Resch, who competed with Smith for the

Battlin' Billy: Around his goal crease, Billy Smith took the rule book into his own hands, and often used his hockey stick to enforce it.

ICE TALK

"THE ONLY THING I EVER TOLD SMITTY WAS TO BE CAREFUL HE DOESN'T HURT SOMEBODY OR HE'LL HAVE TO PAY THE PRICE."

GLENN (CHICO) RESCH, FORMER ISLANDERS TEAMMATE

No. 1 goaltending job as that championship club was maturing. But Resch went to the Colorado Rockies (now the New Jersey Devils) in 1980, leaving Smith as the clear No. 1 goalie with the Islanders dynasty.

He also was the preeminent netminder of the time. Montreal's Ken Dryden had retired as had Boston goalie Gerry Cheevers. Bernie Parent, the Philadelphia Flyers goalie, had to leave the game owing to an eye injury. Grant Fuhr, the splendid netminder who would backstop the Edmonton Oilers' mid-80s Cup teams, had not yet arrived.

Fire on ice

Smith, who had played just five games for the L.A. Kings before being taken by the Islanders in the 1972 expansion draft, guarded the Islanders net for 17 seasons, guarded it with as much competitive fire as any goalie in history.

If an opposing forward crowded him, Smith might chop him in the ankle with his heavy goalie stick. If the player got too aggressive about it, Smith would fight the guy. This often did little for his concentration. But Smith was not about to cede his territory to anyone.

In the 1984-85 season, Smith broke the jaw and cheek bone of Chicago Blackhawks forward Curt Fraser.

"If they changed the rules and made the crease bigger, it would

stop all this cheap stuff," Smith once said.

The NHL was listening. In 1987, two years before Smith retired, a rule change enlarged the goalie crease, which had been rectangular, to a six-foot semicircle. In the 1990s, the league implemented tougher rules on goalie interference.

Smith, quirky, idiosyncratic, more than a little rebellious, had a significant impact on the game.

Tennis and video games

His aggressive play masked an innovative hockey mind. Smith avoided practices if he could, worrying that he could get hurt. He was an avid tennis player, believing it would help a goaltender's footwork.

No traditionalist, Smith played video games, on the theory it would improve hand-to-eye co-ordination.

Almost certainly, the culmination of Smith's unique career came in the 1983 Stanley Cup playoffs, as the Islanders won their fourth straight Cup, beating the talented, callow Edmonton Oilers in four straight games. Smith posted a 2-0 shutout in Game 1 of the series and gave up just six goals in the four games for a goals-against average of 1.50.

Four years after he retired in 1989, Smith was inducted into the Hockey Hall of Fame.

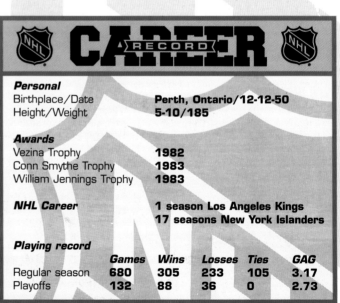

CAREER RECORD

Personal
Birthplace/Date	Perth, Ontario/12-12-50
Height/Weight	5-10/185

Awards
Vezina Trophy	1982
Conn Smythe Trophy	1983
William Jennings Trophy	1983

NHL Career
	1 season Los Angeles Kings
	17 seasons New York Islanders

Playing record

	Games	Wins	Losses	Ties	GAG
Regular season	680	305	233	105	3.17
Playoffs	132	88	36	0	2.73

BRYAN TROTTIER

Indefatigable enthusiasm and dedication marked the career of this model NHL player.

Bryan Trottier is the kind of player who had to have the jersey ripped off his back. No one ever brought as much boyish enthusiasm to an NHL career; no one played so long, so well without losing an ounce of that enthusiasm.

In his rookie season, Trottier scored 32 goals and added 63 assists for 95 points, setting a club record for points by a rookie that still stands.

He went on to litter the Islanders' record book with standards: most career assists (853); most career points (1,353); mosts assists in a season (87); most points by a center (134); most points in a game (8).

Shark attack!

Trottier centered the Trio Grande with right winger Mike Bossy and left winger Clark Gillies. During the early 1980s, the line led the Islanders to four straight Stanley Cups.

He posted six 100-plus point seasons, five of them in a row, with the Islanders and was widely regarded as the game's best centerman during that period.

The line was particularly deadly on the power play, when it joined with defensemen Denis Potvin and Stefan Persson to unleash a precise, often successful attack on the opposition net. At Nassau County Coliseum, at the onset of a power play, the theme from the movie *Jaws* played over the public address system. Shark attack!

Bossy, the sniper, and Potvin, the franchise defenseman, both are in the Hockey Hall of Fame. Trottier's certain entry into the Temple has been delayed for the simple reason that he refused to quit playing.

As his skills declined, so did the fortunes of the Islanders. By

Grand Old Man: Eric Lindros was just two years old when Bryan Trottier was a rookie with the New York Islanders in 1975. Trottier won four Stanley Cups with the Islanders, two more with Pittsburgh.

1989-90, Trottier had been replaced by Pat LaFontaine as the top centerman on the Islanders. A free agent, Trottier signed with the Pittsburgh Penguins in the off-season and found a niche as a fourth-line center with Mario Lemieux's team.

No standing down

Trottier helped the Penguins win two straight Stanley Cups, his fifth and sixth, as a player. He rejoined the Islanders in 1992-93 as an executive, but couldn't stay away from the game.

The following season, he was right back with the Penguins as a sort of playing assistant coach. He played 41 games in 1993-94, his final season. He remains with the Penguins as an assistant coach, close to the game he loves.

His entry into the Hall of Fame is a certainty. He just has to wait the required three years after retirement, which means he probably is on track to enter the shrine in 1997.

During his brilliant career, he was named rookie-of-the-year, twice was a first-team All-Star, won the Art Ross Trophy, the Conn Smythe Trophy and the Hart Trophy as the league's most valuable player.

CAREER RECORD

Personal

Birthplace/Date	Val Marie, Saskatchewan/ 7-17-56
Height/Weight	5-10/195

Awards

Calder Memorial Trophy	1976
Conn Smythe Trophy	1980
Art Ross Trophy	1979
Hart Trophy	1979
First All-Star Team	1978-79

NHL Career

15 seasons New York Islanders
2 seasons Pittsburgh Penguins

Playing record

	Games	Goals	Assists	Points	PIM
Regular Season	1279	524	901	1425	1043
Playoffs	221	71	113	184	277

THE STANLEY CUP
THE ULTIMATE GOAL

It's known as the National Hockey League's second season and it may well be the most exciting post-season tournament in professional sports. The Stanley Cup playoffs stretch from mid-April to mid-June as 16 of the NHL's 26 teams compete for the Stanley Cup, one of the most cherished pieces of sporting silverware in the world. The champion must win four best-of-seven series—16 games out of a possible 28 in total, all played after the 82-game regular season concludes in mid-April.

This annual North American Rite of Spring has unfolded, in various formats, since 1893, one year after Lord Stanley, the Earl of Preston and Governor-General of Canada, donated the challenge cup to symbolize the hockey championship of Canada.

Lord Stanley returned to England without ever seeing a championship game or personally presenting the trophy that bears his name. He wasn't around when the Montreal Amateur Athletic Association hockey club became the first winner of the trophy. He certainly could not have foreseen that his trophy would become the property of the National Hockey League, which did not exist until 1917 and did not assume control of the Stanley Cup competition until the 1926-27 season.

Still, the rich and colorful history attached to the silver cup that Lord Stanley purchased for 10 guineas ($48.67 Cdn) more than lives up to the spirit of the annual hockey competition he envisaged more than 100 years ago.

The institution of the trophy kicked off a parade of legendary performances. In 1904, One-Eyed Frank McGee scored a record five goals in an 11-2 victory for the Ottawa Silver Seven over the Toronto Marlboros. The following year, McGee scored 14 goals for the Silver Seven, who demolished the Dawson City Nuggets 23-2. The Nuggets had journeyed to Ottawa via dogsled, boat and train to challenge for Lord Stanley's Cup.

A special time

The quality of competition has tightened considerably since those early days, and transportation is decidedly less rustic, also. But the mystique of the best four-out-of-seven game final series still holds powerful appeal for hockey fans.

The Stanley Cup final can pit speed and finesse against size and toughness, slick offense versus stingy defense, age against youth and, sometimes, brother against brother. The first time that happened was March 16, 1923 when the Denneny brothers, Cy and Corb, and the Boucher siblings, George and Frank, faced off against each other. Cy and George were members of the Ottawa Senators, Corb and Frank played for the Vancouver Maroons. Ottawa won that game 1-0 and went on to capture the Stanley Cup.

In a playoff game between the Montreal Canadiens and the

Cup of Honor: Lenny McDonald (left), the Calgary Flames' bearded veteran, capped off a 16-year NHL career with a Stanley Cup triumph in 1989.

Quebec Nordiques in the 1980s, Montreal's Mark Hunter missed a golden opportunity to pot an overtime winner at one end, then watched, crestfallen as older brother Dale put the game away for the Nordiques (now the Colorado Avalanche) at the other end.

The Stanley Cup tournament is a special event, when there's no time for injuries to heal, so the great ones simply play through the pain, no matter how excruciating. Hall of Fame defenseman Jacques Laperriere once played the finals with a broken wrist, goaltender John Davidson gritted his teeth and played with a wonky knee in the 1979 finals. Montreal left winger Bob Gainey once completed a playoff series against the New York Islanders with not one but two shoulder separations. And in 1964, Toronto Maple Leafs defenseman Bob Baun scored an overtime winner with a broken ankle in Game

Alberta Magic: Few would have guessed that Wayne Gretzky's fourth Stanley Cup in Edmonton would be his last in an Oiler uniform.

6, then played Game 7 without missing a shift. He then spent two months on crutches recuperating. No doubt, the Stanley Cup ring helped soothe his pain.

The Stanley Cup is about unlikely heroes, like Montreal goalie Ken Dryden being called up from the minors to backstop Montreal to a first-round upset over the heavily favored Boston Bruins in 1971, then going on to win the Conn Smythe Trophy, not to mention the Stanley Cup, both before winning the Calder Trophy as rookie-of-the-year the following season.

It's a showcase for the game's greatest stars, like Maurice (Rocket) Richard, who once scored five goals in a playoff game in 1944. Richard's record of six career playoff overtime goals has stood up for 36 years.

A fitting showcase

In the 1990s, the first round of the playoff tournament has captivated hockey fans, providing some stunning upsets, like the expansion San Jose Sharks knocking out the Detroit Red Wings in seven games in 1994. The Sharks rolled right to the Western Conference semifinal, extending the Toronto Maple Leafs to seven games before losing.

In 1993, the New York Islanders surprised the Washington Capitals in the opening round, then stunned the two-time defending champion Pittsburgh Penguins in the division final, a series victory that helped pave the way for Montreal's surprising Stanley Cup triumph. The Canadiens had fallen behind 2-0 to the talent-rich Quebec Nordiques before winning four straight games to eliminate their provincial rivals from the tournament.

There are those who criticize the Stanley Cup playoffs as far too long, who suggest, not without justification, that hockey is simply not meant to be played in June, taxing the ice-making machinery, the fans' attention span and the players' fitness level.

Few would dare to suggest, however, that the two-month-long tournament is not a fitting showcase for professional hockey. Boring is something the Stanley Cup playoffs most certainly are not.

Lord Stanley never knew what he missed; nor had he any idea how rich a sporting tradition he initiated all those years ago.

FINAL GLORY

The weakened Edmonton dynasty retooled to beat the Boston Bruins in a victory that echoed past glory, but did not herald a new era.

Conn Smythe Goalie: Bill Ranford's netminding heroics led the post-Wayne Gretzky Edmonton Oilers to a Stanley Cup victory in 1990.

The Edmonton Oilers, the NHL's team of the mid-1980s, kicked off the 1990s with their fifth Stanley Cup victory in seven years. They had struggled through 1989 aimlessly, after the trade that shipped their superstar Wayne Gretzky to the Los Angeles Kings.

Now, the Oilers were a re-tooled version of the once-dominant team. Veterans Mark Messier, Glenn Anderson, Kevin Lowe, Jari Kurri, Esa Tikkanen, Charlie Huddy and Randy Gregg were still around. Goaltender Grant Fuhr, injured much of the season, was supplanted by Bill Ranford.

With mid-season acquisitions, general manager Glen Sather had assembled a Kid Line of Adam Graves, Joe Murphy and Martin Gelinas. Peter Klima, gifted but erratic, was aboard for the playoff ride.

The Bruins, as they had been since 1980, were constructed around marvelous defenseman Raymond Bourque, assisted by a small corps of stars that included goaltender Andy Moog, the former Oiler, power forward Cam Neely, center Craig Janney and aging sniper Brian Propp.

A need to prove

Even diminished, the Oilers were not outclassed by the Bruins. Their motivation was to prove they could win a Stanley Cup without Gretzky

Game 1 of the final series was the longest overtime game in finals history and one of the most exciting. The Oilers, on goals by Graves and Anderson, took a 2-0 lead into the third period, which belonged to Bourque. He scored twice, the second with less than 89 seconds remaining in regulation time to force overtime.

When little-used Klima scored the game-winner, at 15:13 of the third overtime period, the clubs were just 4:47 shy of having played the equivalent of two games.

The heat at old, decrepit Boston Garden left everyone drenched in perspiration.

Still drained two nights later, the older Bruins were dumped 7-2, and the outcome of the series seemed assured.

But backed by the brilliant goaltending of Andy Moog, the Bruins posted a surprise 2-1 victory in Game 3. That was their last gasp. They were defeated 5-1 in Game 4 and dismissd 4-1 in the finale in Boston.

Just rewards

Bill Ranford, a former Bruin who had been traded for Moog, won the Conn Smythe Trophy—the hard way. He had been shaky early in the playoffs. From Game 5 of that opening series onward, though, he gave up no cheap goals, establishing himself as a top-rank goalie in the NHL.

★★★★★ RESULTS ★★★★★

	Game	Site	Winner	Score	GWG
May 15	Game 1	Boston	Edmonton	3-2 (OT)	Peter Klima
May 18	Game 2	Boston	Edmonton	7-2	Jari Kurri
May 20	Game 3	Edmonton	Boston	2-1	Greg Johnston
May 22	Game 4	Edmonton	Edmonton	5-1	Glenn Anderson
May 24	Game 5	Boston	Edmonton	4-1	Craig Simpson

1991 Stanley Cup Finals
COMING OUT

Unexpected finalists Minnesota North Stars fell to the Lemieux-led Pittsburgh Penguins offense.

This Stanley Cup final matchup was closer than it might have looked. The North Stars were managed by former Philadelphia Flyers great Bobby Clarke and coached by Bob Gainey, the top defensive forward for the great Montreal Canadiens teams of the 1970s. It took a while for the Clarke-Gainey plan to kick in, but it worked almost to perfection in the playoffs.

The Stars had won fewer regular-season games (27) than any of the teams that qualified for the playoffs, but the pieces of the team puzzle fit nicely together in the post-season.

Goaltender Jon Casey was superb, and ably supported by defensemen like Mark Tinordi and Neil Wilkinson. The forwards were veterans like Bobby Smith, Neal Broten, Brian Propp and Brian Bellows, and young stars like Mike Modano, Dave Gagner and Ulf Dahlen. Gainey had the team playing a sound defensive style.

The Stars surprised most just by advancing to the final, having beaten Chicago, St. Louis and Edmonton.

The Lemieux threat

Most saw this as the North Stars' opportunity to be humiliated by Mario Lemieux and company. Then the North Stars won Game 1.

The Penguins evened the series in Game 2 but they were hardly on a roll. In Game 3, Minnesota grabbed a 2-1 series lead by beating Pittsburgh 3-1.

Lemieux, due to a sore back, didn't play in that game, and just as well—it featured some rough play. Pittsburgh's Stevens received a game misconduct in the third period after he speared an opponent.

Lemieux was back in Game 4, scoring a goal and setting up another as the Penguins evened series at 2-2 with a 5-3 victory.

The Penguins kicked their potent offense into gear in Game 5, rolling to a 4-0 first-period lead. Lemieux scored the first goal and assisted on both of Mark Recchi's goals as the Penguins outshot the Stars 18-7 in the first 20 minutes.

First Cup

The Penguins won their first Stanley Cup in Minneapolis, crushing the Stars 8-0 as Lemieux scored once and added three assists. Lemieux led all scorers in the final series with 12 points, including five goals. He also won the Conn Smythe Trophy as the top performer in the playoffs.

1991 is remembered as the coming-out party for Mario Lemieux and his talented teammates. Jaromir Jagr, a brilliantly creative forward, did not score a single goal in his first Stanley Cup final series.

★★★★ RESULTS ★★★★

	Game	Site	Winner	Score	GWG
May 15	Game 1	Pittsburgh	Minnesota	5-4	Bobby Smith
May 17	Game 2	Pittsburgh	Pittsburgh	4-1	Kevin Stevens
May 19	Game 3	Minnesota	Minnesota	3-1	Bobby Smith
May 21	Game 4	Minnesota	Pittsburgh	5-3	Bryan Trottier
May 23	Game 5	Pittsburgh	Pittsburgh	6-4	Ron Francis
May 25	Game 6	Minnesota	Pittsburgh	8-0	Ulf Samuelsson

A New Dynasty?: When Mario Lemieux led the Pittsburgh Penguins to their first Stanley Cup in 1991 it seemed as if a new era had dawned in the NHL—the Lemieux Era.

VICTORY REPLAY

Mario Lemieux and the Penguins start the playoffs slowly, then roll to eleven straight victories and their second straight Stanley Cup.

Emergent Star: Jaromir Jagr arrived as an NHL star in helping Pittsburgh win a second straight Stanley Cup in 1992.

It was the second time around in the finals for Mario Lemieux and the Pittsburgh Penguins, and they were gathering momentum. Down 3-1 to the Washington Capitals in the first round of the playoffs, they reeled off three straight victories to move past their divisional rivals.

Penguins general manager Craig Patrick had tinkered with the lineup. Gone were Paul Coffey and Mark Recchi. In were defenseman Kjell Samuelsson, power forward Rick Tocchet and winger Shawn McEachern, plus veteran Ken Wregget.

Scotty Bowman, who had been the club's director of scouting, had replaced head coach Bob Johnson, who died in November 1991. Bowman had piloted the Montreal Canadiens to five Stanley Cups in the 1970s.

Tight odds

In Game 1 of the final series, the Blackhawks jumped to a 3-0 first-period lead.

Phil Bourque got one back for the Penguins late in the opening period, but Brent Sutter restored the Blackhawks three-goal lead at 11:36 of the second period. Then the Penguins showed their mettle.

Tocchet and Lemieux sliced the lead to one goal before the end of the second period. And Jaromir Jagr tied the game with his first goal of the finals in the third.

When Blackhawks defenseman Steve Smith was whistled for hooking with 18 seconds left in the game, the Penguins seized the opportunity.

Just 13 seconds before the end of regulation time, Lemieux beat Chicago goaltender Ed Belfour on the power play to win the game for Pittsburgh.

Lemieux was front and center in Game 2, as well, scoring to lift the Penguins to a 3-1 victory and a 2-0 series lead as the final shifted to Chicago Stadium.

Depth of talent

In Game 3, the Penguins showed that they were fully capable of excelling in a tight-checking playoff game by posting a 1-0 victory.

And in Game 4, they won in a 6-5 shootout as the Blackhawks failed to match goals.

The teams entered the third period tied 4-4, but goals by Larry Murphy and Ron Francis gave the Penguins the cushion they needed.

After their slow playoff start, the Penguins had won 11 straight games, including a semifinal sweep of the Boston Bruins.

Lemieux won the Conn Smythe Trophy for the second straight year, the second player to win the playoff MVP award two straight years.

★★★★★ RESULTS ★★★★★

	Game	Site	Winner	Score	GWG
May 26	Game 1	Pittsburgh	Pittsburgh	5-4	Mario Lemieux
May 28	Game 2	Pittsburgh	Pittsburgh	3-1	Mario Lemieux
May 30	Game 3	Chicago	Pittsburgh	1-0	Kevin Stevens
June 1	Game 4	Chicago	Pittsburgh	6-5	Ron Francis

OVERTIME POWERPLAY

Goaltender Patrick Roy—St. Patrick to his Montreal fans—backstops the Canadiens to ten straight overtime victories and a surprise Cup.

Patrick Roy's legend reached its zenith this year as his goaltending keyed ten straight overtime victories by Montreal en route to their 24th Stanley Cup victory. The Canadiens had upset favored Quebec, swept the Buffalo Sabres and beaten the New York Islanders to reach the final series.

Los Angeles, led by Wayne Gretzky, had advanced past the Calgary Flames, Vancouver Canucks and the Toronto Maple Leafs.

In Game 1 of the Stanley Cup final, Luc Robitaille's two goals powered the Kings to a 4-1 victory. In Los Angeles, this was supposed to be the year Gretzky led the Kings to a championship.

All was going well for them, Roy or no Roy, when catastrophe struck. Canadiens captain Guy Carbonneau had noticed that Kings defenseman Marty McSorley used a stick blade whose curvature exceeded the legal one inch limit.

With just 1:45 remaining in the third period and the Kings leading 2-1, referee Kerry Fraser measured the stick. As 18,000 fans and a vast TV audience watched, the blade was shown to be clearly over the limit. McSorley was banished to the penalty box for two minutes.

During the ensuing power play, Montreal defenseman Eric Desjardins beat Kings goalie Kelly Hrudey to tie the game, sending it into overtime.

Just 51 seconds later, Desjardins scored again, lifting Montreal to a 3-2 victory. The series was tied 1-1.

Confidence restored

It gave Montreal new life.

When the series moved to LA, the Canadiens twice extended the Kings to overtime.

Twice in a row, power forward John LeClair scored the gamewinner.

The Canadiens returned to the Forum leading the series 3-1. The demoralized Kings were frustrated by Roy, whose nearly flawless play infused his teammates with confidence.

In Game 5, McSorley, seeking to make amends for his stick gaffe, scored a rare goal to lift the Kings into a 1-1 tie. It wasn't enough.

Kirk Muller, with the Stanley Cup-winning goal, made it 2-1 before the second period was over and Stephan Lebeau padded Montreal's lead with a power-play goal at 11:31 of the period. Paul DiPietro's third-period goal was merely insurance.

The Canadiens clinched the Cup with an emphatic victory in which the Kings managed just 19 shots—only five in the final period— at Roy.

Roy won the Conn Smythe Trophy as the most valuable player in the playoffs, the second time he won the award.

RESULTS

	Game	Site	Winner	Score	GWG
June 1	Game 1	Montreal	Los Angeles	4-1	Luc Robitaille
June 3	Game 2	Montreal	Montreal	3-2 (OT)	Eric Desjardins
June 5	Game 3	Los Angeles	Montreal	4-3 (OT)	Joh LeClair
June 7	Game 4	Los Angeles	Montreal	3-2 (OT)	John LeClair
June 9	Game 5	Montreal	Montreal	4-1	Kirk Muller

Captain Kirk: Montreal's surprise Stanley Cup in 1993 was due in significant part to the gritty play of Kirk Muller.

We Won, We Won

The long-suffering Rangers silenced their many critics by winning their first Stanley Cup championship in fifty four years.

Broadway Championship: Head coach Mike Keenan piloted the Rangers to the Stanley Cup in 1994, 54 years after their previous championship in 1940.

The biggest game in New York's first Stanley Cup triumph in 54 years probably came not in the exciting, final against Vancouver, but in the seven-game semifinal against New Jersey.

It was before Game 6, with the Devils holding a 3-2 series lead, that Rangers captain Mark Messier guaranteed a New York victory to push the series to a seventh game. Then he backed up his prediction with three goals as the Rangers won 4-2 to send the series to a seventh game.

Team for a win

In the final, Vancouver grabbed a 1-0 lead, winning 3-2, but the Rangers methodically rolled to a 3-1 series lead.

Rangers' general manager Neil Smith had carefully constructed a championship team, blending talented draft selections like goalie Mike Richter, Brian Leetch, Alexei Kovalev and Sergei Nemchinov with veterans acquired through trades.

Messier was the centerpiece acquisition, but the cast of players included ex-Oilers like Glenn Anderson, Jeff Beukeboom, Adam Graves, Kevin Lowe, Craig MacTavish and Esa Tikkanen, and role players such as Stephane Matteau, Brian Noonen and Jay Wells.

The Vancouver Canucks, meanwhile, had built their team around Russian speedster Pavel Bure and Trevor Linden, their on-ice leader, who would have to go head-to-head with Messier.

An end to waiting

In Game 5, the Canucks spoiled the party at Madison Square Garden by stunning the Rangers 6-3 as Geoff Courtnall and Bure each scored twice. That meant both teams—and the Cup iself—had to make another trip to Vancouver, where the Canucks tied the series, by posting a 4-1 victory.

The final score in Game 7 was 3-2 for the Rangers, but New York was in command of the game, without question.

Leetch and Graves provided a 2-0 first-period lead, and after Linden's short-handed goal sliced the lead to one goal early in the second, Messier responded with a power-play score in the 14th minute that restored the New York lead to two goals.

Linden's power-play goal at 4:50 of the third period gave the Canucks renewed hope, but the Rangers were able to hold them off to bring the Cup back to their fans for the first time since 1940. The victory touched off days of celebrations and tributes to the Rangers.

Defenseman Leetch won the Conn Smythe Trophy, becoming the first American-born player to do so. He led all playoff scorers with 34 points, including 11 goals.

★★★★★ RESULTS ★★★★★

	Game	Site	Winner	Score	GWG
May 31	Game 1	New York	Vancouver	3-2 (OT)	Greg Adams
June 2	Game 2	New York	NY Rangers	3-1	Glenn Anderson
June 4	Game 3	Vancouver	NY Rangers	5-1	Glenn Anderson
June 7	Game 4	Vancouver	NY Rangers	4-2	Alexei Kovalev
June 9	Game 5	New York	Vancouver	6-3	David Babych
June 11	Game 6	Vancouver	Vancouver	4-1	Geoff Courtnall
June 14	Game 7	NY Rangers	NY Rangers	3-2	Mark Messier

1995 Stanley Cup Finals
DEVILS' TRAP

Once described as a "Mickey Mouse" franchise by Wayne Gretzky, the Devils received their due with a stunning upset over Detroit.

The New Jersey Devils sprung a speed trap on Detroit in 1995 and stopped the flashy Red Wings dead in their tracks in a too-brief Stanley Cup final series. The trap—known as the neutral-zone trap and designed to choke off an opponent's attack in the neutral zone and create turnovers—couldn't have been a surprise to the Red Wings. New Jersey head coach Jacques Lemaire had the Devils using the delayed forechecking system throughout the lockout-shortened 1994-95 season.

The Devils had no easy route to the final. They had withstood the Philadelphia Flyers, who had dismissed the New York Rangers.

The Red Wings, the top team in the league during the 48-game regular season, had cruised to the final, losing just two games in three series along the way.

But the Devils rode the flawless goaltending of Martin Brodeur, the crashing, banging ensemble work of their forwards and the physical play of defensemen like Scott Stevens and Ken Daneyko to the Stanley Cup. And they made it look easy.

No chance

In three of the four series games, the Devils held the potent Red Wings—the likes of Fedorov, Yzerman, Kozlov and Sheppard—to fewer than 20 shots. The Wings managed just seven scores in the four games against New Jersey.

In Game 1, Claude Lemieux scored the gamewinner in the third period. It was his 12th goal of the playoffs and he would score 13 to lead all playoff snipers before the series was over.

In Game 2, the Devils broke open a 2-1 game with three straight third-period goals for a 2-0 lead.

In Game 3, the Devils raced to a 5-0 lead. Fedorov and Yzerman just managed to score power-play goals within the game's final three minutes.

Game 4 was similarly one-sided, as the Devils held the Red Wings to just 16 shots in winning 5-2 again to capture the first Stanley Cup in franchise history.

Red Wings head coach Scotty Bowman termed the defeat "humiliating."

Lemieux won the Conn Smythe Trophy for his steady playoff scoring, and longtime Devils veterans like John MacLean, Bruce Driver, and Ken Daneyko won their first Stanley Cup after years of struggling in mediocrity.

The Devils gained bragging rights in the all-important New York City media market. Long the forgotten franchise, third in the public imagination behind the Rangers and Islanders, it was the Devils' turn to bask in some Stanley Cup glory.

★★★★ RESULTS ★★★

	Game	Site	Winner	Score	GWG
June 17	Game 1	Detroit	New Jersey	2-1	Claude Lemieux
June 20	Game 2	Detroit	New Jersey	4-2	Jim Dowd
June 22	Game 3	New Jersey	New Jersey	5-2	Neal Broten
June 24	Game 4	New Jersey	New Jersey	5-2	Neal Broten

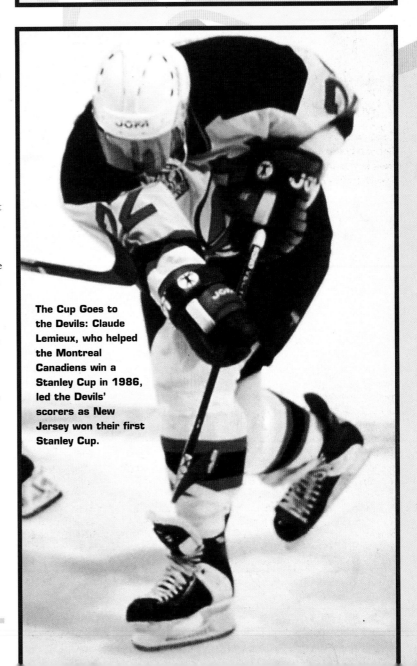

The Cup Goes to the Devils: Claude Lemieux, who helped the Montreal Canadiens win a Stanley Cup in 1986, led the Devils' scorers as New Jersey won their first Stanley Cup.

Avalanche on a Roll

Upstart third-year expansion team Florida Panthers were on a playoff roll to victory until Colorado Avalanche swept their hopes away.

Rush for the Cup: Colorado's Valeri Kamensky couldn't solve Panthers' netminder John Vanbiesbrouck on this rush, but in the end it was Patrick Roy of the Avalanche who won the goalies' duel as the Avalanche swept Florida 4-0 to claim their first Stanley Cup.

The Colorado Avalanche and the Florida Panthers were surprise Stanley Cup finalists in the playoff year that will forever be known as the Year of the Rat. Fans at the Miami Arena brought a new ritual to Stanley Cup play—tossing toy plastic rats onto the ice after a Panthers goal. Rats rained down on the Boston Bruins, Philadelphia Flyers, and Pittsburgh Penguins as each was eliminated.

With nightly miracles by John Vanbiesbrouck in goal, a sound, aggressive defensive system, and total commitment to hard work, the Panthers got on an effective playoff roll—first-year head coach Doug MacLean had them believing they could defeat anyone.

But in the final they confronted a team with far more talent, size, speed, and skill than they could contain.

In Game 1, Tom Fitzgerald gave the Panthers 1-0 first-period lead, but the Avalanche's superior firepower showed up in the second period. Scott Young, Mike Ricci and Uwe Krupp scored consecutive goals in a span of two minutes 49 seconds as momentum shifted irrevocably to Colorado.

Outgunned

The outmanned Panthers were swept aside in Game 2 as Colorado took a 2-0 series lead with a 8-1 win. Swedish forward Peter Forsberg was the scoring star with three goals.

Goaltender Patrick Roy was the key to Colorado's Game 3 victory, a 3-2 squeaker in Miami which saw the toy rats make their first series appearance. Avalanche winger Claude Lemieux, back from a two-game suspension, converted a pass from Valeri Kamensky at 2:44 of the opening period.

Then, at 9:14, Florida's Ray Sheppard prompted the first rat shower, scoring on the power play to tie the game, and Rob Niedermayer scored a 2-1 lead just over two minutes later.

But the Avalanche soon dominated, with Mike Keane scoring at 1:38 and Sakic beating Vanbiesbrouck for the gamewinner on a breakaway at 3:00. A brilliant Roy held off the Panthers until game's end.

Game 4 was a festival of saves by both Roy and Vanbiesbrouck—turning away 119 shots between them over 104 minutes and 31 seconds.

Colorado defenseman Uwe Krupp ended the third-longest game in Stanley Cup history when his slap shot from the right point at 4:31 of the third overtime period handed the Avalanche their first Stanley Cup—and the only rain of rats for the opposing team at the Miami Arena.

The rats symbolized a fairy tale Stanley Cup run for the Panthers. Colorado's performance was embodied by their team captain, Joe Sakic, who led all playoff scorers with 18 goals, 16 assists and 34 points, to earn the Conn Smythe Trophy.

★★★★★ RESULTS ★★★★★

	Game	Site	Winner	Score	GWG
June 4	Game 1	Denver	Colorado	3-1	Mike Ricci
June 6	Game 2	Denver	Colorado	8-1	Rene Corbet
June 8	Game 3	Miami	Colorado	3 -2	Joe Sakic
June 10	Game 4	Miami	Colorado	1-0 (3OT)	Uwe Krupp

Stanley Cup Results 1927-1996 (NHL assumed control of the Cup in 1927)

Year	W/L	Winner	Coach	Runner-up	Coach
1996	4-0	Colorado	Marc Crawford	Florida	Doug MacLean
1995	4-0	NJ Devils	Jacques Lemaire	Detroit	Scott Bowman
1994	4-3	NY Rangers	Mike Keenan	Vancouver	Pat Quinn
1993	4-1	Montreal	Jacques Demers	LA Kings	Barry Melrose
1992	4-0	Pittsburgh	Scott Bowman	Chicago	Mike Keenan
1991	4-2	Pittsburgh	Bob Johnson	Minnesota	Bob Gainey
1990	4-1	Edmonton	John Muckler	Boston	Mike Milbury
1989	4-2	Calgary	Terry Crisp	Montreal	Pat Burns
1988	4-0	Edmonton	Glen Sather	Boston	Terry O'Reilly
1987	4-3	Edmonton	Glen Sather	Philadelphia	Mike Keenan
1986	4-1	Montreal	Jean Perron	Calgary	Bob Johnson
1985	4-1	Edmonton	Glen Sather	Philadelphia	Mike Keenan
1984	4-1	Edmonton	Glen Sather	NY Islanders	Al Arbour
1983	4-0	NY Islanders	Al Arbour	Edmonton	Glen Sather
1982	4-0	NY Islanders	Al Arbour	Vancouver	Roger Neilson
1981	4-1	NY Islanders	Al Arbour	Minnesota	Glen Sonmor
1980	4-2	NY Islanders	Al Arbour	Philadelphia	Pat Quinn
1979	4-1	Montreal	Scott Bowman	NY Rangers	Fred Shero
1978	4-2	Montreal	Scott Bowman	Boston	Don Cherry
1977	4-0	Montreal	Scott Bowman	Boston	Don Cherry
1976	4-0	Montreal	Scott Bowman	Philadelphia	Fred Shero
1975	4-2	Philadelphia	Fred Shero	Buffalo	Floyd Smith
1974	4-2	Philadelphia	Fred Shero	Boston	Bep Guidolin
1973	4-2	Montreal	Scott Bowman	Chicago	Billy Reay
1972	4-2	Boston	Tom Johnson	NY Rangers	Emile Francis
1971	4-3	Montreal	Al McNeil	Chicago	Billy Reay
1970	4-0	Boston	Harry Sinden	St. Louis	Scott Bowman
1969	4-0	Montreal	Claude Ruel	St. Louis	Scott Bowman
1968	4-0	Montreal	Toe Blake	St. Louis	Scott Bowman
1967	4-2	Toronto	Punch Imlach	Montreal	Toe Blake
1966	4-2	Montreal	Toe Blake	Detroit	Sid Abel
1965	4-3	Montreal	Toe Blake	Chicago	Billy Reay
1964	4-3	Toronto	Punch Imlach	Detroit	Sid Abel
1963	4-1	Toronto	Punch Imlach	Detroit	Sid Abel
1962	4-2	Toronto	Punch Imlach	Chicago	Rudy Pilous
1961	4-1	Chicago	Rudy Pilous	Detroit	Sid Abel
1960	4-3	Montreal	Toe Blake	Toronto	Punch Imlach
1959	4-1	Montreal	Toe Blake	Toronto	Punch Imlach
1958	4-2	Montreal	Toe Blake	Boston	Milt Schmidt
1957	4-1	Montreal	Toe Blake	Boston	Milt Schmidt
1956	4-1	Montreal	Toe Blake	Detroit	Jimmy Skinner
1955	4-3	Detroit	Jimmy Skinner	Montreal	Dick Irvin
1954	4-3	Detroit	Tommy Ivan	Montreal	Dick Irvin
1953	4-1	Montreal	Dick Irvin	Boston	Lynn Patrick
1952	4-0	Detroit	Tommy Ivan	Montreal	Dick Irvin
1951	4-1	Toronto	Joe Primeau	Montreal	Dick Irvin
1950	4-3	Detroit	Tommy Ivan	NY Rangers	Lynn Patrick
1949	4-0	Toronto	Hap Day	Detroit	Tommy Ivan
1948	4-0	Toronto	Hap Day	Detroit	Tommy Ivan
1947	4-2	Toronto	Hap Day	Montreal	Dick Irvin
1946	4-1	Montreal	Dick Irvin	Boston	Dit Clapper
1945	4-3	Toronto	Hap Day	Detroit	Jack Adams
1944	4-0	Montreal	Dick Irvin	Chicago	Paul Thompson
1943	4-0	Detroit	Jack Adams	Boston	Art Ross
1942	4-3	Toronto	Hap Day	Detroit	Jack Adams
1941	4-0	Boston	Cooney Weiland	Detroit	Ebbie Goodfellow
1940	4-2	NY Rangers	Frank Boucher	Toronto	Dick Irvin
1939	4-1	Boston	Art Ross	Toronto	Dick Irvin
1938	3-1	Chicago	Bill Stewart	Toronto	Dick Irvin
1937	3-2	Detroit	Jack Adams	NY Rangers	Lester Patrick
1936	3-1	Detroit	Jack Adams	Toronto	Dick Irvin
1935	3-0	Mtl. Maroons	Tommy Gorman	Toronto	Dick Irvin
1934	3-1	Chicago	Tommy Gorman	Detroit	Herbie Lewis
1933	3-1	NY Rangers	Lester Patrick	Toronto	Dick Irvin
1932	3-0	Toronto	Dick Irvin	NY Rangers	Lester Patrick
1931	3-2	Montreal	Cecil Hart	Chicago	Dick Irvin
1930	2-0	Montreal	Cecil Hart	Boston	Art Ross
1929	2-0	Boston	Cy Denneny	NY Rangers	Lester Patrick
1928	3-2	NY Rangers	Lester Patrick	Mtl. Maroons	Eddie Gerard
1927	2-0-2	Ottawa	Dave Gill	Boston	Art Ross

THE ALL-STAR GAME

It's ironic that the NHL All-Star Game, sometimes labeled a non-contact version of hockey, came into being because of an unfortunate incident that ended a player's career. The first, unofficial All-Star game was a benefit for Ace Bailey, who had been gravely injured in a regular-season game between the Toronto Maple Leafs and the Boston Bruins on December 12, 1933.

Bruins' star Eddie Shore had been knocked down while carrying the puck up the ice. Enraged, he charged Bailey, who had not been the culprit, and upended him viciously. Bailey's head struck the ice, knocking him unconscious. Bailey never played again.

On February 14, 1934, the Maple Leafs played a team of NHL All-Stars at Maple Leaf Gardens in a benefit for Bailey. More than $23,000 Cdn. was raised for Bailey, but the format did not exactly capture the imagination of the league's governors.

Two more unofficial All-Star games were staged, both owing to personal tragedy. In November 1937, a game was organized after the death following complications from a broken leg of Montreal Canadiens star Howie Morenz.

And in 1939, a similar game was held to benefit the widow of Babe Siebert, who had drowned that summer.

It's official

The first official All-Star Game was held in 1947, with the reigning Stanley Cup champions, the Toronto Maple Leafs, playing an All-Star team. The Stars won 4-3, establishing the format that would remain for most of the next two decades.

The Dream Game notion was that the true test of just how good the Stanley Cup champions were was to pit the best players from around the league against them. There was one obvious flaw with this set-up. The All-Star team selections often were dominated, understandably, by members of the Stanley Cup champions.

In 1958-59, for example, the Montreal Canadiens placed four players on the first All-Star team and two on the second team. Inevitably, the All-Star team that faced the champions took the ice minus several of its best players.

The league experimented with a different format for two years in the early 1950s, pitting the first All-Star team against the Second Team, but otherwise did not deviate from the Stars against the Stanley Cup champions until 1969.

This was the first All-Star Game following the first major expansion in NHL history, a project that doubled the size of the league from six to 12 teams.

From 1969 through 1971, the All-Star Game pitted the stars from the so-called Original Six against the stars from the six expansion clubs. That period featured the first All-Star Game

held in an expansion city when St. Louis played host to the game in 1970.

The established stars of the East won that game 4-1, but the expansion stars surprised the Original Six when they won the 1971 game in Boston 2-1.

In 1972, the first of a series of realignments shifted the established Chicago Blackhawks into the West Division, and further expansion would continue to alter the makeup of the division.

By 1975, the league had grown to 18 teams, organized into two nine-team conferences: the Prince of Wales Conference; and the Clarence Campbell Conference, named after the longtime president of the NHL.

The Wales did All-Star battle with the Campbells until 1994, when the NHL realigned its conferences and divisions geographically, replacing the Campbell with the Western Conference, and the Wales with the Eastern. The Central and Pacific Divisions comprise the Western Conference, while the Atlantic and Northeast Divisions make up the Eastern.

New trends

The league also had new uniforms designed, in teal and violet colors, and placed new emphasis on the skills competition, a fan-friendly feature the NHL had borrowed from a highly successful skills format used in the National Basketball Association.

The game itself remains an exhibition, a non-contact shootout which showcases plenty of offensive flash but involves little or no bodychecking and little commitment to defense. The goaltenders often have to perform at their best, and just as often they are buried in an avalanche of shots.

Injuries are rare in the All-Star Game, since no one is dishing out any bodychecks. Penalties are rare, too. The 1992 and 1994 games were penalty-free, while the 1993 game involved a single infraction, a minor penalty handed out to defenseman Dave Manson.

The marketing-savvy NHL front office sees the All-Star Game as a chance to market its stars and win new fans. In 1996 the NHL signed a TV deal with Fox, and the network made a splashy, some would say gimmicky, entree into the sport by introducing its FoxTrax puck at the All-Star Game. To TV viewers, the puck appeared with a blue aura highlighting it for greater visibility. Fired at high speed, the blue aura turned into a red rocket and the speed at which the puck was shot was displayed on the screen.

Purists in Canada howled, but the high-tech gimmick certainly drew plenty of free publicity for the league in the United States. The idea seemed harmless enough. After all, the NHL All-Star Game, has never been for purists, anyway.

1990 All-Star Game
Party in Pittsburgh

WALES 12 - CAMPBELL 7

All-Star weekend in Pittsburgh was rife with rumors about a trade, rumors which came discombobulatingly true for center Bernie Nicholls. Once a 70-goal scorer with the Los Angeles Kings, Nicholls found himself a No. 2 pivot in the City of Angels after Wayne Gretzky landed there in 1988. Trying to upgrade their lineup and become a contender, the Kings pulled the trigger on the Nicholls trade on the eve of the All-Star Game, shipping Nicholls to the New York Rangers for feisty winger Tomas Sandstrom and Tony Granato.

Nicholls was not amused.

"If I had known this was going to happen, I would have stayed home," he said.

Home for Lemieux had been Pittsburgh since he was drafted No. 1 overall in 1984. The Penguins franchise was dead-in-the-water at the time, and suffered through four non-playoff seasons even with Lemieux, before qualifying in the 1988-89 season.

The All-Star Game was a coming-out party for Lemieux and the Penguins, and they certainly made the most of it.

Taking over

Just 21 seconds into the game, Lemieux scored his first goal of the game, before the fans' chants of "Mar-io, Mar-io" had died down.

Lemieux scored twice more before the end of the period as the Wales Conference built a 7-2 lead. He finished the game with four goals and the most valuable player trophy as the teams combined for 19 goals, an All-Star record.

"Pittsburgh has really arrived as a hockey city," said Penguins executive Paul Martha. "That's what this is. We are a major hockey market now."

A major hockey market with the game's biggest star, whose performance electrified even the coaching staff.

"I don't think anyone let him take over—he just did," said Pat Burns, who coached the Wales team. "He went out there and took control of everything."

At game's end, Lemieux was still moved by the fans' reception.

"I guess it was special at the beginning of the game when I stepped on the ice," Lemieux said. "I felt pressure at the beginning because I knew the fans were expecting a lot from me. Pittsburgh has been supporting this team for a long time and I'm just happy I was able to give something back to the people."

Perhaps the most significant development in Pittsburgh that weekend did not occur at the Civic Arena, though.

The NHL Players' Association elected former player agent Bob Goodenow to replace Alan Eagleson, who had ruled the association since its inception in 1967.

That development probably was lost on the partying Pittsburgh fans.

Mario's Coming-Out: Mario Lemieux's four-goal performance in the 1990 All-Star game in Pittsburgh was a foretaste of post-season brilliance to come.

Patriots in Chicago

CAMPBELL 11 - WALES 5

Those who attended the 1991 All-Star Game at Chicago Stadium may well remember it more for the roar throughout the national anthems than for the game. The Stadium was renowned for the roar, but the mid-season exhibition came just a few days after the onset of the Persian Gulf War. The 18,472 fans who packed the colorful, old arena that afternoon came prepared to express themselves about the war against Saddam Hussein.

There were plenty of ovations, including one for longtime Chicago star Denis Savard, who had been traded to the Montreal Canadiens, but the building vibrated during the National Anthem, when the fans had other things on their minds.

Many of the players thoughts were elsewhere, also.

"I was standing next to Mark Messier during the national anthems," marveled Wayne Gretzky. "I said to him, 'This is really unbelievable.'

''I've heard it as loud in here before, but never as emotional. The flags of both countries, the banners, the vibrations. You could tell the fans, like us, were thinking of other things."

In the days leading up to the game, Gretzky had even suggested it be cancelled.

"I still feel the same," he said after the game. "It doesn't seem right that we're here having a good time while soldiers are getting killed in the Persian Gulf.

"During intermissions between periods, we came down to the locker room and watched news updates. But there was such a mood in that rink, such patriotism. It was good for hockey. It was a good show, period."

Missed out

The other controversy involved a player not chosen to play in the game, Chicago goaltender Ed Belfour. Campbell coach John Muckler had chosen Bill Ranford, whom he coached with the Edmonton Oilers, and the fans also expressed themselves on that issue.

"Ed-die, Ed-die, Ed-die," they chanted. All game long.

When it was over, an unrepentant Muckler cracked a joke about the heckling.

"I thought Eddie Ranford played a great game," he said.

So did Toronto Maple Leafs' star Vincent Damphousse, who scored four goals for the Campbell Conference to take home the most valuable player award.

Vinny's Day: In 1991, Vincent Damphousse scored four times to earn Most Valuable Player honors.

1992 All-Star Game
Gunning for Goals in Philly

CAMPBELL 10 - WALES 6

The Golden Brett was the star of the show in 1992 in Philadelphia. He scored twice and assisted on another to lead the Campbells over the Wales. This game was not only the typical All-Star no-hitter, it was a game in which no penalties were called, an All-Star Game first. There was nothing to get in the way of five-on-five gunning for goals.

Six goaltenders faced 83 shots in all in this shootout, with Washington Capitals goalie Don Beaupre having the toughest time. He yielded six goals on 12 shots in the second period, as the Campbell Conference built an 8-3 lead. Both of Hull's goals came against Beaupre.

"I didn't have a chance to look up to see which one of their guns was coming at me," said Beaupre. "For a while it seemed like everything was going by me. There were a lot of tips and rebounds and I'm not ready to go through anything like that anytime soon."

Beaupre and the other goalies had the other players' sympathy, for whatever that might have been worth.

"It's totally unfair for goalies," said Wayne Gretzky. "I think everybody understands this game is going to be like that."

Fateful pairing

Four first-time all-stars were able to record goals in Philadelphia: Gary Roberts of the Calgary Flames; Owen Nolan of the Quebec Nordiques; Alexander Mogilny of the Buffalo Sabres; and Randy Burridge of the Washington Capitals.

"It was nice getting on the scoreboard," said Burridge. "I've got the puck in my bag and I'll always have it."

The game was notable for the pairing of Gretzky with Hull, a fantasy pairing that would actually come true years later in St. Louis.

All-Star Theoren: In 1992, Theoren Fleury and the Campbell Conference beat the Wales Conference.

As All-Star teammates, Gretzky and Hull combined for three goals and three assists.

"I've said this a million times—I've always wanted a chance to play with Wayne," said Hull. "Sitting next to Wayne and Stevie Y (Yzerman of the Detroit Red Wings) in the dressing room was unbelievable. Those guys are my idols in this game."

Campbell Blues in Montreal

WALES 16 - CAMPBELL 6

Wayne Gretzky is certainly not a stranger to All-Star games, having been selected a first-team all-star eight times and a second-team player five times. But the spotlight was on him at the All-Star Game in Montreal for an entirely different reason.

Rumors were circulating rapidly that the man many consider the best player in the history of the game was going to be traded to the Toronto Maple Leafs. Los Angeles Kings owner Bruce McNall was forced to hold a news conference to deny everything.

Big deal

Once the controversy subsided and the game began, everybody scored, or so it seemed. Even Brad Marsh, a cautious defenseman for the expansion Ottawa Senators potted one, earning a standing ovation from the Montreal Forum fans.

"Kevin Stevens made a great pass," Marsh said later. "I just put my stick on the ice and it went in off it. I've gone whole seasons without scoring a goal, so any time I do score, it's a big deal."

The goal was all the sweeter for Marsh, who had been embarrassed during the target-shooting portion of the skills competition when he failed to hit a single target in eight tries.

"I knew I was in trouble after I missed the first six," Marsh said. "My excuse is that I'm not supposed to be shooting at targets, anyway."

Mike Gartner took home the MVP award by scoring four goals and adding an assist. The Wales Conference built a 9-0 lead by early in the second period, and a 12-2 lead after 40 minutes of play, as they strafed goalies Ed Belfour and Mike Vernon for six goals each.

Things could have been much worse for the Campbell team when it's considered that Mario Lemieux missed the game.

Lemieux, who had been diagnosed with Hodgkin's Disease four weeks earlier, was undergoing treatment and unable to play. But he was introduced before the game to the fans at the Forum, who gave a five-minute standing ovation to the Montreal-born supberstar.

All-Star Shootout: The teams combined for a record 22 goals in the 1993 All-Star Game, including six in the first period against goalie Ed Belfour.

NHL goes United Nations

EASTERN 9 - WESTERN 8

The NHL had been realigned into Eastern and Western Conferences and hip new uniforms had been designed in time for this game, which was another penalty-free contest. Despite the lopsided result, there was sparkling goaltending, and it was a good thing, considering the teams combined for a record 102 shots.

Mike Richter stopped 19 of the 21 shots the Eastern Conference unleashed at him. Only Paul Coffey and Sandis Ozolinsh beat him.

The acrobatic Richter stopped Vancouver speedster Pavel Bure five times, including twice on breakaways, as the Madison Square Garden fans roared their approval.

"I didn't want to come into this game and not be tested," said Richter. "You're playing against the best in the world. If they pepper you with a bunch of shots and you're feeling good, it's fantastic. You want more."

More was what the winning Eastern Conference team got—more money. The victory was worth $5,000 U.S. for each winning player as the NHL decided to sweeten the pot for All-Star participants in an effort to add some competitive zip to the often tepid game.

"If they're giving you $5,000, you might as well try to win it," reasoned Rangers defenseman Brian Leetch.

Still, the All-Stars do have one unwritten rule, no matter how competitive they or the league might try to intensify things: no hitting.

"We didn't do any checking but at least we got into each other's way," said Chicago defenseman Chris Chelios, with a laugh.

The game also illustrated the growing international make-up of the NHL. Among the participants there were five Russians, two Latvians, a Czechoslovakian, a Finn, eight Americans and 24 Canadians.

One of the Latvians—Sandis Ozolinsh—and one of the Russians—rookie Alexei Yashin—each scored two goals. Yashin's second was the gamewinner for the Eastern Conference.

"It was all luck," said Yashin, the only rookie in the game.

Some of his peers—notably Wayne Gretzky—didn't agree with Yashin.

"He's a tremendous talent," said Gretzky. "I see a lot of Mario (Lemieux) in him.

Beginner's Luck: Alexei Yashin, the only rookie in the game, scored two goals including the winner in 1994.

"He's got good puck sense and Mario's size. To be doing what he's doing on an expansion team (Ottawa) is a credit to him, along with his coming over from Russia for his first year."

For his part, Gretzky had two assists, giving him 19 points lifetime in All-Star competition, tying Gordie Howe's record for points in All-Star games. Gretzky, though, collected his 19 points in 14 games, compared to 23 appearances for Howe.

FoxTraxing in Boston

EASTERN 5 - WESTERN 4

The 1995 All-Star Game was one of the casualties of the lockout-shortened 1994-95 season. The 1996 All-Star was held in Boston, but not at historic Boston Garden, which had officially closed before the season began.

Literally inches away from the funky, intimate Garden, the Bruins owners had built the FleetCenter, a state-of-the-art, 17,565-seat amphitheater.

The center of attention during the game, at least for fans watching on Fox, was a high-tech puck the network had designed to enhance viewers' ability to follow the disk in the heat of the action.

The FoxTrax puck, fashioned with infrared-emitting diodes, gave off a pale blue haze as it slid about the ice in its debut.

When a player teed up a shot at 120-kilometres-an-hour or faster, the puck became a red rocket as it zoomed netward, with a comet-like tail, describing its flight path for the viewers.

The puck was a public relations smash as the NHL and Fox generated plenty of media attention.

Hockey purists in Canada sniffed at the innovation, but Fox, attempting to boost interest in the sport across the United States, was encouraged by the fancy puck.

Local hero

The game, meanwhile, provided the perfect ending for Bruins fans, and gave them a chance to salute one of the game's greatest stars, Boston captain and wheelhorse defenseman Ray Bourque, who was playing in his 14th All-Star Game.

The early thunder in the game belonged to goaltender Martin Brodeur, who pitched a shutout in the first period, stopping 12 shots from the best of the West. The Buffalo Sabres goaltender, Dominik Hasek, faced 13 shots for the Eastern team in the third period, giving up just one goal.

It was a relatively low-scoring affair, as these things go, but the final one was a masterpiece.

That one came at 19:23 of the final period, when Bourque beat Toronto Maple Leafs goalie Felix Potvin to hand the victory to the Eastern team, take the MVP award and bask in the heat of an enormous ovation from the Boston fans.

Hometown Hero: Boston Bruins defenseman Ray Bourque thrilled the Boston fans when he scored the winner in 1996.

All-Star Game Results 1947-1996

Year	Venue	Score	Coaches
1996	Boston	Eastern 5, Western 4	Doug MacLean; Scott Bowman
1994	New York	Eastern 9, Western 8	Jacques Demers; Barry Melrose
1993	Montreal	Wales 16, Campbell 6	Scott Bowman; Mike Keenan
1992	Philadelphia	Campbell 10, Wales 6	Bob Gainey; Scott Bowman
1991	Chicago	Campbell 11, Wales 5	John Muckler; Mike Milbury
1990	Pittsburgh	Wales 12, Campbell 7	Pat Burns; Terry Crisp
1989	Edmonton	Campbell 9, Wales 5	Glen Sather; Terry O'Reilly
1988	St. Louis	Wales 6, Campbell 5(OT)	Mike Keenan; Glen Sather
1986	Hartford	Wales 4, Campbell 3(OT)	Mike Keenan; Glen Sather
1985	Calgary	Wales 6, Campbell 4	Al Arbour; Glen Sather
1984	New Jersey	Wales 7, Campbell 6	Al Arbour; Glen Sather
1983	NY Islanders	Campbell 9, Wales 3	Roger Neilson; Al Arbour
1982	Wash.	Wales 4, Campbell 2	Al Arbour; Glen Sonmor
1981	Los Angeles	Campbell 4, Wales 1	Pat Quinn; Scott Bowman
1980	Detroit	Wales 6, Campbell 3	Scott Bowman; Al Arbour
1978	Buffalo	Wales 3, Campbell 2 (OT)	Scott Bowman; Fred Shero
1977	Vancouver	Wales 4, Campbell 3	Scott Bowman; Fred Shero
1976	Philadelphia	Wales 7, Campbell 5	Floyd Smith; Fred Shero
1975	Montreal	Wales 7, Campbell 1	Bep Guidolin; Fred Shero
1974	Chicago	West 6, East 4	Billy Reay; Scott Bowman
1973	New York	East 5, West 4	Tom Johnson; Billy Reay
1972	Minnesota	East 3, West 2	Al McNeill; Billy Reay
1971	Boston	West 2, East 1	Scott Bowman; Harry Sinden
1970	St. Louis	East 4, West 1	Claude Ruel; Scott Bowman
1969	Montreal	East 3, West 3	Toe Blake; Scott Bowman
1968	Toronto	Toronto 4, All-Stars 3	Punch Imlach; Toe Blake
1967	Montreal	Montreal 3, All-Stars 0	Toe Blake; Sid Abel
1965	Montreal	All-Stars 5, Montreal 2	Billy Reay; Toe Blake
1964	Toronto	All-Stars 3, Toronto 2	Sid Abel; Punch Imlach
1963	Toronto	All-Stars 3, Toronto3	Sid Abel; Punch Imlach
1962	Toronto	Toronto 4, All-Stars1	Punch Imlach; Rudy Pilous
1961	Chicago	All-Stars 3, Chicago 1	Sid Abel; Rudy Pilous
1960	Montreal	All-Stars 2, Montreal 1	Punch Imlach; Toe Blake
1959	Montreal	Montreal 6, All-Stars 1	Toe Blake; Punch Imlach
1958	Montreal	Montreal 6, All-Stars 3	Toe Blake; Milt Schmidt
1957	Montreal	All-Stars 5, Montreal 3	Milt Schmidt; Toe Blake
1956	Montreal	All-Stars 1, Montreal 1	Jim Skinner; Toe Blake
1955	Detroit	Detroit 3, All-Stars 1	Jim Skinner; Dick Irvin
1954	Detroit	All-Stars 2, Detroit 2	King Clancy; Jim Skinner
1953	Montreal	All-Stars 3, Montreal 1	Lynn Patrick; Dick Irvin
1952	Detroit	1st Team 1, 2nd Team 1	Tommy Ivan; Dick Irvin
1951	Toronto	1st Team 2, 2nd Team 2	Joe Primeau; Hap Day
1950	Detroit	Detroit 7, All-Stars 1	Tommy Ivan; Lynn Patrick
1949	Toronto	All-Stars 3, Toronto 1	Tommy Ivan; Hap Day
1948	Chicago	All-Stars 3, Toronto 1	Tommy Ivan; Hap Day
1947	Toronto	All-Stars 4, Toronto 3	Dick Irvin; Hap Day

All-Star Hockey Mosts

Most Games Played
23   Gordie Howe, from 1948 through 1980.

Most Goals
12   Wayne Gretzky, in 15 appearances.

Most Points, One Game
6   Mario Lemieux, Wales, 1988 (3 goals, 3 assists)

Most Goals In One Game
4   Wayne Gretzky, Campbell, 1983
      Mario Lemieux, Wales, 1990
      Vincent Damphousse, Campbell, 1991
      Mike Gartner, Wales, 1993

Most Goals, Both Teams, One Game
22   Wales 16, Campbell 6, 1993 at Montreal

THE HOCKEY HALL OF FAME

The building that houses the state-of-the-art Hockey Hall of Fame in Toronto is a former Bank of Montreal that was built in the previous century. It's appropriate that the National Hockey League showcases its rich history in a vintage 1885 building. After all, the first recorded advertisement for a hockey game comes from the same era, having been placed in the *Montreal Gazette* in 1875.

The game that came to be known as hockey had been played for decades across Canada by that time, in a variety of forms, with a variety of names. Its 'invention' was a product of rural isolation and the need for some activity to enliven the months-long winter.

Unlike baseball, though, hockey has no Abner Doubleday, no personage who can be said, however inaccurately, to have invented the game, no bucolic equivalent of Cooperstown to cherish as the cradle of the game.

Numerous hockey historians make cases for the game originating in, variously, Kingston, Ontario, or Montreal or a certain rural pond in Nova Scotia. Which claim is the most legitimate? Flip a coin.

But if there is no one mythology surrounding the location of the Hockey Hall of Fame it doesn't seem to matter. The ultra-modern facility is fraught with lore, rich in tradition, bursting with memories.

Golden memories

The Hall fills 51,000 square feet of space at BCE Place in downtown Toronto, a modern skyscraper that incorporates the century-old former bank building into its sprawling complex.

The displays include a surprisingly life-like re-creation of the fabled Montreal Canadiens dressing room in the old Forum, a large collection of the many strikingly artistic protective masks worn by the league's goaltenders over the years, and interactive displays that enable visitors, for example, to try their hand at play-by-play description of some of the game's golden moments.

The centerpiece of the building, which opened on 18 June 1993, is the Great Hall, a magnificent dome-ceilinged room that proudly showcases the plaques honoring the members as well as the NHL's glittering family of trophies.

Hall of Honor: The great rotunda in the Hockey Hall of Fame is a fitting setting for the plaques honoring the greats of the game.

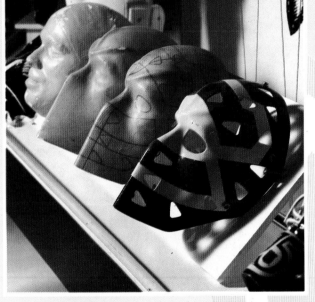

Art on Ice: NHL goalies express their individuality—and personality—in the way they decorate their facial protection.

The most famous trophy in the collection, of course, is the Stanley Cup, donated by Lord Stanley in 1893, the oldest trophy continuously competed for by professional athletes in North America.

The plaques honor the Hall of Fame's 304 members: 207 players; 84 builders (coaches, general managers, owners) and 13 referees and linesmen.

There also are 55 members from the media—broadcasters and print reporters—whose work helped raise awareness about, helped foster the mythology of the game.

The broadcast members are awarded the Foster Hewitt Memorial Award, named after the legendary play-by-play man whose "He shoots, he scores" became a recreational rink mantra for all Canadian hockey fans. The print members are awarded the Elmer Ferguson Memorial Award. Ferguson, who worked for the Montreal Herald, covered the 1917 meeting at which the NHL was formed, and followed the game for years afterward.

Honor for a league

The Hall of Fame was first established in 1943, its early members first honored in 1945. But a permanent location to house the legacy of the game wasn't found until 26 August 1961, when the collection was set up in a building on the grounds of the Canadian National Exhibition on Toronto's lakeshore.

The current location updates the museum for the 1990s and the coming century. Which is not surprising for the Hall of Fame of a league that has more than quadrupled in size in the past 30 years.

Inductees are honored at a special ceremony held each fall. In November 1995, six new members entered the Hall: players Larry Robinson of the Montreal Canadiens and Los Angeles Kings, and Fred Joseph (Bun) Cook of the New York Rangers; Bill Torrey, architect of the great New York Islanders team that won four straight Stanley Cups in the 1980s; and Dr. Gunther Sabetzki, the former head of the International Ice Hockey Federation.

Two media members also were honored: Brian MacFarlane, a longtime TV and radio broadcaster; and Jack Gatecliffe, who covered junior and professional hockey for the *St. Catharines Standard*.

Inspirational Leader: Bobby Clarke overcame limited natural ability and diabetes through sheer hard work and dedication to become the key player on the Philadelhia Flyers in the 1970s.

JEAN BELIVEAU: center. A native of Victoriaville, Quebec, Beliveau became a star center with the Quebec Aces of the Quebec Senior League. Le Colisée in Quebec, where the Aces played their games, was nicknamed the House that Beliveau Built, but it wasn't his hockey home for long. In 1952, Beliveau joined the Montreal Canadiens, who held his pro rights. He remained with them for his entire 18-year NHL career, and led the Canadiens to ten Stanley Cup victories. He was the first winner of the Conn Smythe Trophy as the most valuable player in the playoffs and twice won the Hart Trophy. He retired after leading the Canadiens to the Stanley Cup in 1970-71, having played 1125 NHL games and scored 507 goals.

HECTOR (TOE) BLAKE: left winger. coach. Blake played 578 NHL games, scoring 235 goals and adding 292 assists. The left wing beside center Elmer Lach and right winger Maurice Richard on the legendary Punch Line, Blake was nicknamed the Old Lamplighter for his scoring prowess. Many regard him as the best coach in the history of the NHL. For 13 seasons he coached the Canadiens, who won eight Stanley Cups under his regime, including five straight from 1956-60. He retired after coaching his eighth Cup victory in 1968.

MIKE BOSSY: right winger. As a junior star, Bossy was considered a soft player, a one-dimensional scorer whose offensive skills would be muted in the NHL, whose defensive skills would be a liability. The Montreal Canadiens, among other teams, passed on Bossy in the Entry Draft and lived to regret it. Bossy became the best right winger in the NHL in the 1980s, scoring 573 goals in just 752 regular-season games. For nine straight years, he scored 50 or more goals. He was the sniper on the Trio Grande—a line with Bryan Trottier at center and Clark Gillies at left wing. Bossy added 85 goals in 129 playoff games as he helped the New York Islanders win four straight Stanley Cup championships from 1980-83. Chronic back trouble forced him into retirement in 1987.

JOHNNY BOWER: goaltender. Scar-faced Bower didn't make it to the NHL for good until he was 34. He played 11 seasons for the Toronto Maple Leafs, helping them win four Stanley Cups, including the fabled upset in 1967 when an aging Toronto team beat the favored Montreal Canadiens. Bower and Terry Sawchuck shared the goaltending duties that season, as well as the Vezina Trophy as the best netminding duo in the league. He retired after the 1969-70 season, the only one in which he wore a protective mask.

SCOTTY BOWMAN: coach. general manager. He apprenticed in the Montreal Canadiens system under Sam Pollock before becoming the coach of the expansion St. Louis Blues, whom he led to three straight Stanley Cup finals. Repatriated to the Canadiens as head coach in 1971, Bowman led them to five Stanley Cup victories. He worked for the Sabres from 1979 to 1987 but didn't return to the Stanley Cup final until 1992, with the Penguins, replacing the late Bob Johnson as head coach. Now the head coach of the Detroit Red Wings, Bowman is the most successful coach in NHL history with well over 800 victories.

CLARENCE CAMPBELL: NHL president, 1947-78. Campbell was a Rhodes Scholar and won the Order of the British Empire after working as a prosecutor with the Canadian War Crimes Commission in Germany. He is remembered mostly as the man who suspended Maurice (Rocket) Richard after he slugged linesman Cliff Thompson in March 1955. Campbell's presence at the Forum on March 16, 1955 touched off a riot by outraged Montreal fans. But Campbell withstood that storm. His most notable achievement came in 1968, when he oversaw the expansion of the NHL from six to 12 teams. Before he retired in 1978, the league had grown to 18 teams.

Scarface: Bruins goaltender Gerry Cheevers had symbolic stitches painted onto his mask to represent wounds averted because he wore a mask.

GERRY CHEEVERS: goaltender. Starting goalie for the Boston Bruins in the Bobby Orr-Phil Esposito era. Known as a great money goaltender, Cheevers was at his best in the playoffs. He helped Boston win the Stanley Cup in 1970 and 1972.

BOBBY CLARKE: center, coach, general manager. In 1968-69, Clarke piled up 137 points with the Flin Flon Bombers of the Western Hockey League, but many teams were leery of his diabetic condition and he was taken 17th overall in the NHL entry draft. He proved the skeptics wrong, playing 15 NHL seasons for the Philadelphia Flyers, winning the Hart Trophy three times and leading the Flyers to two straight Stanley Cups in the early 1970s. He was the first player on a post-1967 expansion team to score 100 or more points in a season. His grit, determination and leadership were central to the Flyers becoming the first expansion club ever to win the Stanley Cup.

YVAN COURNOYER: right winger. Cournoyer's speed earned him the nickname 'The Roadrunner,' but he was anything but birdlike. His speed came from thickly muscled legs that teammate Ken Dryden once compared to "two enormous roasts spilling over his knees." When he joined the Montreal Canadiens in 1963-64, Cournoyer was used as a power-play specialist. He developed into one of the most explosive forwards in the game, scoring 428 goals in 16 seasons, and helping Montreal win ten Stanley Cups. He was the Canadiens captain for their four-straight Stanley Cup run in the 1970s.

MARCEL DIONNE: center. Dionne was chosen second overall behind Guy Lafleur in the 1970 entry draft and played most of his career in brilliant obscurity. After racking up 366 points in four seasons with Detroit, Dionne was traded to the Los Angeles Kings, where he quietly piled up points for years, centering the Triple Crown Line with wingers Charlie Simmer and Dave Taylor. He won a scoring championship with the Kings and ended his 18-year career with 731 goals and 1,040 assists, but no Stanley Cup victories.

KEN DRYDEN: goaltender. Dryden, 23-year-old law student and a 6-foot-4, 210-pound giant, backstopped the Montreal Canadiens to a surprise Stanley Cup victory in 1970-71 after playing just six regular-season games with the club. He was awarded the Conn Smythe Trophy as the most valuable player in the playoffs, and followed that up by winning the Calder Trophy (rookie-of-the-year) the next season. Dryden played eight seasons for the Canadiens, helping them win six Stanley Cups, while winning the Vezina Trophy five times. He retired after the 1978-79 season, after helping the Canadiens win a fourth straight Cup. On March 2, 1971, he made hockey history when he faced brother Dave Dryden of the Buffalo Sabres. The pair were the first goaltending brothers ever to face each other in goal.

PHIL ESPOSITO: center, coach, general manager. Esposito was a competent, but

The Roadrunner: Montreal Canadiens sniper Yvan Cournoyer used blazing speed to zoom past opponents and score big goals.

unremarkable center for the Chicago Blackhawks when he was traded, with Ken Hodge and Fred Stanfield, to the Boston Bruins in 1967 for Hubert (Pit) Martin, Jack Norris and Gilles Marotte. Esposito blossomed as a Bruin, becoming the first player to score more than 100 points in a season. He won five scoring titles in eight-and-a-half seasons in Boston, where he and Bobby Orr led the Bruins to two Stanley Cups. He won two Hart Trophies and scored 55 goals or more in five straight seasons. He played 18 seasons in all, scoring 717 goals and adding 873 assists. He retired in 1981, finishing his career as a New York Ranger.

BILL GADSBY: defenseman. Gadsby played standout defense for Chicago, New York Rangers and the Detroit Red Wings for 20 seasons over three decades, stretching from 1946-47 to 1965-66. Gadsby was fortunate to have a career at all. When he was 12, he and his mother

were returning from England when the ship they were traveling on was torpedoed and sunk. He was rescued after spending five hours in the frigid Atlantic. In 1952, he overcame a bout of polio so severe doctors told him he would never play again. He played—well enough to be named an All-Star seven times. Strangely, he never won a Stanley Cup.

BERNARD (BOOM-BOOM) GEOFFRION: left wing. Geoffrion earned his nickname by becoming the first to consistently use the slap shot as an offensive weapon in the 1950s. He won the Calder Trophy in 1952 and led the NHL in scoring in 1955. He was the second player, after teammate Maurice Richard, to score 50 goals in a season and helped Montreal win five Stanley Cups. He frequently played the point (defense) on the power play to take advantage of his booming shot. He also coached, briefly, for the New York Rangers, Atlanta Flames and Montreal Canadiens.

ED GIACOMIN: goaltender. "Ed-die, Ed-die" was the chant at Madison Square Garden during Giacomin's decade as the No. 1 goaltender for the Rangers in the late 1960s and early 1970s. Giacomin shared the Vezina Trophy and won 226 games for the Rangers, while endearing himself to the tough Garden fans with his acrobatic style.

DOUG HARVEY: defenseman. Many consider Harvey, who played 20 NHL seasons from 1947-48 to 1968-69, the best defenseman in the history of the game. He won the Norris Trophy as the league's best defenseman seven times and helped the Montreal Canadiens win six Stanley Cups. He was the point man on the great Montreal power-play unit that included Jean Beliveau, Maurice (Rocket) Richard, Dickie Moore and Bernard (Boom-Boom) Geoffrion. The power-play unit was so effective that the NHL altered its rules so that a penalized player could leave the penalty box before his two minutes was up if the opposing team scored a goal. It was said of Harvey that he was so skilled he could control the tempo of a game, speeding its pace or slowing it down to suit the situation.

GORDIE HOWE: right winger. Howe, a physically powerful, awesomely talented but shy and humble farm boy from Floral, Saskatchewan, fully earned the nickname Mr. Hockey. Howe played 26 seasons, 34 pro seasons in all, covering five decades from 1946-47 to 1979-80. He played 1767 NHL games, scored 801 goals, added 1049 assists. At one time, he held NHL records for most games played, most goals, assists, and points in both regular season and playoffs. He became the first NHLer over the age of 50 to score a goal and the first to play on a line with his sons, Mark and Marty.

GLENN HALL: goaltender. The man who became known as Mr Goalie didn't earn the title for nothing. Hall played 18 seasons—ten with Chicago—and was named an All-Star 11 times. He led the NHL in shutouts for six seasons, played in 115 Stanley Cup playoff games and set a league record for most consecutive games by a goalie—502, stretching from 1955 to November 7, 1962. He finished his remarkable career sharing goaltending duties with fellow Hall of Famer Jacques Plante in St. Louis, where he backstopped the Blues to three straight Stanley Cup final appearances.

BOBBY HULL: left winger. Blond-haired and dimple-cheeked handsome and built like an Adonis, Hull also had blazing speed (29.7 mph top speed) and a frighteningly hard slap shot that once was clocked at 118.3 mph. Hull quickly became known as The Golden Jet in the NHL. He scored 610 goals in a 16-year NHL career during which he became the first player ever to record more than one 50-goal season (he had five). He won the Art Ross Trophy as the league's top scorer three times, the Lady Byng Trophy once, the Hart twice. He led the Blackhawks to the Stanley Cup in 1961, the first of his 50-goal seasons. He was the first big-name superstar to jump to the World Hockey Association when he signed a $1 million Cdn.. contract with the Winnipeg Jets.

GEORGE (PUNCH) IMLACH: coach, general manager, Toronto Maple Leafs, Buffalo Sabres. Imlach was a bundle of superstitions and hockey acumen who piloted the Maple Leafs to four Stanley Cups in the 1960s. In 1970-71 he gave the expansion Buffalo Sabres instant credibility when he became their first coach and general manager. Imlach was instantly recognized by his trademark lucky fedoras. His superstition prevented him from changing suits when his team was on a winning streak.

GUY LAFLEUR: right winger. Lafleur, lightning-fast, creative and possessed of a

Ed-die, Ed-die, Ed-die: On-ice acrobatics were the hallmark of goaltender Ed Giacomin, one of the stars of some fine New York Rangers teams in the 1970s.

wicked slap shot was the NHL's dominant scorer of the 1970s. He was the first to score 50 goals or more in six consecutive seasons and six straight 100-point seasons. He also was the youngest player in history to score 400 goals and attain 1,000 points. He helped the Canadiens win five Stanley Cups, including four straight during his heyday from 1976-79.

TED LINDSAY: left winger. Terrible Ted Lindsay, one of the toughest players the NHL has ever seen, played on the famous Production Line with Gordie Howe and center Sid Abel. He helped the Red Wings win four Stanley Cups from 1948 to 1955. Lindsay channelled his combativeness into setting up the NHL Players' Association, which many believe led to his being traded to the Chicago Blackhawks in 1957.

FRANK MAHOVLICH: left winger. The man better known to hockey fans as The Big M possessed a booming slap shot and perhaps the smoothest, most powerful skating stride the game has ever seen. He scored 48 goals as a 23-year-old with Toronto in 1961 and helped the Maple Leafs win four Stanley Cups in the 1960s. Traded to Detroit in 1968, Mahovlich played on a line with Gordie Howe and Alex Delvecchio. Detroit traded him to Montreal in 1971 and The Big M set a playoff scoring record with 27 points and 14 goals to lead the Canadiens to the Stanley Cup. He also helped the

Canadiens win the Cup in 1973.

LANNY MCDONALD: right winger. McDonald scored 500 goals and added 506 assists in his 16-year career with Toronto, Colorado and Calgary. McDonald teamed up with Sittler as a potent one-two punch with the Maple Leafs until club owner Harold Ballard traded him to Colorado, largely out of spite. McDonald concluded a distinguished career in style, scoring a goal in Calgary's Cup-winning game against the Montreal Canadiens in 1989, the only Cup victory of his career.

STAN MIKITA: center. Born in Czechoslovakia, Mikita entered the NHL as a feisty, clever centerman, but he underwent a transformation into a gentlemanly player winning the Art Ross, Hart and Lady Byng trophies in 1967 and 1968, the first player ever to win all three in a single season. He is credited with introducing the curved stick blade to the NHL, by accident, it turns out. An angry Mikita tried to snap his stick blade by closing the door to the team bench on it. The stick bent, but did not break, and Mikita discovered it enhanced his shooting immensely.

FRANK NIGHBOR: center, defenseman. They called Nighbor the Pembroke Peach and he is credited with perfecting the poke check. He played 13 seasons in the NHL, from 1917-18 to 1929-30. He won five Stanley Cups, one with the Vancouver Millionaires in 1915, four more with the Ottawa Senators. In 1923, he became the first winner of the Hart Trophy as the NHL's most valuable player. In 1925, he was the first recipient of the Lady Byng Trophy, awarded to the league's most sportsmanlike player.

BOBBY ORR: defenseman. Played junior hockey for the Oshawa Generals and joined the Boston Bruins, at age 18, in 1966-67. Orr, one of the fastest skaters in the NHL in his time, revolutionized the defense position. With his quick acceleration, excellent straightahead speed and lateral mobility, Orr played defense like a point guard in basketball. More often than not, it was Orr who led the Bruins' offensive attacks, dishing a pass off to a teammate, or going end to end to take a shot on goal. He scored 296 goals in his 13 NHL seasons and was the first defenseman to score more than 40 goals and record more than 100 points in a season. He was the first defenseman to win the Conn Smythe Trophy. He also won the Norris Trophy eight times, the Hart three times and twice won the league scoring championship. He led the Bruins to two Stanley Cups. His career was foreshortened by a series of knee injuries.

BRAD PARK: defenseman. Contemporary of Orr and Potvin. Park played 17 years in the NHL, never for a team that missed the playoffs; but never for a team that won the Stanley Cup. He was named a first-team All-Star five times and became the second defenseman in NHL history to record 500 assists—after Orr. He scored 213 goals and added 683 assists in his career, which, like Orr's, was plagued by knee injuries. Early in his career, Park revived the seemingly lost art of the open-ice body check. Often cast in the shadow of first Orr, then Denis Potvin, Park was a superb two-way defenseman.

GILBERT PERREAULT: center. Won two Memorial Cups while a member of the Montreal Junior Canadiens. Perreault was the first draft pick of the Buffalo Sabres, for whom he played his entire 17-year career. Perreault centered the dangerous French Connection line with wingers Rene Robert and Richard Martin, amassing 1,336 points (512 goals) in his brilliant career. A virtuoso performer, Perreault was a strong, fast, slightly bow-legged skater, whose head

and shoulder fakes and quicksilver stickhandling mystified opponents. The Sabres built a credible NHL franchise in Buffalo around Perreault, who retired after the 1987-88 season.

JACQUES PLANTE: goaltender. Plante redefined his position. He was the first to roam away from the goal crease to handle loose pucks in the corners and along the end boards. After he suffered a nasty facial cut in a game in 1959, Plante donned a protective mask of his own design and, over the protests of his coach, Toe Blake, wore one from then on. Plante played 19 years in the NHL, with Montreal, New York, Toronto, St. Louis and Boston, but his years in Montreal were his finest. He won seven Vezina Trophies, six Stanley Cups and one Hart Trophy during his career.

DENIS POTVIN: defenseman. After a brilliant five-year junior career with the Ottawa 67s that Potvin began as a 14-year-old, the defenseman joined the New York Islanders as their indisputable franchise player. He led the Islanders to four straight Stanley Cups in the early 1980s. Potvin, a rugged, highly skilled player, chafed at comparisons with Orr. When his 15-year career was over, Potvin had recorded more goals (310), assists (742) and points (1,052) than any defenseman in NHL history.

Big Bird: Larry Robinson was one of the famous Big Three defenseman in Montreal, with Guy Lapointe and Serge Savard in the 1970s.

MAURICE RICHARD: right winger. The Rocket, as he was known, was a passionate presence on the ice who often saved his most brilliant performances for the most dramatic of circumstances. Among the 82 playoff goals he scored, 18 were gamewinners, six of those in sudden-death overtime. He was the first player to score 50 goals in 50 games in a single season and the first to score 500 in his career. He scored 544 goals during his career, won eight Stanley Cups and won the Hart Trophy. Ironically, the man many consider the league's best-ever pure scorer, never won the Art Ross Trophy as the leading NHL's leading scorer.

TERRY SAWCHUCK: goaltender. Many consider Sawchuck to be the best goalie who ever played in the NHL. He posted an NHL-record 103 shutouts during his 21-year career, which saw him play for Detroit, Toronto, Boston, Los Angeles and New York Rangers. In 1952, Sawchuck carried the Red Wings to a Stanley Cup, posting four shutouts in Detroit's eight straight victories, and allowing just five goals overall. Sawchuck won the Vezina Trophy three times, including one award he shared with Johnny Bower for Toronto in 1967.

DARRYL SITTLER: center. Sittler was the heart and soul of some exciting Toronto Maple Leafs teams in the 1970s. He is remembered, as much as anything, for one brilliant night when he scored six goals and added four assists in an 11-4 Maple Leafs victory over the Boston Bruins in 1976. The same year, he scored five goals in a playoff game against the Flyers. He was the first member of the Maple Leafs to score 100 points in a season. He finished his career with 484 goals.

VLADISLAV TRETIAK: goaltender. In a perfect world, Tretiak, the brilliant goaltender for the Soviet Red Army and Soviet national teams, might have played for the Montreal Canadiens, who held his NHL rights. As a 20-year-old, Tretiak established himself as an excellent goaltender in the eight-game Canada-Soviet Summit Series in 1972. Viktor Tikhonov, the legendary Soviet coach, pulled Tretiak after the first period in the famous Miracle on Ice loss to the U.S. team at the Winter Olympics in 1980 in Lake Placid. Tikhonov would admit later this was his biggest regret as a coach.

HOCKEY HALL OF FAME MEMBERSHIP ROSTER
(PLAYERS ONLY)

SID ABEL: center, Detroit Red Wings (1938-43 and 1945-52), Chicago Blackhawks (1952-54). Inducted 1969.

JACK ADAMS: forward, Toronto Arenas (1917-19), Toronto St. Pats (1922-26), Ottawa Senators (1926-27). Inducted 1959.

SYL APPS: center, Toronto Maple Leafs (1936-43 and 1945-48). Inducted 1961.

GEORGE ARMSTRONG: center, Toronto Maple Leafs (1949-71). Inducted 1975.

IRVINE (ACE) BAILEY: forward, Toronto St. Pats (1926-27), Toronto Maple Leafs (1927-34). Inducted 1975.

DAN BAIN: forward, Winnipeg Victorias (1895-1902). Inducted 1945.

HOBEY BAKER: forward, Princeton University (1910-1914). Inducted 1945.

BILL BARBER: right winger, Philadelphia Flyers (1972-84). Inducted 1990.

MARTY BARRY: forward, NY Americans (1927-28), Boston Bruins (1929-35), Detroit Red Wings (1935-39), Montreal Canadiens (1939-40). Inducted 1965.

ANDY BATHGATE: right winger, NY Rangers (1952-63), Toronto Maple Leafs (1963-65), Detroit Red Wings (1965-67), Pittsburgh Penguins (1967-68 and1970-71). Inducted 1978.

JEAN BELIVEAU: center, Montreal Canadiens (1950-51 and 1952-71). Inducted 1972.

CLINT BENEDICT: goaltender, Ottawa Senators (1912-24), Montreal Maroons (1924-30). Inducted 1965.

DOUG BENTLEY: forward, Chicago Blackhawks (1939-44 and 1945-52), NY Rangers (1953-54). Inducted 1964.

MAX BENTLEY: forward, Chicago Blackhawks (1940-43 and 1945-48), Toronto Maple Leafs (1947-53), NY Rangers (1953-54). Inducted 1966.

HECTOR (TOE) BLAKE: left winger, Montreal Maroons (1934-35), Montreal Canadiens (1935-48). Inducted 1966.

LEO BOIVIN: defenseman, Boston Bruins (1954-66), Detroit Red Wings (1965-67), Pittsburgh Penguins (1967-69), Minnesota North Stars (1968-70). Inducted 1986.

DICKIE BOON: forward, Montreal AAAs (1899-03), Montreal Wanderers (1904-06). Inducted 1952.

MIKE BOSSY: right winger, New York Islanders (1977-87). Inducted 1991.

EMILE (BUTCH) BOUCHARD: defenseman, Montreal Canadiens (1941-1956). Inducted 1966.

FRANK BOUCHER: forward, Ottawa Senators (1921-22), NY Rangers (1926-38 and 1943-44). Inducted 1958.

GEORGE BOUCHER: forward, Ottawa Senators (1915-1929), Montreal Maroons (1928-31), Chicago Blackhawks (1931-32). Inducted 1960.

JOHNNY BOWER: goaltender, NY Rangers (1953-55 and 1956-57), Toronto Maple Leafs (1958-70), Vancouver Canucks (1954-55). Inducted 1976.

RUSSELL (DUBBIE) BOWIE: forward, Montreal Victorias (1898-1908). Inducted 1945.

FRANK BRIMSEK: goaltender, Boston Bruins (1938-43 and 1945-49), Chicago Blackhawks (1949-50). Inducted 1966.

HARRY (PUNCH) BROADBENT: forward, Ottawa Senators (1912-15 and 1918-24 and 1927-28), Montreal Maroons (1924-27), NY Americans (1928-29). Inducted1962.

WALTER (TURK) BRODA: goaltender, Toronto Maple Leafs (1936-43 and 1945-52). Inducted 1967.

JOHN BUCYK: left winger, Detroit Red Wings (1955-57), Boston Bruins (1957-78). Inducted 1981.

BILLY BURCH: forward, Hamilton Tigers (1922-25), NY Americans (1925-32), Boston/Chicago (1932-33). Inducted 1974.

HARRY CAMERON: forward, Toronto Blue Shirts (1912-16), Montreal Wanderers (1916-17), Toronto Arenas (1917-19), Ottawa Senators (1918-19), Montreal Canadiens (1919-20), Toronto St. Pats (1919-23). Inducted 1962.

GERRY CHEEVERS: goaltender, Toronto Maple Leafs (1961-62), Boston Bruins (1965-72 and 1975-80). Inducted 1985.

FRANCIS (KING) CLANCY: defenseman, Ottawa Senators (1921-30), Toronto Maple Leafs (1930-37). Inducted 1958.

AUBRY (DIT) CLAPPER: defenseman, Boston Bruins (1927-47). Inducted 1947.

BOBBY CLARKE: center, Philadelphia Flyers (1969-84). Inducted 1987.

SPRAGUE CLEGHORN: forward, Montreal Wanderers (1911-17), Ottawa Senators (1918-21), Toronto St. Pats (1920-21), Montreal Canadiens (1921-25), Boston Bruins (1925-28). Inducted 1958.

NEIL COLVILLE: forward, NY Rangers (1935-42 and 1944-49). Inducted 1961.

CHARLIE CONACHER: forward, Toronto Maple Leafs (1929-38), Detroit Red Wings (1938-39), NY Americans (1939-41).

ALEX CONNELL: goaltender, Ottawa Senators (1924-31 and 1932-33), Detroit Falcons (1931-32), NY Americans (1933-34), Montreal Maroons (1934-35 and 1936-37). Inducted 1958.

BILL COOK: forward, Saskatoon Crescents (1921-26), NY Rangers (1926-37). Inducted 1952.

FRED JOSEPH (BUN) COOK: forward, Boston Bruins/New York Rangers (1926-37). Inducted 1995.

ART COULTER: defenseman, Chicago Blackhawks (1931-36), NY Rangers (1935-42). Inducted 1974.

YVAN COURNOYER: right winger, Montreal Canadiens (1963-79). Inducted 1982.

BILL COWLEY: forward, St. Louis Eagles (1934-35), Boston Bruins (1935-47). Inducted 1968.

RUSTY CRAWFORD: forward, Quebec Bulldogs (1912-17), Toronto Arenas (1917-19), Ottawa Senators (1917-18), Vancouver Maroons (1925-26). Inducted 1962.

JACK DARRAGH: forward, Ottawa Senators (1910-1924). Inducted 1962.

ALLAN (SCOTTY) DAVIDSON: forward, Toronto Blueshirts (1912-14). Inducted 1950.

CLARENCE (HAP) DAY: defenseman, Toronto St. Pats (1924-26), Toronto Maple Leafs (1926-37), NY Americans (1937-38). Inducted 1961.

ALEX DELVECCHIO: center, Detroit Red Wings (1950-74). Inducted 1977.

CY DENNENY: forward, Toronto Shamrocks (1914-15), Toronto Arenas (1915-16), Ottawa Senators (1916-28), Boston Bruins (1928-29). Inducted 1959.

MARCEL DIONNE: center, Detroit Red Wings (1971-75), LA Kings (1975-87), NY Rangers (1987-89). Inducted 1992.

GORDIE DRILLON: forward, Toronto Maple Leafs (1936-42), Montreal Canadiens (1942-43). Inducted 1975.

GRAHAM DRINKWATER: forward, Montreal AAAs (1892-93), Montreal Victorias (1893, 1895-98), McGill University (1894-95), Montreal Victorias (1899).

KEN DRYDEN: goaltender, Montreal Canadiens (1970-73 and 1974-79). Inducted 1983.

WOODY DUMART: forward, Boston Bruins (1935-42 and 1945-54). Inducted 1992.

TOMMY DUNDERDALE: forward, Winnipeg Victorias (1906-08), Toronto Shamrocks (1909-10), Quebec Bulldogs (1910-11), Victoria Aristocrats 1911-15 and 1918-23), Portland Rosebuds (1915-18), Saskatoon/Edmonton (1923-24). Inducted 1974.

BILL DURNAN: goaltender, Montreal Canadiens (1943-50). Inducted 1964.

MERVYN (RED) DUTTON: defenseman, Montreal Maroons (1926-30), NY Americans (1930-36). Inducted 1958.

CECIL (BABE) DYE: forward, Toronto St. Pats (1919-26), Hamilton Tigers (1920-21), Chicago Blackhawks (1926-28), NY Americans (1928-29), Toronto Maple Leafs (1930-31) Inducted 1970.

PHIL ESPOSITO: center, Chicago Blackhawks (1963-67), Boston Bruins (1967-76), NY Rangers (1975-81). Inducted 1984.

TONY ESPOSITO: goaltender, Montreal Canadiens (1968-69), Chicago Blackhawks (1969-84). Inducted 1988.

ARTHUR FARRELL: forward, Montreal Shamrocks (1896-1901). Inducted 1965.

FERNIE FLAMAN: defenseman, Boston Bruins (1944-51 and 1954-61), Toronto Maple Leafs (1950-54). Inducted 1965.

FRANK FOYSTON: forward, Toronto Blueshirts (1912-16), Seattle Metros (1915-24), Victoria Aristocrats (1924-26), Detroit Cougars (1926-28). Inducted 1958.

FRANK FREDERICKSON: forward, Victoria Aristocrats (1920-26), Boston Bruins (1926-29), Detroit Falcons (1926-27 and 1930-31), Pittsburgh Pirates (1928-30). Inducted 1958.

BILL GADSBY: defenseman, Chicago Blackhawks (1946-54), NY Rangers (1954-61), Detroit Red Wings (1961-66). Inducted 1970.

BOB GAINEY: left winger, Montreal Canadiens (1973-89). Inducted 1992.

CHUCK GARDINER: goaltender, Chicago Blackhawks (1927-34). Inducted 1945.

HERB GARDINER: defenseman, Montreal Canadiens (1926-29), Chicago Blackhawks (1928-29). Inducted 1958.

JIMMY GARDNER: forward, Montreal AAAs (1900-03), Montreal Wanderers (1903-11), New Westminster Royals (1911-13), Montreal Canadiens (1913-15). Inducted 1962.

BERNARD (BOOM BOOM) GEOFFRION: left winger, Montreal Canadiens (1951-64), NY Rangers (1966-68). Inducted 1972.

EDDIE GERARD: forward, Ottawa Victorias (1907-08), Ottawa Senators (1913-23). Inducted 1945.

EDDIE GIACOMIN: goaltender, NY Rangers (1965-76), Detroit Red Wings (1975-78). Inducted 1987.

ROD GILBERT: forward, NY Rangers (1960-78). Inducted 1982.

BILLY GILMOUR: forward, Ottawa Senators (1902-06 and 1908-09 and 1915-16), Montreal Victorias (1907-08). Inducted 1962.

FRANK (MOOSE) GOHEEN: defenseman, St. Paul Athletic Club (1914-28). Inducted 1952.

EBBIE GOODFELLOW: forward, Detroit Cougars (1928-30), Detroit Falcons (1930-33), Detroit Red Wings (1933-43). Inducted 1963.

MIKE GRANT: defenseman, Montreal Victorias (1893-1902). Inducted 1950.

WILF (SHORTY) GREEN: forward, Hamilton Tigers (1923-25), NY Americans (1925-27). Inducted 1962.

SI GRIFFIS: forward, Rat Portage Thistles (1902-06), Kenora Thistles (1906-07), Vancouver Millionaires (1911-19). Inducted 1950.

GEORGE HAINSWORTH: goaltender, Montreal Canadiens (1926-33 and 1936-37), Toronto Maple Leafs (1933-37). Inducted 1961.

GLENN HALL: goaltender, Detroit Red Wings (1952-53 and 1954-57), Chicago Blackhawks (1957-67), St. Louis Blues (1967-71). Inducted 1975.

JOE HALL: forward, Winnipeg Victorias (1903-05), Quebec Bulldogs (1905-06 and 1910-17), Brandon (1906-07), Montreal AAAs (1907-08), Montreal Shamrocks (1907-08 and 1909-10), Montreal Wanderers (1908-09), Montreal Canadiens (1917-19). Inducted 1961.

DOUG HARVEY: defenseman, Montreal Canadiens (1947-61), NY Rangers (1961-64), Detroit Red Wings (1966-67), St. Louis Blues (1967-69). Inducted 1973.

GEORGE HAY: forward, Chicago Blackhawks (1926-27), Detroit Cougars (1927-30), Detroit Falcons (1930-31), Detroit Red Wings (1932-34). Inducted 1958.

RILEY HERN: goaltender, Montreal Wanderers (1906-11). Inducted 1962.

BRYAN HEXTALL: forward, NY Rangers (1936-44 and 1945-48). Inducted 1969.

HARRY (HAP) HOLMES: goaltender, Toronto Blueshirts (1912-16), Seattle Metros (1915-17 and 1918-24), Toronto Arenas (1917-19), Victoria Aristocrats (1924-26), Detroit Cougars (1926-28).

TOM HOOPER: forward, Rat Portage Thistles (1901-05), Kenora Thistles (1906-07), Montreal Wanderers (1907-08), Montreal AAAs (1907-08). Inducted 1962.

REGINALD G. (RED) HORNER: defenseman, Toronto Maple Leafs (1928-40). Inducted 1965.

TIM HORTON: defenseman, Toronto Maple Leafs, 1949-70), NY Rangers (1969-71), Pittsburgh Penguins (1971-72), Buffalo Sabres (1972-74). Inducted 1977.

GORDIE HOWE: right winger, Detroit Red Wings (1946-71), Houston Aeros (1973-77), New England Whalers (1977-79), Hartford Whalers (1979-80). Inducted 1972.

SYD HOWE: forward, Ottawa Senators (1929-30 and 1932-34), Philadelphia Quakers (1930-31), Toronto Maple Leafs (1931-32), St. Louis Eagles (1934-35), Detroit Red Wings (1934-46). Inducted 1965.

HARRY HOWELL: defenseman, NY Rangers (1952-69), Oakland Seals (1969-70), LA Kings (1970-73). Inducted 1979.

ROBERT MARVIN (BOBBY) HULL: left winger, Chicago Blackhawks (1957-72), Winnipeg Jets (1972-80), Hartford Whalers (1979-80). Inducted 1983.

BOUSE HUTTON: goaltender, Ottawa Senators (1898-1904). Inducted 1962.

HARRY HYLAND: forward, Montreal Shamrocks (1908-09), Montreal Wanderers (1909-11 and 1912-17), New Westminster Royals (1911-12), Montreal/Ottawa (1917-18). Inducted 1962.

DICK IRVIN: forward, Portland Rosebuds (1916-17), Regina Capitals (1921-25), Portland Capitals (1925-26), Chicago Blackhawks (1926-29). Inducted 1958.

HARVEY (BUSHER) JACKSON: forward, Toronto Maple Leafs (1929-39), NY Americans (1939-41), Boston Bruins (1941-44). Inducted 1971.

IVAN WILFRED (CHING) JOHNSON: defenseman, NY Rangers (1926-37), NY Americans (1937-38). Inducted 1958.

ERNIE JOHNSON: forward, Montreal Victorias (1903-05), Montreal Wanderers (1905-11), New Westminster Royals (1911-14), Portland Rosebuds (1914-18), Victoria Aristocrats (1918-22). Inducted 1952.

TOM JOHNSON: defenseman, Montreal Canadiens (1947-48 and 1949-63), Boston Bruins (1963-65). Inducted 1970.

Aurel Joliat: forward, Montreal Canadiens (1922-38). Inducted 1947.

Gordon (Duke) Keats: forward, Toronto Blue Shirts (1915-17), Edmonton Eskimos (1921-26), Boston & Detroit (1926-27), Detroit & Chicago (1927-28) Chicago Blackhawks (1928-29). Inducted 1958.

Leonard (Red) Kelly: defenseman, center, Detroit Red Wings (1947-60), Toronto Maple Leafs (1960-67). Inducted 1969.

Ted (Teeder) Kennedy: forward, Toronto Maple Leafs (1942-55 and 1956-57). Inducted 1966.

Dave Keon: center, Toronto Maple Leafs (1960-75), Hartford Whalers (1979-82). Inducted 1986.

Elmer Lach: center, Montreal Canadiens (1940-54). Inducted 1966.

Guy Lafleur: right winger, Montreal Canadiens (1971-85), NY Rangers (1988-89), Quebec Nordiques (1989-91). Inducted 1988.

Edouard (Newsy) Lalonde: forward, Montreal Canadiens (1910-11 and 1912-22), NY Americans (1926-27). Inducted 1950.

Jacques Laperriere: defenseman, Montreal Canadiens (1962-74). Inducted 1987.

Jack Laviolette: defenseman, Montreal Nationals (1903-07), Montreal Shamrocks (1907-09), Montreal Canadiens (1909-18). Inducted 1962.

Hugh Lehman: goaltender, New Westminster Royals (1911-14), Vancouver Millionaires (1914-26), Chicago Blackhawks (1926-28). Inducted 1958.

Jacques Lemaire: left winger, center, Montreal Canadiens (1967-79). Inducted 1984.

Percy LeSueur: goaltender, Ottawa Senators (1905-14), Toronto Shamrocks (1914-15), Toronto Blueshirts (1915-16). Inducted 1961.

Herbie Lewis: forward, Detroit Cougars (1928-30), Detroit Falcons (1930-33), Detroit Red Wings (1933-39). Inducted 1989.

Ted Lindsay: left winger, Detroit Red Wings (1944-58 and 1964-65), Chicago Blackhawks (1957-60). Inducted 1966.

Harry Lumley: goaltender, Detroit Red Wings (1943-50), Chicago Blackhawks (1950-52), Toronto Maple Leafs (1952-56), Boston Bruins (1957-60).

Mickey MacKay: forward, Vancouver Millionaires (1914-19 and 1920-24), Vancouver Maroons (1924-26), Chicago Blackhawks (1926-28), Boston & Pittsburgh (1928-29), Boston Bruins (1929-30). Inducted 1952.

Frank Mahovlich: left winger, Toronto Maple Leafs (1956-68), Detroit Red Wings (1968-71), Montreal Canadiens (1971-74). Inducted 1981.

Joe (Phantom) Malone: forward, Quebec Bulldogs (1908-09 and 1910-17), Waterloo (1909-10), Montreal Canadiens (1917-24), Hamilton Tigers (1921-22). Inducted 1950.

Sylvio Mantha: defenseman, Montreal Canadiens (1923-36), Boston Bruins (1936-37). Inducted 1960.

Jack Marshall: forward, Winnipeg Victorias (1900-01), Montreal Victorias (1901-03), Montreal Wanderers (1903-05 and 1906-07 and 1909-12 and 1915-17), Montreal Shamrocks (1907-09), Toronto Tecumsehs (1912-13), Toronto Ontarios (1913-14), Toronto Shamrocks (1914-15). Inducted 1965.

Fred Maxwell: forward, Winnipeg Monarchs (1914-16), Winnipeg Falcons (1918-25). Inducted 1962.

Lanny McDonald: right winger, Toronto Maple Leafs (1973-80), Colorado Rockies (1980-82), Calgary Flames (1982-89). Inducted 1992.

Frank McGee: forward, Ottawa Senators (1902-06). Inducted 1945.

Billy McGimsie: forward, Rat Portage Thistles (1902-03 and 1904-06), Kenora Thistles (1906-07). Inducted 1962.

George McNamara: defenseman, Montreal Shamrocks (1907-09), Halifax Crescents (1909-12), Waterloo (1911), Toronto Tecumsehs (1912-13), Ottawa (1913-14), Toronto Shamrocks (1914-15), Toronto Blueshirts (1915-16), 228th Battalion (1916-17). Inducted 1958.

Stan Mikita: center, Chicago Blackhawks (1958-80). Inducted 1983.

Richard (Dickie) Moore: left winger, Montreal Canadiens (1951-63), Toronto Maple Leafs (1964-65), St. Louis Blues (1967-68). Inducted 1974.

Paddy Moran: goaltender, Quebec Bulldogs (1901-09 and 1910-17), Halleybury Comets (1909-10). Inducted 1958.

Howie Morenz: forward, Montreal Canadiens (1923-34 and 1936-37), Chicago Blackhawks (1934-36), NY Rangers (1935-36). Inducted 1945.

Bill Mosienko: forward, Chicago Blackhawks (1941-55). Inducted 1965.

Frank Nighbor: center, Ottawa Senators (1915-29), Toronto Maple Leafs (1929-30). Inducted 1947.

Reginald Noble: forward, Toronto Arenas (1917-19), Toronto St. Patricks (1919-25), Montreal Maroons (1924-27), Detroit Cougars (1927-32), Detroit & Montreal (1932-33). Inducted 1962.

Buddy O'Connor: forward, Montreal Canadiens (1941-47), NY Rangers (1947-51). Inducted 1988.

Harry Oliver: forward, Boston Bruins (1926-34), NY Americans (1934-37). Inducted 1967.

Bert Olmstead: left winger, Chicago Blackhawks (1948-51), Montreal Canadiens (1950-58), Toronto Maple Leafs (1958-62). Inducted 1985.

Robert (Bobby) Orr: defenseman, Boston Bruins (1966-76), Chicago Blackhawks (1976-79). Inducted 1979.

Bernard Parent: goaltender, Boston Bruins (1965-67), Philadelphia Flyers (1967-71 and 1973-79), Toronto Maple Leafs (1970-72). Inducted 1984.

Brad Park: defenseman, NY Rangers (1968-76), Boston Bruins (1976-83), Detroit Red Wings (1983-85). Inducted 1988.

Lester Patrick: forward, Brandon (1903-04), Westmount (1904-05), Montreal Wanderers (1905-07), Edmonton (1907-08), Renfrew Cream Kings (1909-10), Victoria Aristocrats (1911-16 and 1918-22), Spokane (1916-17), Seattle Metros (1917-18), Victoria Cougars (1925-26), NY Rangers (1927-28). Inducted 1947.

Joseph Lynn Patrick: forward, NY Rangers (1934-43 and 1945-46). Inducted 1980.

Gilbert Perreault: center, Buffalo Sabres (1970-87). Inducted 1990.

Tom Phillips: forward, Montreal AAAs (1902-03), Toronto Marlboroughs (1903-04), Rat Portage Thistles (1904-06), Kenora Thistles (1906-07), Ottawa Senators (1907-08), Vancouver Millionaires (1911-12). Inducted 1945.

Pierre Pilote: defenseman, Chicago Blackhawks (1955-68), Toronto Maple Leafs (1968-69). Inducted 1975.

Didier Pitre: forward, Montreal Nationals (1903-05), Montreal Shamrocks (1907-08), Renfrew Millionaires (1908-09), Montreal Canadiens (1909-23). Inducted 1962.

Jacques Plante: goaltender, Montreal Canadiens (1952-63), NY Rangers (1963-65), St. Louis Blues (1968-70), Toronto Maple Leafs (1970-73), Boston Bruins (1972-73). Inducted 1978.

Denis Potvin: defenseman, NY Islanders (1973-88). Inducted 1991.

Walter (Babe) Pratt: defenseman, NY Rangers (1935-43), Toronto Maple Leafs (1942-46), Boston Bruins (1946-47). Inducted 1966.

Joe Primeau: defenseman, Toronto Maple Leafs (1927-36). Inducted 1963.

Marcel Pronovost: defenseman, Detroit Red Wings (1949-65), Toronto Maple Leafs (1965-70). Inducted 1978.

Bob Pulford: center, Toronto Maple Leafs (1956-70), LA Kings (1970-72). Inducted 1991.

Harvey Pulford: defenseman, Ottawa Senators (1893-1908). Inducted 1945.

Bill Quackenbush: defenseman, Detroit Red Wings (1942-49), Boston Bruins (1949-56). Inducted 1976.

Frank Rankin: forward, Stratford (1906-09), Eaton's Athletic Association (1910-12), St. Michaels' (1912-14). Inducted 1961.

Jean Ratelle: center, NY Rangers (1962-76), Boston Bruins (1975-81). Inducted 1985.

Chuck Rayner: goaltender, NY Americans (1940-41), Brooklyn Americans (1941-42), NY Rangers (1945-53). Inducted 1973.

Kenneth Joseph Reardon: defenseman, Montreal Canadiens (1940-42 and 1945-50). Inducted 1966.

Henri Richard: center, Montreal Canadiens (1955-75). Inducted 1979.

Maurice (Rocket) Richard: right winger, Montreal Canadiens (1942-60). Inducted 1961.

George Richardson: forward, 14th Regiment (1906-13), Queens University (1908-09). Inducted 1950.

Gordon Roberts: forward, Ottawa Senators (1909-10), Montreal Wanderers (1910-16), Vancouver Millionaires (1916-17 and 1919-20), Seattle Metropolitans (1917-18). Inducted 1971.

Larry Robinson: defenseman, Montreal Canadiens (1972-90), Los Angeles Kings (1990-92). Inducted 1995.

Art Ross: forward, Westmount (1904-05), Brandon (1906-07), Kenora Thistles (1906-07), Montreal Wanderers (1907-09 and 1910-14 and 1917-18), Halleybury Comets (1909-10), Ottawa Senators (1914-16). Inducted 1945.

Blair Russel: forward, Montreal Victorias (1899-1908). Inducted 1965.

Ernie Russell: forward, Montreal AAAs (1904-05), Montreal Wanderers (1905-08 and 1909-14). Inducted 1965.

Jack Ruttan: forward, Armstrong's Point (1905-06), Rustler (1906-07), St. Johns College (1907-08), Manitoba Varsity (1909-12), Winnipeg (1912-13). Inducted 1962.

Serge Savard: defenseman, Montreal Canadiens (1966-81), Winnipeg Jets (1981-83). Inducted 1986.

Terry Sawchuck: goaltender, Detroit Red Wings (1949-55 and 1957-64 and 1968-69), Boston Bruins (1955-57), Toronto Maple Leafs (1964-67), LA Kings (1967-68), NY Rangers (1969-70). Inducted 1971.

Fred Scanlan: forward, Montreal Shamrocks (1897-1901), Winnipeg Victorias (1901-03). Inducted 1965.

Milt Schmidt: center, Boston Bruins, 1936-42 and 1945-55). Inducted 1961.

Sweeney Schriner: forward, NY Americans (1934-39), Toronto Maple Leafs (1939-43 and 1944-46). Inducted 1962.

Earl Seibert: defenseman, NY Rangers (1931-36), Chicago Blackhawks (1935-45), Detroit Red Wings (1944-46). Inducted 1963.

Oliver Seibert: forward, Berlin Dutchmen (1900-06). Inducted 1961.

Eddie Shore: defenseman, Boston Bruins (1926-40). Inducted 1947.

Steve Shutt: left winger, Montreal Canadiens (1973-1984), LA Kings (1985). Inducted 1993.

Albert Charles (Babe) Siebert: defenseman, Montreal Maroons (1925-32), NY Rangers (1932-34), Boston Bruins (1933-36), Montreal Canadiens (1936-39). Inducted 1964.

Joe Simpson: defenseman, Edmonton Eskimos (1921-25), NY Americans (1925-31). Inducted 1962.

Darryl Sittler: center, Toronto Maple Leafs (1970-82), Philadelphia Flyers (1982-84), Detroit Red Wings (1984-85). Inducted 1989.

Alf Smith: forward, Ottawa Senators, 1894-1908), Kenora Thistles (1906-07). Inducted 1962.

Billy Smith: goaltender: LA Kings (1971-72), NY Islanders (1972-89). Inducted 1993.

Clint Smith: forward, NY Rangers (1936-43), Chicago Blackhawks (1943-47). Inducted 1991.

Reginald Joseph (Hooley) Smith: forward, Ottawa Senators (1924-27), Montreal Maroons (1927-36), Boston Bruins (1936-37), NY Americans (1937-41). Inducted 1972.

Tommy Smith: forward, Ottawa Victorias (1905-06), Brantford Indians (1908-10), Cobalt Silver Kings (1909-10), Galt (1910-11), Moncton (1911-12), Quebec Bulldogs (1912-16 and 1919-20), Ontarios (1914-15), Montreal Canadiens (1916-17). Inducted 1973.

Allan Stanley: defenseman, NY Rangers (1948-55), Chicago Blackhawks (1954-56), Toronto Maple Leafs (1958-68), Philadelphia Flyers (1968-69). Inducted 1981.

Barney Stanley: forward, Vancouver Millionaires (1914-19), Calgary Tigers (1921-22), Regina Capitals (1922-24), Edmonton Eskimos (1924-26). Inducted 1962.

Jack Stewart: defenseman, Detroit Red Wings (1938-43 and 1945-50), Chicago Blackhawks (1950-52).

Nelson Stewart: forward, Montreal Maroons (1925-32), Boston Bruins (1932-35 and 1936-37), NY Americans (1935-40). Inducted 1962.

Bruce Stuart: forward, Ottawa Senators (1898-1902 and 1908-11), Quebec Bulldogs (1900-01), Montreal Wanderers (1907-08). Inducted 1961.

William Hodgson (Hod) Stuart: forward, Ottawa Senators (1898-1900), Quebec Bulldogs (1900-06), Montreal Wanderers (1906-08). Inducted 1945.

Frederick (Cyclone) Taylor: forward, Ottawa Senators (1907-09), Renfrew Cream Kings (1909-11), Vancouver Millionaires (1912-21 and 1922-23). Inducted 1947.

Cecil R. (Tiny) Thompson: goaltender, Boston Bruins (1928-39), Detroit Red Wings (1939-40). Inducted 1959.

Vladislav Tretiak: goaltender, Central Red Army (1969-84), Soviet National Team (1969-84). Inducted 1989.

Harry Trihey: forward, Montreal Shamrocks (1896-1901). Inducted 1950.

Norm Ullman: center, Detroit Red Wings (1955-67), Toronto Maple Leafs (1967-75), Edmonton Oilers (1975-77). Inducted 1982.

Georges Vezina: goaltender, Montreal Canadiens (1910-26). Inducted 1945.

Jack Walker: forward, Toronto Blueshirts (1912-15), Seattle Metros (1915-24), Victoria Cougars (1924-26), Detroit Cougars (1926-28). Inducted 1960.

Marty Walsh: forward, Ottawa Senators (1907-12). Inducted 1962.

Harry (Moose) Watson: defenseman, St. Andrews (1915), Aura Lee Juniors (1918), Toronto Dentals (1919), Toronto Granites (1920-25), Toronto Sea Fleas (1931). Inducted 1962.

Ralph C. (Cooney) Weiland: forward, Boston Bruins (1928-32 and 1935-39), Ottawa Senators (1932-34), Detroit Red Wings (1933-35). Inducted 1971.

Harry Westwick: forward, Ottawa Senators (1894-98 and 1900-08), Kenora Thistles (1906-07). Inducted 1962.

Fret Whitcroft: forward, Kenora Thistles (1906-08), Edmonton (1908-10), Renfrew Cream Kings (1909-10). Inducted 1962.

Gordon Allan (Phat) Wilson: forward, Port Arthur War Veterans (1918-20), Iroquois Falls Eskimos (1921), Port Arthur Bearcats (1923-33). Inducted 1962.

Lorne (Gump) Worsley: goaltender, NY Rangers (1952-63), Montreal Canadiens (1963-70), Minnesota North Stars (1969-74). Inducted 1980.

Roy Worters: goaltender, Pittsburgh Pirates (1925-28), NY Americans (1928-37), Montreal Maroons (1929-30). Inducted 1969.

Glossary of Hockey Terms

Art Ross Trophy: Awarded to the player who wins the scoring championship during the regular season.
Assist: A pass that leads to a goal being scored. One or two, or none, may be awarded on any goal.
Backchecking: Skating with an opponent through the neutral and defensive zones to try to break up an attack.
Backhand: A pass or shot, in which the player cradles the puck on the off- or backside of the stick blade and propels it with a shoveling motion..
Back pass: A pass left or slid backwards for a trailing teammate to recover.
Blocker: A protective glove worn on the hand a goaltender uses to hold his stick so that the goalie can deflect pucks away from the net.
Blue lines: The lines, located 29 feet from each side of the center red line, which demarcate the beginning of the offensive zone.
Boarding: Riding or driving an opponent into the boards. A two- or five-minute penalty may be assessed, at the referee's discretion.
Boards: Wooden structures, 48 inches high, topped by plexiglass fencing, that enclose the 200 feet by 85 feet ice surface.
Bodycheck: Using the hips or shoulders to stop the progress of the puck carrier.
Breakaway: The puck carrier skating toward the opposition's net ahead of all the other players.
Butt-Ending: Striking an opponent with the top end of the hockey stick, a dangerously illegal act that brings a five-minute penalty.
Calder Memorial Trophy: Awarded to the goaltender, defenseman or forward judged to be the best first-year, or rookie, player.
Central Scouting Bureau: An NHL agency that compiles statistical and evaluative information on all players eligible for the Entry Draft. The information, which includes a rating system of all players, is distributed to all NHL teams.
Charging: Skating three strides or more and crashing into an opponent. Calls for a two-minute or five-minute penalty at the referee's discretion.
Conn Smythe Trophy: Awarded to the top performer throughout the Stanley Cup playoffs.
Crease: A six-foot semicircular area at the mouth of the goal that opponents may not enter. Only the goaltender may freeze the puck in this space.
Crossbar: A red, horizontal pipe, four feet above the ice and six feet long across the top of the goal cage.
Crosschecking: Hitting an opponent with both hands on the stick and no part of the stick on the ice. Warrants a two-minute penalty.
Defensemen: The two players who form the second line of defense, after the goalie. Defensemen try to strip opponents of the puck in their own zone and either pass to teammates or skate the puck up-ice themselves to start an attack. When retreating from the opponent's zone, defensemen move back toward their zone by skating backwards, facing the oncoming opponents.
Deflection: Placing the blade of the stick in the path of a shot on goal, causing the puck to change direction and deceive the goaltender. A puck may also deflect off a player's skate or pads.
Delay of game: Causing the play to stop by either propelling the puck outside the playing surface or covering it with the hand. Warrants a two-minute penalty.
Delayed penalty: An infraction, signaled by the referee's upraised right hand, but not whistled until the offending team regains possession of the puck. During the delay, the other team can launch a scoring attack, sometimes by replacing their goaltender with a skater. If the team scores during the delay, the penalized player does not sit out his penalty.
Elbowing: Striking an opponent with the elbow. Calls for a two-minute penalty.
Entry Draft: An annual event, at which all 26 NHL teams submit claims on young players who have not signed professional contracts. The talent pool consists of players from the Canadian junior leagues, U.S. high schools and universities and European elite and junior leagues.
Faceoff: A play that initiates all action in a hockey game, in which the referee or a linesman drops the puck onto a spot between the poised stick blades of two opponents. Marks the start of every period, also occurs after every goal and every play stoppage.
Fighting: Players dropping their gloves and striking each other with their fists. Calls for a five-minute penalty and ejection for the player who instigated the fisticuffs.
Forechecking: Harassing opponents in their own zone to try to gain possession of the puck.
Forwards: Three players—the center and the left and right wingers—comprise a hockey team's forward line. The forwards are primarily attackers whose aim is to score goals.
Frank J. Selke Trophy: Awarded to the player judged the best defensive forward in the NHL.
Goal: A goal is scored when the puck completely crosses the red goal line and enters the net.
Goals-Against-Average (GAG): Average number of goals a goaltender surrenders per game. Determined by multiplying the total number of goals allowed by 60 and dividing that figure by the total number of minutes played.
Goaltender: A heavily padded player who protects his team's goal.
Hart Memorial Trophy: Awarded to the player judged the most valuable to his team during the NHL regular season.
Hat Trick: One player scoring three goals in one game. A player who scores three consecutive goals in one period is said to have scored a 'natural' hat trick.
High sticking: Carrying the stick above the shoulder level. Calls for a faceoff if a player strikes the puck in this fashion. Calls for a two- or five-minute penalty if a player strikes an opponent with his stick.
Holding: Using the hands to impede the progress of an opponent. Two-minute penalty.
Hooking: Using the blade of the stick to impede an opponent. Two-minute penalty.
Icing the puck: Shooting the puck from one side of the center red line so that it crosses the opponent's red goal line. Calls for a play stoppage and a faceoff in the offending team's zone.
Interference: Using the body or stick to impede an opponent who is not in possession of the puck or was the last one to touch it. Two-minute penalty.
James Norris Memorial Trophy: Awarded annually to the player who is judged to be the best defenseman in the NHL.
Kneeing: Using the knee to check an opponent. Two-minute penalty.
Lady Byng Trophy: Awarded to the player who best combines playing excellence with sportsmanship.
Linesmen: Two on-ice officials responsible for calling offside, icing and some infractions, such as too many men on the ice. Linesmen drop the puck for faceoffs excluding those after a goal has been scored.
Neutral zone: The area of the ice surface between the two blue lines and bisected by the center red line.
Neutral-zone trap: Also called the delayed forecheck. A checking system designed to choke off offensive attacks in the neutral zone and enable the defensive team to regain possession of the puck.
Offside: A player who crosses the opposition blue line before the puck does is offside. Play is stopped when this occurs and a faceoff is held outside the blue line. A player also is offside if he accepts a pass that has crossed two lines (e.g. his team's blue line and the center red line). When this occurs, play is stopped and a faceoff is held at the point where the pass was made.
Original Six: In common usage, it refers to the six NHL teams in the pre-1968 expansion era: Toronto Maple Leafs; Montreal Canadiens; Boston Bruins; New York Rangers; Chicago Blackhawks; Detroit Red Wings.
Overtime: During regular-season play, teams play a five-minute, sudden-death overtime period if the score is tied at the end of regulation time. Teams play as many 20-minute sudden-death overtime periods as is necessary to reach a final result during the entire playoff schedule. Sudden-death means the game is over as soon as a goal is scored.
Penalty: A rules infraction which results in a player serving a two- or five-minute penalty in the penalty box, or in expulsion from the game. The penalized player's team must play one man short while he serves a minor or major penalty, but is not so handicapped if the player is assessed a ten-minute misconduct. The player cannot play until his time is up, but the team continues at full on-ice strength. A player assessed a game misconduct penalty cannot play for the rest of the game.
Penalty kill: A four- or three-man unit of players assigned to prevent the opposition from scoring while a teammate serves a two- or five-minute penalty.
Penalty Shot: Called when an attacking player, on a breakaway, is illegally prevented from getting a shot on goal. The puck is placed at center ice and the fouled player skates in alone on the goaltender.
Period: A 20-minute segment, during which time the clock stops at every play stoppage. A hockey game consists of three stop-time periods.
Playing Roster: A team may only dress 18 skaters and two goaltenders for each NHL game.
Plus-Minus: A 'plus' is credited to a player who is on the ice when his team scores an even-strength or shorthanded goal. A 'minus' is given to a player who is on the ice when an opponent scores an even-strength or shorthanded goal. A player's plus-minus total is the aggregate score of pluses and minuses. It is a barometer of a player's value to his team.
Point man: A player, usually a defenseman, who positions himself along the blue line near the boards and orchestrates an attacking team's offensive zone strategy. Often teams try to isolate the point man for a shot on goal.
Pokecheck: A sweeping or poking motion with the stick used to take the puck away from an opponent. Perfected by Frank Nighbor of the Ottawa Senators teams in the 1920s.
Power play: A situation in which one team has one or two more players on the ice than the other team, owing to penalties assessed. It provides the attacking team with an excellent opportunity to create quality scoring chances.
Puck: A vulcanized rubber disk, three inches wide and one inch thick. Game pucks are kept on ice before and during a game, which hardens them even more and helps them slide more quickly.
Rebound: A puck bouncing off the boards, the goaltender or the goalposts. A rebound gives an attacker a second chance for a dangerous shot on goal.
Red line: The red, center line dividing the ice surface in half. In junior and professional hockey, the red line is used to determine icing calls and offside passes. It is not used in U.S. college hockey.
Referee: The chief on-ice official at a hockey game. The referee calls all penalties except too many men on the ice and controls the flow of the game.
Roughing: Excessive pushing and shoving that has not escalated to the level of fisticuffs. Two-minute penalty.
Rink: A surface 200 feet by 85 feet on which a game of hockey is played.
Save: Occurs when a goalie uses his blocker, goalie stick, catching glove or pads to prevent a puck from entering the goal.
Scout: A man or woman who travels to junior, college and high school games, evaluating players who will be available in the Entry Draft. NHL teams also have pro scouts, who evaluate the play of opposing teams.
Shift: The period of time—usually 35-45 seconds—that a player spends on the ice playing the game. Normally a player will play several shifts each period. Some players log as much as 30 minutes in ice time in any given game.
Shot On Goal: Any deliberate attempt by a player to shoot the puck into an opponent's net that, without the intervention of the goaltender, would have scored a goal. Therefore, a shot that hits a goalpost or the crossbar and bounces away, is not a shot on goal.
Shutout: A game result in which the opponent does not score a goal, usually owing to excellent work by the goaltender.
Slap shot: Shooting the puck by swinging the hockey stick through the disk, in a manner similar to a golf swing, except with the hands several inches apart on the stick.
Slashing: Swinging a stick at an opponent. Two-minute penalty.
Slot, The: The area in the offensive zone directly in front of the crease, extending back between the two faceoff circles, about halfway toward the blue line. Teams work hard to create scoring opportunities inside this area.
Spearing: Using a stick as a weapon, jabbing it, like a spear, into an opponent. Five-minute penalty, with expulsion at the discretion of the referee.
Stanley Cup: A silver trophy, originally donated by Lord Stanley, Earl of Preston in 1893 to be emblematic of Canadian hockey supremacy. Since 1926 only NHL teams have competed for the trophy.
Stickhandle: Manipulating the puck back and forth, or any direction, with the blade of the stick in order to deceive an opponent and carry the puck up the ice.
Tip-In: A goal that results when one player shoots on net and a teammate, positioned near the crease, uses his stick to redirect the puck past the goaltender.
Vezina Trophy: Awarded annually to the player judged to be the best goaltender in the NHL.
Wrist shot: Shooting the puck by sweeping the stick along the ice, snapping the wrists on the follow-through.
Zamboni: The box-like, motor-powered vehicle used to resurface the ice in all NHL arenas. The machine collects the snow that builds up during a period of play and lays down a fresh coat of water, providing a smooth ice sheet to begin each period.

INDEX